Ralph Snodsmith's

Fundamentals
of
Gardening

RALPH SNODSMITH'S
FUNDAMENTALS
OF
GARDENING

---- Plus ----
Questions and Answers from
The Garden Hotline®

R. L. SNODSMITH ORNAMENTAL HORTICULTURE, INC.
New York

Grateful acknowledgment is made to the Cornell Cooperative Extension publication Guide to Pest Management Around the Home and Larry Newey for the illustration Insects and Injury (page 184), and to Guide to Pest Management Around the Home for Disease Symptoms (page 187).

This writing does not make or imply endorsement of any product mentioned. When using any product, check the product label, which is the final word with respect to the use of a product, or check with the manufacturer or supplier for updated information. Changes in pesticide regulations occur constantly, and human errors are still possible. These recommendations are not a substitute for pesticide labeling. Please read the label before applying any pesticide.

Library of Congress Cataloging-in-Publication Data is available 2006901446.

Snodsmith, Ralph, 1939
      Ralph Snodsmith's Fundamentals of Gardening / Ralph Snodsmith.
            p. cm.
      Includes index.
      ISBN 0-940239-06-X

Printed in the United States of America

Revised Edition, 2006

10 9 8 7 6 5 4 3 2 1

Printed by UniGraphic Color Corporation   Unigraphic color corporation

ILLUSTRATIONS BY LYDIA VISCARDI

Cover designed by Nelson Vanderhoff

CONTENTS

PREFACE

I HEARD ONCE THAT retirement is doing what you love to do best. If that is true, then I was close to retirement at a very early age. Horticulture was a name and discipline I learned later in life, but my introduction to it started with a summer job, at the age of nine, mowing grass on a thirty-two acre estate in my hometown of Mt. Vernon, Illinois. Day after day and week after week I walked behind an 18-HP Locke mower, cutting a swath that was thirty inches wide. It was a job that never seemed to get done because by the time I mowed from one edge of the estate to the other, it was time to go back and start again. But I loved the work, the smell of the freshly mowed grass, and the fact that I was outdoors. As the years went by, my summer job continued and I did other things, such as planting flowers, trimming hedges, and pruning trees and shrubs. I remember one year being given a very fine pair of pruning shears by my employer, along with the admonition "not to lose them." Well, I did lose them and the price of the next pair of shears came out of my paycheck. I suspect that was a lesson that stayed with me all my life because I'm always reminding people to invest in quality equipment and to take good care of their tools.

My formal education, when I really began to learn "the difference between the roots and shoots," began at the University of Illinois, Department of Floriculture and Ornamental Horticulture, where I learned from books, from great instructors, and by doing. To this day, my education continues in the same way. I grow flowers and vegetables, experimenting every year with a few new varieties. Various house plants come and go between home and greenhouse. Outdoor plants, trees and shrubs, are a part of my everyday living. So when a caller to *The Garden Hotline®* tells me about his tomato problems or his lawn problems or his tree problems, chances are I have had that same or similar experience at one time of another and I can relate to him *and* his problem. When a woman's voice tells me over the phone that her hanging asparagus plant has little bugs on the stems or foliage, I think I know what she is talking about because *my* asparagus has probably had that same problem.

I have been fortunate to have had great mentors and I must mention them here, and thank them: Dr. Pascal P. Pirone, plant pathologist, of the New York Botanical Garden and author of *Tree Maintenance*; Dr. Warren T. Johnson, entomologist, of Cornell University and author of *Insects That Feed on Trees and Shrubs*; and the late Thomas H. Everett, horticulturist and teacher, and author of the ten-volume *The New York Botanical Garden Illustrated Encyclopedia of Horticulture*.

All of my adult like has been spent helping people with their plant problems. When I was the county agricultural agent for Cornell Cooperative Extension, I spent all of my time analyzing plant problems or giving education programs to groups in an effort to prevent problems. As director of the Queens Botanical Garden I was again in a position to offer educational programs to people in the community who were interested in learning more about floriculture and ornamental horticulture. In this position I was even able to provide visual and other sensory interpretations for using plants in the environment. And guest lecturing at the New York Botanical Garden has provided a special reward for me. The thousands of students who have taken the "Fundamentals of Gardening" course have been there because they have the desire to learn, not just because they have to take the class.

In attempting to help people with their plants, I find many times that people's lack of basic knowledge regarding plants is what causes the roadblocks in communication. Television presentations usually provide the luxury of having the plant on hand for visual reference. But usually I am taking questions from people by telephone when they call while listening to *The Garden Hotline* on the radio. Without my actually seeing the plant, I have to start with the assumption that the caller knows little about the subject at hand. Very quickly though, through the caller's tone and terminology, I am able to discern if he or she knows that a branch is a branch or a root is a root. The soil a plant grows in can make such a difference too, and here again, we must each understand what the other is

talking about. Sometimes soil doesn't even contain "soil" as we commonly think of it.

I want people to become aware of their plants and their surroundings. For instance, if a tree is planted to grow and shade the house, I hope that it will be a tree that will grow tall enough to do the job. How much water does a plant need? Since water is such a precious resource for both man and plants, it seems to me that a little planning should go into the choice of plants. And when that house plant, vegetable plant, bush, tree, shrub, or whatever needs pruning, I would like people to know that there are better times and better ways to prune. I want people to understand that when they use a mulch, they are doing more than decorating around a plant. They are improving life in the soil, conserving precious moisture, and reducing pesky weeds, the gardener's nemesis. I also want people to understand that one "bug" does not constitute an invasion; however, when it is necessary to use a control, they absolutely must read the label.

As a communicator and a teacher, I want to help people understand the simple basics of plants so that they can then build on that knowledge and go as far in their quest as they might wish, whether it is to successfully grow one plant or one million plants.

I

—

PLANT
PHYSIOLOGY

IF YOU WANT TO BE A GARDEN SLEUTH with the detective skills of Sherlock Holmes, you must fully understand how a plant grows. You must know the difference between the roots and the shoots. Each part of the plant acts out its own important role in the growth process.

Witness the experience I had as County Agricultural Agent in suburban New York. I was asked to make a "house call" to pronounce some trees dead. A new home-owner had purchased fifty dormant, bare-root poplar trees from a mail-order nursery. The trees had been guaranteed to grow; in fact, the company had promised to replace any trees that failed, if verified by a horticultural authority's signature on the guarantee certificate. I was certain I knew exactly what had happened. The young trees must have dried out in transit or in the cold-storage warehouse. I decided to make that house call.

The bare-root poplars were three-foot "whips," sticks with no soil on the roots and no leaves on the stems. The trees had been shipped during the dormant season, with the roots packed in moist peat moss.

When I drove into the driveway of the new home, I had to bite my lip to keep from laughing. Poplar trees had been planted down one side of the property line, across the backyard line, and up the other side; fifty poplars, and every one of them planted upside down. The twisted, dried-out roots had been mistaken for tree branches. All the plants were dead, I think murdered. The "death certificate" initiated this gardener's education in the differentiation of "the roots from the shoots."

PHYSICAL MAKE-UP

To understand how a plant grows and to become your own "plant doctor," you must have some knowledge of a plant's physical components. All gardeners, indoor and out, must recognize four basic parts of the plant: roots, stems, leaves, and cones or flowers. The roots, stems, and leaves are primarily vegetative, concerned with securing raw minerals, manufacturing food, transporting minerals and food, and growing. The cones or flowers primarily produce seeds. We grow seeds to produce more seeds for future plant-ings, as well as for aesthetic and nutritional value; cut flowers decorate our tables; and fried squash blossoms complement our dinner plates.

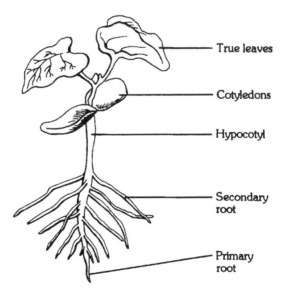

True leaves

Cotyledons

Hypocotyl

Secondary root

Primary root

Dicot Plant from Seed

THE ROOTS

Let's start with the roots and become experts from the ground up. Though there are internal differences between monocot (one seed-leaf, or cotyledon) and dicot (two seed-leaves, or dicotyledons) roots, the first root to emerge from the seed is the radical, or primary root. The primary root often develops into a taproot, a single, elongated root with limited lateral root growth that usually grows

downward. Carrots, which we grow for nutrition, develop a primary taproot and so do those invasive dandelions. Secondary roots originate within the primary root and could be the smaller roots extending outward from the main carrot taproot.

Tap Root System

Many other plants develop root systems lacking a dominant taproot and grow roots of similar size in all directions: a fibrous root system. Grain crops like rice and wheat, and grasses like bluegrass and crabgrass, all produce a fibrous root system. One single mature specimen can have hundreds of miles of roots per plant.

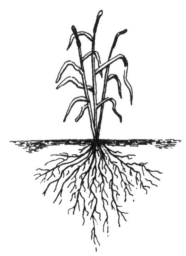

Fibrous Rood System

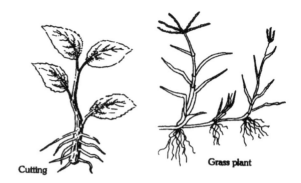

Cutting

Grass plant

Adventitious Roots

Adventitious roots—roots that occur in unusual or abnormal places—do not develop from the primary root. They're best illustrated by a stem used in vegetative propagation. You will find adventitious roots developing from the base of a cutting or at the node of a prostrate stem. Examine a cutting that has rooted. You will notice small, fibrous roots sprouting from the wounded area and the outer tissue of the stem. Now examine an ivy stem growing along the ground. Roots at the nodes, the point where leaves are or have been attached, and roots from the inner node areas, spaces between the nodes, attaching the ivy stem to the soil are also adventitious. Some plants, such as corn, develop aerial adventitious roots for support; we call these prop roots.

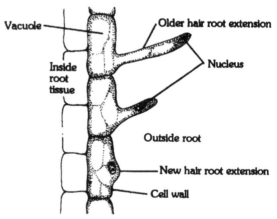

Vacuole

Older hair root extension

Inside root tissue

Nucleus

Outside root

New hair root extension

Cell wall

**Hair Root Development
(Root Epidermis)**

Hair roots really are not roots at all, but extensions of the single cells called root epidermis, the outer covering of the root. Hair roots are short-lived and are replaced continuously. They're located just above the area of cell elongation and protected by the root cap at the very tip of the root. The root-cap cells protect the growing root meristem cells that are making new roots.

FUNCTIONS OF THE ROOTS

The functions of the roots are primarily four-fold: (1) absorption of water and dissolved minerals from the soil; (2) anchorage of the plant; (3) conduction of water and dissolved minerals from the root to the stem and from the stem to the root; (4) storage of food.

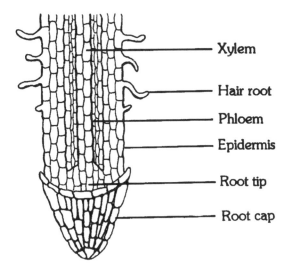

Root Cross Section

Labels on diagram: Xylem, Hair root, Phloem, Epidermis, Root tip, Root cap

Absorption

The absorption of water and dissolved minerals is primarily a task for hair roots. The uptake of water by these specialized single cells is dictated by the plant's rate of transpiration, soil temperature, concentration of salts (minerals) in the soil water, and available water in the soil. Too little water in the soil causes the plant to wilt. If this condition is not remedied, the plant reaches its "permanent wilting point", which is death.

Anchorage

The function of anchorage is self-explanatory. Roots anchor a plant to its growing medium. Whether it lives in a flower pot or outdoors in a garden, the two types of root systems that concern us are the taproot and the fibrous root. The carrot is an excellent example of a plant with a taproot; its ability to anchor is phenomenal. If you have ever tried to pull a carrot root from the ground without loosening the soil first, you know what I mean. If you haven't, try it some day. In most growing conditions, the carrot taproot is anchored so well that it simply snaps off at ground level.

The dandelion plant, that pretty yellow flower that comes uninvited to a beautiful lawn, is another example of a taproot. The dandelion's fleshy taproot, if pulled, generally breaks off just a few inches below the surface and sends up two or more plants in its place. The giant hickory and many oak family members develop a taproot, too.

The fibrous root system, in contrast to the taproot, is a multiple of many roots. If you were to wash the soil from a fibrous root system, it might resemble a major road map; interstate highways would symbolize the primary roots, smaller highways would symbolize the secondary roots, and smallest roads would symbolize the hair roots. Examples of plants with fibrous root systems are tomato, eggplant, pepper, Kentucky bluegrass, impatiens, philodendron, Swedish ivy, dogwood, rhododendron, and azalea, to name a few.

Conduction

The root system also functions to conduct water and dissolved minerals through the tiny hair roots up to the stem and to translocate manufactured sugars, the building blocks for new cells, back to the growing root tips. Water and dissolved minerals entering the hair roots travel to the growing stem through the vascular system in both the secondary roots and the primary root. Without the root system, there would be little or no flow of nutrients and water into the plant. The return, through the vascular system, of manufactured food to the growing cells of the root, supplies necessary energy for cell initiation and development.

Food Storage

The fourth critical function of the root system is food storage. Individual cells in the root system store manufactured food along with water, dissolved minerals, and inorganic chemicals for plant growth. Some plants are able to store massive quantities of food in their primary root system. Others must store their food in their secondary fibrous root system. Mother Nature provides wonderful safeguards: for us, she has conveniently packaged food in the carrot, beet, rutabaga, or turnip. For trees and shrubs, she has packaged some food in their root systems. Food manufactured during the growing season is translocated to the root system for storage, and carried back to the growing point the following season.

FUNCTIONS OF THE STEM

Stem functions are generally threefold: (1) to conduct minerals and water from the root to the leaf and manufactured food from the leaf back to the root; (2) to store food; (3) to support and produce leaves and flowers. The main stem and its branches are the skeleton of the plant.

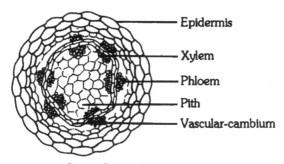

Stem Cross Section: Dicot

Conduction

Water, dissolved minerals, and manufactured food are carried up and down the stem through a complex group of tissues—xylem and phloem—called the vascular system. If either complex tissue is functioning improperly, due to disease or physical damage, the plant will not grow.

Food storage

Food is also stored in stem cells. The tender morsels of asparagus you eat are stems. Stems containing cells with chlorophyll manufacture food as well. Stems contain the "womb" for developing leaves and flowers.

FUNCTIONS OF THE LEAVES

From the plant's point of view, leaves are more than pretty shade-makers or edibles. They are more like assembly-line workers who contribute the building blocks to the end product: plant growth. Individual chlorophyll-containing cells within the leaves manufacture food from water, minerals and carbon dioxide. This process is, of course, photosynthesis.

From the gardener's point of view, a plant's foliage may be an end in itself. It could be intended to shade your patio, to be lettuce for a crisp salad, or to become cascading foliage

in a hanging basket to substitute for window drapes. In gardening, plants with different foliage characteristics also provide contrast in landscaping. The light green foliage of the ground-covering pachysandra can make the dark-green, broad-leafed foliage of a rhododendron much more outstanding. We can also brighten a flower garden by planting the colorfully leaved coleus, or enliven the vegetable patch with red cabbage and ruby lettuce.

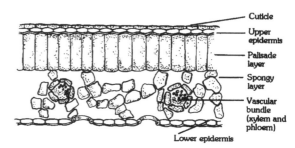

Leaf Cross Section

FUNCTIONS OF THE FLOWERS AND CONES

The fourth part of the plant is the flower and/or cone. Its function is primarily reproduction. Flowers and cones produce seeds necessary for Mother Nature's cycles of growth. Most of our vegetable plants, like tomatoes, eggplants, and peppers, have male and female parts within each flower; consequently, one plant by itself can produce fruit.

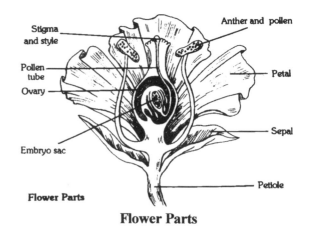

Flower Parts

Some plants have only male or only female parts in their flowers. American holly and skimmia require both male and female plants

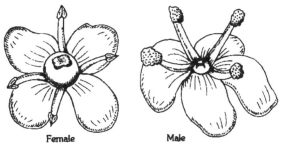

Holly Flowers: Comparison

in close proximity for production of their colorful fruit. The cucumber family produces both male and female flowers, but they are borne on the same plant. We obtain many of our edible fruits from the flowers. We grow flowers for their aesthetics, to grace our tables or to brighten our windows. Sensible Mother Nature makes sure flowers serve also to attract pollinators such as insects and birds.

THE CELL

Now, let's break down the plant into one of its smallest portions: the cell. Cells come in many sizes; from 1/25,000 inch to 1/250 inch. There are exceptions though. The nettle family may have a single cell as long as eight inches. It's estimated that there could be fifty million cells in one single apple leaf. From this, I believe it is quite evident that billions or even trillions of cells exist in an average plant.

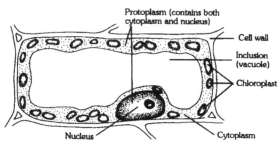

Plant Cell: Basic Parts

A Typical Cell

A typical cell has three basic parts: (1) the cell wall; (2) the protoplasm; (3) the inclusion. The cell wall consists primarily of carbohydrates, and gives support and form to the plant. It is permeable to water, which passes through the cell walls as needed.

The protoplasm is the living portion of the cell, and contains substances necessary for life. Its major components are the nucleus and the cytoplasm. The nucleus is the command center, the brain, which transmits all cell division and genetic instructions for the plant's identity. All decisions are made in the nucleus. Some cells become flower buds, some cells become new roots, and some cells clone themselves, performing the same function generation after generation.

The cytoplasm contains the dissolved minerals. Suspended in the cytoplasm are elements which produce the beautiful foliage colors we experience: chlorophyll, the green; xanthophyll and carotene, the beautiful yellows; chromoplasts, the red, yellow and orange often found in many of the beautiful fruit skins; and leucoplasts, the colorless pigments that retain starches. Leucoplasts are present in roots and white asparagus.

The inclusion, or vacuole, in the cell contains nonliving material. It is often called the junkyard or the wastecan of the cell. In this part of the cell, the plant stores for future growth. When the nucleus decides on certain building materials, a message courses through the plant, summoning to action the building blocks stored in the vacuole. Through chemical reaction, these nutrients are fed to the growing tissue.

Liquid in the vacuole does not contain pure water, but a "cell sap" of highly diluted substances. Pigments suspended in the "cell sap" sap are called anthocyanins, and yield the yellow coloration of poppy flowers, and the red, purple, and blue petals of many other flowers, as well as the red roots and leaves of garden beets.

TISSUE

A group of cells working together to perform the same function is a tissue. The tree's outer layer of cells (epidermal cells) forms bark tissue.

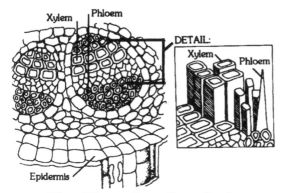

Plant Tissue: Stem Cross Section

ORGAN

An organ is a composition of various tissues; for example, leaves and stems. Plants are comprised of both simple and complex tissues.

Simple tissues consist of only one kind of cell, such as: (1) the epidermis (the outer cover of the leaves, stems, and roots); (2) the parenchyma (contains chloroplasts and manufactures food); (3) the sclerenchyma (provides the fiber and the strength necessary for the hard walnut shell); (4) cork (waterproof cells that die soon after they form).

Complex tissues contain more than one kind of cell. The xylem and phloem are two examples of such important complex tissues. Together they form the backbone of the vascular system. Xylem tissue primarily carries water, dissolved minerals, and chemical substances from the roots to the stems and leaves. In flowering plants, xylem tissue contains four different types of cells. Two types, the trachieds and vessel elements, actually conduct the liquids. The other cells, parenchyma and fiber, provide internal support. Phloem tissue, consisting of sieve tube members, companion cells, parenchyma, and fibers, conducts manufactured food to the roots and throughout the plant. A simple way to remember the vascular system's direction of flow is: "xylem up and phloem down."

Another complex tissue is the meristematic tissue, the growing tissue found in the cambium layer. All growth originates from the meristematic tissue: new roots, shoots, bark, flowers, leaves, cones, and so on.

You must now agree to the extreme importance of knowing the difference between the roots and the shoots. Each part of the plant, whether it be roots, stems, leaves, flowers or cones, has its very particular function.

PHYSIOLOGICAL PROCESSES

A plant's physiological processes basically revolve around water, whose importance cannot be denied. Better than 70 percent of each plant is water. Water maintains a cell's turgidity (firmness from the cell's being filled with water); it provides form and support to plant cells. Without water, each cell would collapse; the plant would first wilt and then die. Water is a constituent of protoplasm (the living part of the cell), and required for food manufacturing, that is, photosynthesis. Water provides a medium for moving minerals, such as sulphur, calcium, potassium, magnesium, boron, phosphorus, and nitrogen, throughout the plant. And, water is a medium for chemical reactions.

Water enters the plant mainly through its hair roots in the same process by which a sponge soaks up water: imbibition. Water also enters the plant through osmosis, which depends on several conditions: diffusion of water from high to low concentration; difference in concentration; and degree of cell membrane permeability. Water can move into the plant by capillary action, too; this is simply a pumping action.

Transpiration—The Cooling System
Let us examine the physiological process of transpiration, the release of water vapor from aerial portions of the plant. Transpiration is the cooling system. In my opinion, if you can learn to adjust the transpiration rate of your plants, whether they be little seedlings, vegetable transplants, gardenias in bud, petunias on the windowsill, or hanging baskets of philodendrons, you will successfully become a "green thumb."

There are many external and internal factors that affect the plant's transpiration rate. External factors include light, temperature, relative humidity, air circulation, and soil conditions like temperature and moisture.

The rate of transpiration (the giving off of water through those aerial parts) can be reduced simply by reducing light on the foliage. When light is absorbed by leaf tissue, heat is generated, and water serves to cool the leaf. If less light strikes the foliage, less water is needed for transpiration. The rate of transpiration is also reduced if the temperature around the plant is decreased. Cooler air holds less water. Increased humidity around foliage allows more water to remain in the leaf. Reducing air movement around foliage will greatly decrease the rate of evaporation, or transpiration, from the leaf. Reducing air movement increases humidity immediately adjacent to the leaf, causing less water to be lost. Keeping the soil cool and moist reduces stress within the plant cells and slows down transpiration.

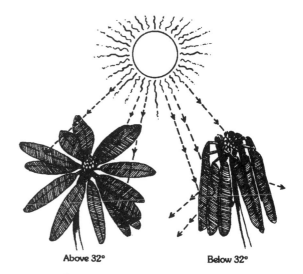

Transpiration: Rhododendron

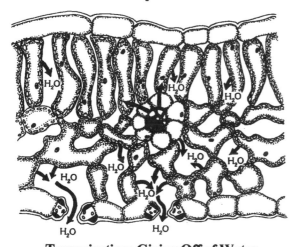

Transpiration: Giving Off of Water

Internal factors, those natural to the plant, also affect the rate of transpiration. The heavy layer of cutin, manufactured by the epidermal cells, waxes the leaf's surface, making it shine and making it better able to retain water. As the cutin deteriorates, the rate of transpiration increases. The vertical or horizontal position of the leaf also affects transpiration. On a cold day, look out the window at a rhododendron shrub. Its leaves are vertical, not horizontal, and they're tightly rolled. Nature got those leaves out of the direct sunlight, consequently reducing the rate of transpiration. Leaves that are horizontal and directly exposed to the light

labor to increase their transpiration rate, because light absorbed by their green cells creates heat energy and greater water requirements for the cooling system.

Another internal factor, the stomata, affects the rate of transpiration. The stomata, protected by the guard cells, are tiny openings generally found on the bottom of the leaf. Guard cells open and close the individual stomata, and thereby increase or decrease water vapor loss from the leaf. During stressful events, such as high temperatures, the stomata close to reduce water loss.

Leaf drop also controls transpiration. Many troubled plants drop foliage. A good example is the *Ficus benjamina*, the little-leafed or weeping fig grown by many of us in our homes and offices. When the weeping fig moves from a greenhouse environment (humidity of 60 to 80 percent or even higher) to the home or office, which may be as dry as the Sahara desert (5 percent or less), foliage will drop. It is Mother Nature's way of shutting down the rate of transpiration to protect the plant. In the greenhouse environment, the root system developed adequate hair roots to supply needed moisture for growth activity to upper parts of the plant. In a drier environment, the plant's root system needs to develop more hair roots to absorb additional moisture. Until then, the lack of adequate hair roots means the plant cannot absorb enough moisture to compensate for the changed environment.

Through transpiration alone, a plant can give off thousands of gallons of water a year.

An average apple tree can pump off eighteen hundred gallons of water in one growing season.

Water is necessary, period. If you are planning an extended vacation, make adequate arrangements for watering your plants; equip them with mechanical devices or give your neighbor a key and watering instructions.

METABOLIC PROCESSES

Metabolic processes involve chemical changes within the plant. Without these chemical changes, the growth of leaves, stems, flowers, fruits and roots will not occur. No one process is more important than another, but let's start with photosynthesis.

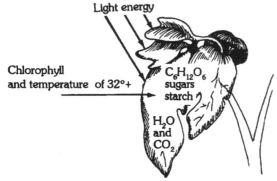

Photosynthesis: Food Manufacturing

Photosynthesis combines carbon dioxide and water in the presence of light, chlorophyll and above-freezing temperature, to make sugars (glucose and fructose) and an oxygen-gas byproduct. Sugars are the building blocks of the plant.

Respiration, or food utilization, is another metabolic process of the plant. It generates heat, unlike the process of photosynthesis. Through the stomata, oxygen is inhaled by the plant. The attack begins on the sugars, which break down to the basic elements of water and carbon dioxide. This process occurs in all plant cells, even dormant ones. Respiration parallels the oxidation reaction which turns a tin can to rust. When oxygen makes contact with the metal, rust occurs. Similarly, respiration processes significantly affect a plant's chemical bonds. During periods of low light, a reduced temperature helps balance the opposing forces of respiration and photosynthesis. Your plants may not grow as well, but they might not die quite as fast, either.

Assimilation, the third metabolic process, is the plant's mysterious ability to form living protoplasm from nonliving elements.

NUTRIENTS AND THEIR USES IN THE PLANT

Mineral nutrients used in plant growth fall into two general classifications: macronutrients and micronutrients. They include sixteen essential elements. Macronutrients are used in large quantities and are further distinguished by their place in a primary or secondary subgroup. The primary macronutrients are major mineral elements: nitrogen; phosphorus; and potassium.

Nitrogen encourages vegetative growth and improves the green color of foliage. It also increases flower size and the plumpness of seeds. Nitrogen tends to govern the utilization of potassium, phosphorus, and other elements, and plays an important role in the plant's protein development. Nitrogen shortage causes stunted growth in a plant, whose maturity is much delayed. You might also see a general yellowing of foliage. Too much nitrogen can cause excessive, vegetative growth. While this might be desirable in lettuce production, it would be undesirable for tomato plants where green foliage production superseded the setting of flowers and fruit.

Phosphorus is used extensively in cell division and in formation of fats and albumen. Phosphorus is present during oxidation, the conversion of starches to sugars. Phosphorus significantly aids growth of a strong stem and extensive root system. Plants deficient in phosphorus may have reduced yields of flowers, fruits, and seeds. In some cases, leaves and stems may be purplish in color. Vegetable plants like tomato, eggplant, and pepper all require phosphorus in their diet. If this mineral element is inadequate, you may have a nice green plant without fruit.

Potassium is used to grow longer and denser root systems, and to delay maturity. Potassium is essential to starch formation and translocation, as well as for chlorophyll formation. Soils deficient in potassium often develop poorly rooted crops and plants with less resistance to disease.

Secondary macronutrients—used in somewhat lesser quantities than primary mineral elements—are calcium, sulfur, and magnesium. Calcium is needed for cell wall, protoplasm, and protein formation, and for root development. Sulfur is found in certain amino acids and vitamins. It provides the flavors in the cruciferous (mustard) plant family, and in onions. Magnesium is needed for chlorophyll formation and neutralizing organic acids. Without adequate magnesium, chlorosis (a failure of chlorophyll development due to a nutrient deficiency) may occur in older leaves.

So-called trace, or minor, elements are micronutrients. They include the other seven mineral elements known to affect plant growth: iron, boron, manganese, molybdenum, copper, chlorine, and zinc. Each one of these elements, even in minute amounts, must be present for proper cell development and growth.

Iron is necessary for chlorophyll formation and to manufacture carbohydrates and proteins. You may have used an iron-containing plant food to cure yellowing leaves on your gardenia. If an iron deficiency had been the culprit, the leaves would green-up in just a few days.

Boron helps to reduce internal disorders in the plant. In small quantities, its presence is essential for the development of terminal shoots, elimination of extreme brittleness in the stem, and general vigor or upkeep of plant tissues. A minor-element test analysis can reveal a need for boron, even if the shortage is as small as one tablespoon per acre.

Manganese is important in making chlorophyll and forming sugars within the plant. A deficiency of manganese may be seen in a network of dark-green veins on a light-green background of leaf tissue.

The remaining minor elements are used in developing everything from the roots to the shoots, including flowers and cones.

Carbon, hydrogen, and oxygen are nonmineral elements essential to plant growth. They are taken from the air, water, and soil. Carbon comes from carbon dioxide used in photosynthesis and from respiration of organisms in the soil. Hydrogen is supplied by soil water. Oxygen is obtained from both water and air.

Without the proper elements, a plant's metabolic processes would cease to be; nutrition is essential for life.

QUESTIONS AND ANSWERS

1. **Q. My local nursery sells evergreens. The ad says to plant conifers for use as a windbreak. What does *coniferous* mean?**
   A. Coniferous means cone-bearing, such as firs, hemlocks, spruce, pines, and Douglas fir; these are evergreen plants, plants that retain their foliage year-round. Conifers are often recommended for windbreaks.

2. **Q. What causes winterkill on boxwood?**
   A. One cause is low temperature. The chief cause for winterkill, however, is very bright, warm sunshine in the early spring of the year while the ground is still frozen. Frozen soil does not allow roots to take up adequate moisture to keep leaf and stem cells turgid. There are many complex physiological factors involved.

3. **Q. How do different vines climb?**
   A. Sweet peas climb by coiling tendrils; English ivy by clinging rootlets; Boston ivy by adhesive disks; and wisteria by stems which twine.

4. **Q. A description in my garden catalog refers to plants as being deciduous. What does *deciduous* mean?**
   A. Deciduous trees and shrubs are those that shed their leaves in the autumn. Forsythia, apple, lilac, dogwood, and maple trees are examples of plants that drop their foliage annually. Beech and some oak trees retain their dry leaves through the winter, but they are still referred to as deciduous trees.

5.   Q. **The poinsettia plant I saved from last Christmas took forever to bloom. What was wrong?**
      A. Unless you provided total darkness for your plant, it was probably exposed to too many long days of sunlight in the fall. Next fall, put the plant in total darkness from six P.M. until eight A.M. every day for forty days, starting October 1. These controlled "days" and "nights" will initiate the flower buds.

6.   Q. **Every summer, I take some of my potted plants out of my house and put them on a sunny deck, but their leaves scorch. How can I prevent the scorching?**
      A. If they are plants that will put up with direct sun, for the first week they are outside keep them in a partially shaded location before putting them in the direct rays of sun. It takes time for the chlorophyll in the leaf cells to realign. Chlorophyll in the plant tissue acts as a solar collector.

7.   Q. **The leaves of my *Rhododendron maximum* and *Rhododendron roseum elegans* droop and curl into a cigar shape when it is cold outside during winter. Does this signal a problem with the plant?**
      A. No. It *is* a sign the temperature is below freezing outside. Curling and drooping of foliage is nature's way of reducing transpiration.

8.   Q. **After the last frost date in the spring, I place many of my foliage plants outside for their summer vacation. The new leaves produced while they are growing outside are bigger than those that developed during the winter indoors. Why?**
      A. The leaf size is directly related to the growing environment. During the summer months, humidity is greater than it is indoors during winter. High humidity makes moisture in the plant usable for growth, as opposed to being used for the cooling process, transpiration. Increasing the humidity indoors will grow larger leaves during winter.

9.   Q. **How can you tell when indoor plants need a rest?**
      A. Observe them closely and read about the culture of your specific plants. When a plant such as *Ficus benjamina* has been actively growing for six months or so, it may show signs of needed rest by yellowing and dropping leaves. At that time, check the plant for cultural problems including invasions of spider mites, scale insects, and/or mealybugs. If these are not the cause, allow the plant to rest by reducing nutrient applications and allowing it to dry longer between waterings. *Ficus benjamina, Ficus elastica, Dracaena marginata*, and many varieties of palms are classic examples of plants that rest now and again.

10.   Q. **How do you "rest" a plant?**
      A. Cut back on the watering, stop fertilizing, and lower the temperature. Mother Nature allows northern plants to rest by becoming dormant in winter. Many spring-flowering bulbs—tulips, daffodils, and crocus, for example—become dormant in summer to overcome the summer drought period. Many tropical plants rest by suspending growing activities during the dry period of the season.

11.   Q. **During mid to late summer, my tomatoes crack open just before they are ripe enough to pick. Why do tomatoes crack open?**
      A. Tomatoes split when the weather is very hot and dry, and following very moist weather or a period of heavy watering. During the dry period, the epidermal (outer) cells of the skin of the tomato fruit stop or slow in growth. They become "hardened-off." When moisture becomes available again, it is translocated into the fruit, resulting in the expansion of the inner cells. Due to the hardened-off condition of the outer cells, they cannot expand sufficiently to compensate for the water pressure within the fruit. When the internal pressure becomes too great, the fruit split. Keeping the soil moist at all times will help prevent cracking.

12. **Q. What is the cambium ring?**

    A. It is the microscopic layer, usually one to two cells thick, between the bark and the wood of a woody plant. It contains the meristematic tissue from which new growth originates. If you cross-section a twig or branch on a tree or shrub, you will note that it has bark, a large area of sapwood and heartwood, and a small area of pith at the center. The cambium ring is located between the bark and the area of sapwood and heartwood. The thickness of these layers will vary in various trees and shrubs.

13. **Q. My neighbor has a camellia bush that produces many blossoms each year. Mine produces lush green leaves but no flowers. Why?**

    A. Light exposure is most likely the answer. Possibly your plant is in too-dense a shade. Camellias appreciate protection from strong sun, but must have bright light in order to set flower buds. Also, you may be using a plant food with too much nitrogen nutrition, which stimulates leaf development instead of flowers.

14. **Q. My Cooperative Extension Agent formerly known as the County Agricultural Agent recommended that I plant crown vetch as a ground cover in an area exposed to full sun that has no supplemental water available. He says it will help enrich the soil. The catalog describes it as a legume. What is a legume?**

    A. Crown vetch is an excellent ground cover for a sunny, dry location. It, along with beans and peas from the vegetable patch and clovers in the lawn, are examples of legumes. Leguminous plants belong to the pea family. Legumes attract bacteria, which collect nitrogen and store it on their roots. When the small nodules on the roots decay, they add nitrogen to the soil.

15. **Q. I want to propagate rhododendrons, azaleas, boxwood, and holly from cuttings. Why is it recommended to cut back or remove leaves before inserting them in a rooting medium?**

    A. The answer is simple. It is to reduce transpiration, the lose of moisture through the aerial parts of the plant (leaves). Until the evergreen cutting develops roots, it is important to conserve as much moisture in the cells as possible.

16. **Q. Tomato plants, eggplants, and peppers always seem to wilt immediately after being planted in my sunny vegetable garden. Is there anything, besides watering and shading, that will reduce wilting of new transplants?**

    A. Reduce leaf surface of the new plant by pinching or trimming off some of the leaves. Having fewer leaves on the plant will reduce transpiration, thus allowing the plant to become more quickly established.

17. **Q. Can an antitranspirant spray be used to reduce wilting on my newly planted vegetables and flowers?**

    A. An antitranspirant spray can be applied to the aboveground parts to reduce moisture loss through the foliage, potentially reducing wilting. It slows evaporation of moisture from both the leaf surface and the stomata. Before applying the antitranspirant, read the label for recommended rates and directions.

18. **Q. A mail-order catalog states that my new fruit trees and forsythia shrubs will be shipped in a dormant condition. What is meant by *dormant*?**

    A. Plants are dormant when they are not actively growing. In deciduous trees and shrubs, it is the period between when the leaves fall in the autumn and the beginning of leaf growth in the spring.

19. **Q. Last year, the fruit growers in my area blamed the price increase of apples, peaches, and pears on what they called June drop. What's that?**

    A. "June drop" is a term used by many growers when small fruits drop from the tree prematurely. It is the physiological reaction caused by one of several factors: poor

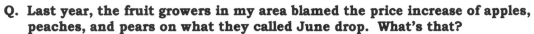

pollination, excessive fruit set (more fruit than the plant stem can sustain), rapid fluctuation of temperatures, dry weather, or even insects or diseases.

20. **Q. Before I dedicate part of my gardening space to growing a fruit orchard, can June drop be avoided?**
    A. You can reduce June drop by hand pulling approximately 50 percent of the tiny developing fruit from the tree shortly after fruit set. In the fruit-growing industry, a thinning-agent spray is used to cause a given percentage of the fruit to drop, thus allowing the balance of the fruit to develop fully. Thinning agents are generally not available to the home grower, because they must be applied under exacting guidelines and conditions. If they are misused, all of the fruit will drop.

21. **Q. Every spring, my peach trees blossom beautifully and set what appears to be thousands of new fruits. About the middle of June, almost all of them fall to the ground. What causes this?**
    A. This is a very common problem with peaches and apricots. Again, it's a case of June drop. Your problem actually started last year when the blossoms for the next season were developed. In spring, when air temperatures are cool and humidity is high, fruit trees set fruit if properly pollinated. Generally, there is adequate moisture available in the soil to start development of the fruit. As air temperature rises and soil begins to dry, plants cannot take up adequate moisture to sustain all of the developing fruit. In an effort to reduce this demand for moisture within the plant, the abscission layer forms, and fruit drops. Your peach tree simply set and started to develop more fruit than it could sustain under the existing growing conditions.

22. **Q. What is the abscission layer?**
    A. A group of thin-walled cells located across the base of the leaf or fruit petiole. The layer is located where the leaf or fruit petiole joins the stem. It is a function of this layer to stop the flow of water and dissolved minerals into a maturing leaf or fruit, causing drop.

23. **Q. The cultural directions on the hardy mums I planted last year said to pinch out the terminal bud when it reached six inches in height during spring, in order to make the plant branch. What is the "terminal bud"?**
    A. It is the topmost bud on a shoot or stem. Pinching out the growing tip—the terminal bud—causes lateral or side buds to grow.

24. **Q. What are anthers?**
    A. Anthers are the pollen-bearing parts of the flower. They often appear as saclike appendages at the tip of the stamen. Together, anthers and stamens are often referred to as the "male" part of the flower.

25. **Q. What are stigmas?**
    A. Stigmas are the receptive portion of the style to which pollen from the anthers adheres. They may be hairy in texture or coated with a sticky substance which helps ensure pollination.

26. **Q. What is the pistil of a flower?**
    A. It is the seed-bearing organ of the flower, consisting of the stigma, the style, and the ovary.

27. **Q. I planted a bed of *Skimmia japonica* some years back but have never had the bright red berries develop after flowering. What is wrong?**
    A. You probably have all male plants. *Skimmia japonica* is a species that produces only male or female flowers on a given plant. A rule-of-thumb ratio for planting male and female skimmia: one male to ten females.

28. **Q. It has been recommended that I plant a strawberry patch by using stolons. What is a stolon?**

A. The strawberry "runner" is a stolon. It is a branch or stem that grows prostrate along the surface of the soil. When it comes into contact with the soil, the stem becomes rooted, can be pruned from the main plant, dug up, and transplanted as an independent plant. Strawberry, forsythia, and Bermuda grass all can be reproduced by stolons.

29. **Q. What is a rhizome?**

A. A rhizome is an underground branch or stem, differentiated from roots by the presence of nodes and internodes where both roots and shoots may emerge. Rhizomatous *Iris* (bearded type), sugar cane, lily of the valley, quack grass, and bamboo propagate by rhizomes.

30. **Q. Will a bulb bloom if it is planted upside down?**

A. Yes, Mother Nature is very forgiving, but it is not the recommended thing to do. The stem will turn upward and the roots will grow downward if the bulb is sideways or planted upside down.

31. **Q. Even though my zebra plant has its bright-yellow flower, it is shedding its leaves from the bottom up. It looks rather strange, a tall, skinny stem with two leaves and a flower at the top. How can I prevent this from happening?**

A. Leaf drop from the zebra plant is probably due to lack of moisture in the air, and erratic watering. Improve the growing conditions by providing at least 50 percent humidity, keep the soil evenly moist, place it where it will receive strong north light, and keep it at average room temperature.

32. **Q. The gardenia I recently purchased from a local greenhouse had fat, green flower buds at the tips of every stem. They looked as if they were all about to open. After just a few days in my home, the buds all fell off. Why?**

A. Bud dropping was primarily due to the change in growing conditions. The flower buds had been developing in a bright-light condition with high humidity. Increase the humidity and keep the night temperature in the low sixties. Keep the soil slightly moist at all times, *not* allowing it to dry between waterings.

33. **Q. Just as the buds on my gardenia plant that I have been growing indoors for the past two years get ready to open, they start to turn brown and/or fall off. How can I prevent this?**

A. The problem is referred to as "bud drop." During winter months, lack of adequate sunlight and low humidity are the culprits. Too much overhead watering after the buds have set can also cause the gardenia buds to drop. Gardenias grown in pots should regularly receive an acid-type fertilizer containing iron, applied according to the label directions. To stop bud drop, keep the gardenia in a uniform temperature of 60 to 62 degrees, in good light, and maintain a high humidity.

34. **Q. The pachysandra ground cover planted under my Norway maple is light green in color instead of a rich, dark green. Does it need feeding?**

A. The light-green color may be due to lack of nitrogen and iron. Apply a high-nitrogen fertilizer containing chelated iron, and water it in. This application should turn the pachysandra dark green in only a matter of a few days.

35. **Q. When I place my potted amaryllis on a table about three feet from the window, the stalk of the flower leans toward the window. Why?**

A. The amaryllis is responding to the light source. Place the plant closer to the center of the window so the plant will be exposed to light on all sides. Turn the plant 180 degrees each day. This will reduce the curved-stem growth habit. This reaction to light is called phototropism.

36. **Q. My American holly blooms with tiny white flowers every spring, but does not produce berries. What is wrong?**
   A. To produce berries on holly there must be male and female plants within close proximity of one another. Most growers recommend planting a male and female plant no more than twenty feet apart. When the plant blooms next spring, compare the blossoms to a known male and female blossom to identify which one you are growing.

37. **Q. The plants in my windowless office are losing more leaves than they are producing. Would it help to put the lights on a timer to give them more light at night?**
   A. Additional light will reduce the period of respiration and lengthen the time for photosynthesis. A total of fourteen to sixteen hours of artificial light may be necessary to reverse the decline of your plants.

38. **Q. Will lowering the temperature at night be helpful to my house plants?**
   A. Most of our house plants have enjoyed the energy crisis. The lower night temperatures reduce the rate of respiration.

39. **Q. My African violets bloom very poorly during December and January, even though I have them near a bright window. Why?**
   A. African violets bloom in relation to the quantity and quality of light they receive. During the months in question, the days are too short and the quality of light is at its lowest. Provide additional light to keep them in bloom.

40. **Q. The leaves on my *Rhododendron maximum* loose their shine over winter. Why?**
   A. The cuticle layer, which contains the waxy natural substance called cutin, wears away due to weather.

41. **Q. The older leaves on my *Ficus elastica*, large-leaf rubber plant, look dull and dirty. They have lost their shine. Should I apply a "plant-shine" product to make them more lustrous?**
   A. The luster can be restored with plant-shine products available from your local florist or garden center. Their use may necessitate more frequent cleaning, as they tend to attract dust. Read and follow label directions for use.

42. **Q. My large-leaf rubber plant has a wrapping around the new bud that is forming at the top of the plant. Should I remove the wrap to help the leaf emerge?**
   A. No. This wrapping, called the sheath, is important to the development of a healthy leaf. Leaf growth will cause the sheath to separate and drop from the plant at the proper time.

43. **Q. The pyracantha, or firethorn, growing on the sunny side of my house did not produce a good crop of reddish-orange berries this year. Does it need fertilizer?**
   A. The problem may not be a lack of nutrients. Pyracanthas often produce heavy crops of berries every other year. If nutrients are needed, apply a fertilizer high in phosphorus. Phosphorus stimulates flowering and fruiting.

44. **Q. What kind of soil should I use for my Martha Washington and walnut geraniums to get blooms? They haven't bloomed, either winter or summer, for several years?**
   A. Soil type should have no effect on the blooming ability of geraniums, as long as growth is normal. The problem is one of improper growing temperatures. *Pelargonium domesticum* (Martha Washington and fancy-leafed types) only form flower buds at temperatures below 60 degrees.

45. **Q. What does it mean when a plant is turgid?**
A. Turgidity refers to a cell that is firm because it is filled with water.

46. **Q. What is cutin?**
A. Cutin is the waxy substance on the outer epidermal cell wall that retards moisture loss and gives the leaf its shiny characteristic.

47. **Q. Every time I water my dieffenbachia, I turn the pot so the plant will not have a crooked stem. It always seems to grow with a bend in the stem. What causes that to happen?**
A. The plant is responding to the light source. Phototropism is the bending or movement of leaves and stems toward the light. It is due to the expansion of cells caused by the movement of auxins—natural growth hormones—to the shady side of the stem or leaf.

48. **Q. What is evapotranspiration?**
A. It is the term representing the total loss of water through both evaporation from the soil and transpiration from the cell structure of the plant. Knowing the rate of evapotranspiration provides a guide for calculating irrigation needs of agricultural crops.

49. **Q. I have large flowers on my zucchini plants but no fruit. Why not?**
A. The zucchini is probably still producing all male flowers. It is not unusual for members of the cucurbit family to start the season by producing all male flowers. Be patient. When the zucchini starts producing flowers on long petioles (male flowers) and flowers on very short petioles (female flowers), you will have fruit.

50. **Q. I have been growing a lemon citrus plant in a container next to a large glass door for many years, but it has not produced one flower. I feed it with a citrus plant food according to the label directions, and the foliage is in excellent condition. How can I get it to bloom?**
A. Your citrus needs more light. Increase the period of light by using plant lights to provide longer days and increase the intensity of light by moving the plant into more direct sunlight during the day. Citrus needs quality light in order to bloom.

51. **Q. Will it damage *Ficus benjamina* to let it wilt between waterings? I use the drooping of the leaves as an indicator for water need.**
A. A slight loss of turgidity in the petioles attaching the leaves to the stem is generally not a critical time for the plant. Be sure to provide water within a day or so of the initial wilting.

52. **Q. What is a root cap?**
A. The root cap is a mass of hard cells protecting the growth point (apical meristem) of the root from mechanical injury by soil particles.

II

SOILS

MANY TIMES I HAVE HEARD the saying, "You can't make a silk purse out of a sows ear." To me, that means you can't turn something inferior into something magnificent. Well, that sure isn't true when it comes to soils. Soil is the one external factor of the physical environment over which you can exert major control. A poor soil can be converted into a good growing medium. You may not be able to turn bronze into gold, but you can turn dead soil into live soil.

Whether it is all-purpose potting soil for your house plants or an acre of land in the countryside, you need to understand the physical properties and limitations of the soil. A good gardener will be sure to learn all he can about the soil he has for a growing medium. Engineers and architects use soils as building materials to support buildings, bridges and highways. As gardeners, we use soil to provide support for our plants and to store nutrients for growth.

What is soil? Soil is a living, dynamic system both fragile and perishable. Soil is sand, silt and clay particles along with organic matter, air, and water. A good garden soil typically contains 45 percent sand, silt and clay particles, 5 percent organic matter, 30 percent air and 20 percent water. This literally means that soil is made of solids, liquids, and gases.

Knowing the size of sand, silt, and clay particles is important to you, because particle size helps identify your soil type. A soil scientist figured out a way to compare and understand the size differences among these particles: If magnified, a sand particle would be equivalent to the Empire State Building, a silt particle to a large house, and a clay particle to a cigar box. Particle sizes within soil types are indeed significantly varied.

Particle sizes for sand range from 0.02 to 2 millimeters in diameter; for silt particles, from 0.002 to 0.02 millimeters in diameter; and for clay particles, any size less than 0.002 millimeters in diameter.

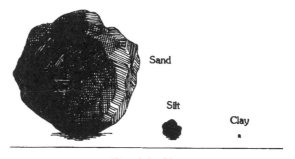

Particle Size

A quick hand test indicates which particles are in your soil. Place a couple spoonfuls of dry soil in the palm of your hand and then vigorously rub your hands together. If the soil feels gritty, sand is present. If, when you rub your hands together, the feel is silky or like baby powder, clay is in your soil.

Sand, silt, and clay particles blended together make a soil aggregate. Left totally undisturbed, this mixture would be of evenly distributed particle sizes. If disturbed by vibration, the larger particles remain on top and the smallest particles settle to the bottom.

Remember the box of popcorn you purchased the last time you went to the movies? The box was filled to the top, and you even added extra salt. By the time you walked to your seat, the box of popcorn had been bumped several times by the person standing in front of you. You might have noticed that your first handful of popcorn was of fully popped kernels. As you ate your way through the box, the kernels seemed to get smaller. By the time you got to the bottom of the box, all you could find were a few unpopped kernels and lots of salt.

The same would happen if you mixed together sand, silt and clay particles, and shook them vigorously. To build a good soil

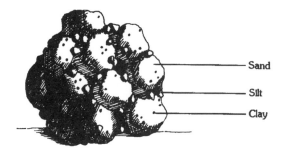

Aggregate: A Cluster of Soil Particles

aggregate where the small particles would not settle, add something to act as cement. Organic matter, which should be about 5 percent of your soil aggregate, does just that. The end product of decaying organic matter is humic acid. This brown, sticky, gelatinous liquid acts as cement, bonding soil particles together, as well as holding them apart. Soil particles thoroughly coated with humic acid will show little compaction from rain or foot traffic. The decayed organic matter also gives soil a dark, rich, brown color.

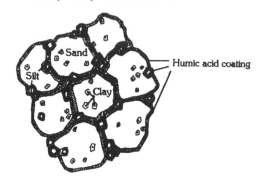

Humic Acid: The Soil Cement

It is difficult to tell how much humic acid is in a soil sample, particularly in a wet sample. Moist soil usually looks dark in color. To test for humic acid, place a small amount of moist soil in your hand and rub both hands together again. You will probably see a very dark, dirty mess on your hands. Wait a few minutes for the moisture on your skin to dry and look again. You may be surprised. The dark, dirty mess may have changed to a light-gray or tan color, indicating very little humic acid in the soil sample.

SOIL CLASSIFICATIONS

Whether you have a coarse, sandy soil, often found near the beach, or a very-fine-particle clay soil for gardening, it is necessary to understand some of the soil's characteristics. Soil classifications are abundantly different. Sandy soil is generally extremely coarse. It is nonabsorbent when it comes to water, and extremely porous. Water penetrates a sandy soil very rapidly. If you were to pick up a handful of dry sand, squeeze it, then open your hand, the sand particles would simply fall apart and slip through your fingers. "Deserts of shifting sand" is an apt description of sand's instability.

A clay soil, at the other extreme, is very, very fine; the particles are ultra-microscopic in size and retain huge quantities of water. After a heavy rain, clay soil can take hours or days to drain. It is almost impermeable by water and impervious to air.

Do you remember all the "mud" you tracked into the house when you were a kid? You were demonstrating another characteristic of clay soil: It's very sticky. When handling wet clay soil, billions of clay particles stick to your hands. This sticky characteristic makes clay particles very desirable for forming bricks and clay flower-pots. The manufacturer takes wet clay particles not coated with humic acid, forces the air from between the particles, and then dries them. By forcing air from between the ultramicroscopic particles, a very tight clay structure is obtained. For this reason, wet clay soils are not recommended for gardening. You don't want to make bricks in your garden—you want to grow plants.

In between the classifications of clay soils and sandy soils are loam soils. They are a combination of sand and clay particles. Silt soils found in river beds and delta regions are also loam soils.

Adequate pore space must exist for soil to obtain the adequate proportion of air to water. Pore space is the area between individual particles. When dry, pore space holds air; when wet, it holds water. A happy medium allows plants to grow healthy, vigorous roots. As stated previously, the balance should be somewhere in the neighborhood of 20 percent water and 30 percent air.

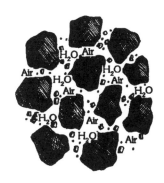

Soil Pore Space: Air and Water

Gravity has a great effect on the water supply in soil. In garden soil, gravitational force pulls water down to the water table. In a container, it pulls water into the drip pan or saucer below. The film strength of water counteracts the force of gravity and lets a fine coat of water surround each particle. The field capacity, or water-holding capacity, of your soil measures the amount of water left in the soil after gravity has pulled out all that it can; field capacity is generally measured twenty-four hours after water was applied. You can test the field capacity of water in your soil by pouring a given volume of water through a dry soil sample, and then measuring the amount of water that exits the sample. If you have a balanced soil mix of sand, silt, and clay particles, your field capacity should be approximately 20 percent water and 30 percent air, after gravity has acted. This water is available for root consumption, up to a point. Roots in soil will continue to draw out water until the supply depletes, at which time the plant will wilt and die. The plant has reached its permanent wilting point. Though there would still be a very small amount of water left in the micropores of the soil particles, it is not available to the plant. The amount of water between field capacity and the permanent wilting point is what the plant can use.

SOIL COMPACTION

Previously, we mentioned compaction: making bricks by forcing out air from between the particles. In gardening, we have two types of compaction to combat: one caused by physical action and the other caused by lack of organic matter in the soil. Physical compaction can result from overhead irrigation sprinklers. The impact disturbs soil particles and rearranges them. Soil with inadequate organic matter to bond particles together separates and becomes compacted. After a heavy rain, look at the soil surface as it begins to dry. If the surface develops a crust, you are seeing compacted soil particles. Recently tilled or cultivated soil is especially susceptible to crusting.

The surface of soil in a window box or flowerpot can exhibit the same compaction symptom if your watering can has no spray head or nozzle to break the force of a direct stream of water. We'll discuss solutions for compaction in container gardening in more detail when we discuss watering and mulching.

Foot traffic also causes soil to compact. Walking on wet soils separates and rearranges soil particles. Take a look at the corner where your driveway and sidewalk intersect. Almost no one stays on the sidewalk, so crossing the corner means stepping on the soil or sod. The soil seems to be wearing away, showing a depression or dished-out area. The physical pressure of a foot on soil, particularly when soil is wet, pounds soil particles tighter and tighter together. Physical compaction can be corrected by tilling or spading the soil. Time these corrective measures with care; remember, if you handle wet soil, you make bricks.

In regions where freezing and thawing alternate, Mother Nature exerts herself to correct physical compaction. Ice crystals formed between soil particles actually spread them apart and break up the soil aggregate. I had a very dramatic experience that illustrates nature's correction of physical compaction.

Shortly after we purchased our home, we decided to drill a water well behind our house. There was no way we could get the drilling rig to this area without driving across my neighbor's property. The property had been an open meadow for many years, so the soil was in no way physically damaged. The time of year was late fall, and we had had no appreciable precipitation. The soil was dry. The well-drilling rig was enormous—it had to weigh at least thirty tons. The driver headed across the field, but not for long; the truck wheels sank into the sod, right up to the axle. A tow truck and winch pulled the drilling rig out of the field. Much to my dismay, we had created two, twenty-four-inch-deep trenches in my neighbors field. That was real compaction!

Needless to say, my neighbor was upset, to put it mildly. He wanted me to purchase screened topsoil immediately, fill in the trenches, and then reseed the area with bluegrass. I told my neighbor it was too late to reseed, and that new topsoil would only erode over winter. We eventually compromised, and I agreed to do the repairs in the spring.

Come spring, my neighbor and I surveyed the field. It looked as if someone had filled the trenches during the winter. Except for a slight depression where minor erosion had occurred, the trenches were almost filled to capacity with soil. All I had to do was spread a few shovelsful of new soil, rake it level, and reseed the damaged area.

The lesson: Because I live in an area where soil freezing and thawing recurs many times during winter, thanks to compaction-correcting ice crystals between soil particles, any trenches I might have filled in the fall would have become two long mounds rising across my neighbor's field.

If I had lived where no freezing and thawing cycles could be expected, the solution would have been either to fill the trenches with new soil or to break up the compacted soil by tilling or spading. Either way, it would have been lots of extra work.

The other major cause of compaction is inadequate organic matter in the soil. To alleviate compaction, organic matter must be in its final state: humic acid—totally decomposed organic matter. Soil particles not surrounded by humic acid will slip into a solid mass when exposed to the pressures of rain, irrigation, or physical traffic. The less movement of soil particles, the less compaction.

Soils extremely high in partially decomposed organic matter generally have a fluffy texture. Imagine walking through a forest. Underfoot, you feel a spongy response to the pressure of your feet. Pull away the fresh leaves on the surface and put your hand on the soil. If the forest has lived for a considerable length of time, you should be able to easily work your hand four or five inches into the soil. The upper layer is almost pure decaying organic matter that eventually turns into humic acid. The forest floor is Mother Nature's ready-made compost pile. This demonstrates that compaction due to too little organic matter can be alleviated by adding great quantities of composted organic matter to garden soils or potting mixes.

SOIL PROFILE

A quick look at the layers of soil lining a hole twenty-four to thirty-six inches deep can be quite an education. In fact, if you are about to purchase a new piece of property, I think such a look is a must. Since your home will probably be your largest investment, I encourage you to obtain permission to examine the soil before you purchase a property. After all, you would test-drive a car and try on a pair of shoes before you bought them.

Your U.S. Soil Conservation District may have a soils map to guide your expectations. Upon examination, the soil color near the top of the hole may be darker than that of soil at the bottom of the hole. If this is the case, the soil has probably not been disturbed for many years. Decaying organic matter left by plants, leaves, and roots growing on the surface turns into humic acid and penetrates through the soil particles; color indicates the soil's condition. If this color differentiation is not obvious, you look deeper. If digging the hole unearths an aluminum object with BUD printed on it, you might be about to purchase property made of fill. At this point, hiring a professional soils engineer may be in order.

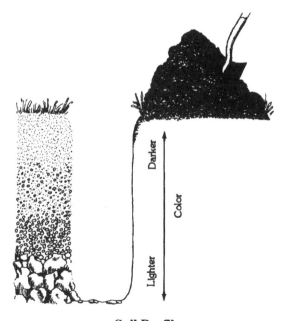

Soil Profile

SOIL CHEMISTRY

Soils are the storage warehouse for nutrients. Remember learning about negative and positive charges in chemistry? Take two magnets and put the positive ends together. What happens? They repel. Put the positive and negative ends together, and they attract. This is how soil particles and nutrients get together.

Potassium chloride is a good example of positive and negative bonding. The potassium ion is positive (+); the chloride is negative (-); they freely combine to form potassium chloride (KCl). Soils containing clay and/or humic acid are usually negatively charged. When potassium chloride is added to the soil and dissolved in water, potassium ions are freed. When the positive ions pass by a soil particle of clay or a soil particle coated with humic acid, they are attracted to its negative ions. The potassium will stay

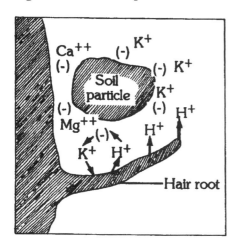

Soil Chemistry: Ion Exchange

until it can be absorbed by the root system or replaced by another ion.

When a young plant is put into soil, it has to receive nutrients to grow. Hair roots on the root system do the work. As the root system spreads out through the soil, the hair roots produce carbonic acid, which contains the hydrogen (H+) ion. The hair roots exchange the hydrogen ion for the potassium ion and then absorb potassium for the plant's use. The procedure is done over and over as the plant takes up nutrients. Other nutrients are assimilated in the same way. Calcium, magnesium, and sodium ions are exchanged with hydrogen ions.

Most soils low in organic matter content, by definition, have fewer negative ions and a low ion exchange capacity. This deficiency of negative ions leads to a soil that has little ability to store food. Sandy soils have few negative ions and generally require more frequent applications of fertilizer than do other types of soil. Water-soluble nutrients applied to a sandy soil are washed through it by rain and irrigation, because sand has little ability to store mineral ions. Inorganic slow release and organic plant foods are often recommended for gardening in sandy soils, because they are not readily water soluble and don't leach through the sand with the first rain.

Perhaps you have heard the old adage: "If one will do it, two will do it better." Well, this does not apply to feeding plants. If one ounce is recommended, two will *not* do it better. Over-fertilizing with one particular element can cause deficiencies of other needed elements, as the excessive one occupies all the negative charges on soil particles and other ions will simply pass through.

NUTRIENT ANALYSIS

In order to know which nutrient elements your plants need, it is necessary to inventory soil elements at the present time. The primary test for nitrogen, phosphorus, and potassium is known as the "complete soil test for nutrients." Amounts of the three major nutrient elements are diagnosed and allow you to adjust your fertilizing practices to fit particular plants' needs.

I highly recommend an additional soil-nutrient analysis, particularly if you have been growing the same or a similar crop in the same area, year after year. This test is for secondary and minor or trace elements. Growing plants year after year, in the same spot in the garden or in the same soil in a container, slowly depletes the soil of its nutrients and may result in poor growth.

There are soil-testing kits, available through garden-supply catalogs and local garden centers, for the major primary elements and for the secondary and trace elements. If you follow the directions explicitly, you can accomplish a complete analysis with relative ease. Because the testing is somewhat time-consuming, you may want to have your soil samples analyzed by a professional soil-testing laboratory. There are specific, recommended procedures for preparing soil samples for testing by a professional lab. Check with your local Cooperative Extension Association or the soils laboratory at your state university for recommendations of soil-testing laboratories in your area. Whether you wish to test your soil yourself or have it done professionally, don't wait to the last minute. It may take some time to find a supply for all the nutrients that your soil might be missing. One more point: Keep good records of your test analysis and what you do to correct any deficiencies. This information will give you a reference point for future testing.

SOIL MANAGEMENT

Improving and managing soil is a real science, one which all gardeners should undertake. Good soil management includes matching the crop to the soil, adding organic matter, rotating crops, erosion control, and the proper use of lime and fertilizer.

I don't know how many times gardeners have explained to me that they have tried, time and time again, to grow a specific plant in their garden, with nothing but poor results. It just might be that they did not match the plant to the soil conditions. The soil may be too alkaline or too acid for a particular species of plant. Azaleas and rhododendrons prefer acid soil conditions, while asparagus roots enjoy more alkalinity. Drainage and permeability may not be adequate for root development, the cause of many crop failures of carrots and other root crops. It doesn't pay to try to grow carrots in a hard, clay soil.

Organic matter is an essential soil component, and whether you are an indoor or outdoor gardener, there will be many times when you need to add organic matter to your soil. It not only gives color to the soil and holds particles together, but it increases moisture-holding-capacity and ability of the soil to hold more nutrients. Any soil management scheme must include the addition of organic matter to the soil. It can be added by physically tilling or spading well-rotted compost, peat moss, steer manure, or

other matter into the soil. Organic matter can also be grown into the soil. Planting a cover crop of annual rye late in the fall and spading it into the soil in spring is an easy way to incorporate beneficial organic matter. Every time you grow a plant, the roots from that plant decay in the soil and become humic acid.

Rotation of crops will help reduce the likelihood of nutrient deficiencies. In the vegetable patch, you might grow peas in a given area one year to restore the nitrogen balance. The next year you might grow corn, a crop that enjoys the nitrogen build-up. Another benefit of crop rotation is natural control of insect pests and diseases. This will be explored in much greater detail in Chapter VIII, Integrated Pest Management (IPM).

Soils management also includes keeping the soil in place, erosion control. Let's hope that we learned our lesson from the "dust bowl" days of the 1930s. It is a *must* that we prevent erosion by rain and wind. The best control is to keep a healthy cover crop growing over the soil surface. Other practices that will reduce or eliminate erosion include, for large-scale agriculture: no-till or strip cropping; contour tillage; and terracing. For the smaller garden, employ such practices as using mulches, cover crops, and terracing. For the deck or patio container-grower, erosion control might be accomplished just by moving the container out of the wind and rain.

Lime is the adjustment valve for soil. Lime alters nutrient release and activates bacterial action. In order to find out how much lime is necessary in the garden or in that flowerpot, a simple "pH test" is used. This tests for the hydrogen ion concentration in the soil—that is, soil acidity or alkalinity. The pH scale ranges from zero, which is extremely acid, to seven, which is neutral, to fourteen, which is very basic or alkaline. Of any tests done for soil, the pH or acidity test will pay the greatest dividends, and is the least expensive.

You can purchase a pH soil-test kit at your local garden center and perform the function yourself. Simply remove the upper two inches of soil before taking the soil sample. Otherwise, extraneous organic material and residues from nutrients could adversely affect the test. Take multiple soil samples about four to five inches deep (about a cup) from each garden area, mix them thoroughly, and allow them to air-dry. Results obtained from testing wet soil can vary greatly, so it is best to use dry soil samples. In a small garden area it is all right to mix your samples for a single test. For a large garden area, where different crops are being grown each with different soil pH requirements, it is advisable to test separate samples. Remember, some crops like acid soil and some like it more alkaline.

It is not necessary to do an annual pH test, but if you have had to substantially adjust the pH of the soil, I recommend it. Soil pH changes gradually, and six months may pass before results are visible. Soil pH tests based on a color-chart comparison cannot be done by a color-blind person. In this case, you can use an electronic pH meter for your test. There are several meters that not only test for pH but also test for primary nutrients.

Changes in pH may occur because of leaching. The natural process of rainwater percolating down through the soil carries calcium ions out of the soil. Another natural influence on soil pH is the removal of calcium by the crop. A man-made influence, acid rain, depending on its source of pollutants, can lower the soil pH dramatically.

Lime comes basically in two forms: limestone and hydrated lime. Limestone, the regular agricultural lime, is calcium carbonate. Hydrated lime or burnt lime is calcium hydroxide and calcium oxide. Limestone can be added at any time of the year. It takes a long period of time, generally six months, for it to change the pH of the soil. So, don't instantly repeat your pH test. Hydrated lime, on the other hand, will provide an instant change. Hydrated lime is generally not used in gardening because it can cause root burn and death of the plant if applied improperly.

You may have had the experience of applying lime to your lawn on a windy day. When finished, you looked like a snow-white polar bear. Probably you applied a bag of pulverized limestone, the least expensive but very powdery. One product on the market,

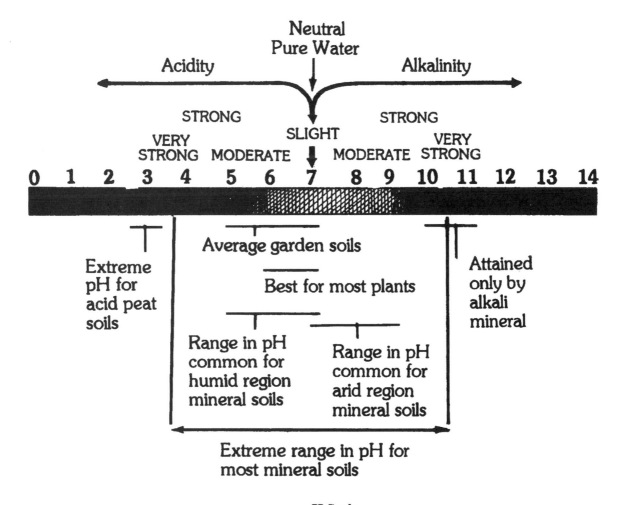

pH Scale

called pelletized lime, provides uniformity in size and eliminates most of the dust problem. Once the bonding agent used to make pellets from the pulverized lime has been moistened, the very fine granules make contact with the soil and begin their reaction. Of any garden practice, adding lime, if it is necessary, can give the biggest bang for your buck. If soil is too acid, applying nutrients may do no good. Mineral elements are so tightly bound to the soil's negative charges that they are not available to the plant. With a properly adjusted pH or soil acidity, the fertilizer you add can provide fantastic results.

Adjusting the soil pH downward from an alkaline level will release mineral elements such as manganese, iron, and zinc for plant consumption. A high pH is typical in arid regions where calcium is abundant in the soil. In the garden, elemental sulfur, ferrous sulfate, and calcium sulfate can be added to the soil to lower the pH to a more desirable level. For your house plants and container-grown ornamentals, mixing acid-forming decomposed organic matter such as pine needles, leaf compost, or shredded bark in your soil mix will lower the soil pH.

The adjustment valve for encouraging growth of desirable soil bacteria and organisms, lime is often overlooked. Changing the pH of the soil to a desirable level can promote beneficial bacteria, fungi, algae, and soil insect life, all essential to decomposing dead organic matter in the soil.

When you go to the garden center or plant shop, you notice a multitude of fertilizer formulations on the shelf; all say "theirs" is the best. Are you confused? Well, it might be simpler than you think. On any fertilizer being sold as a complete formula, the label displays three numbers separated by dashes. An example is 10-6-4. This means the nutrient content of the fertilizer is 10 percent nitrogen (N), 6 percent available phosphorus (P_2O_5), and 4 percent available potassium (K_2O). These are known as the NPK numbers, and always reflect the same order of nutrients: nitrogen, phosphorus and potassium. You will find many complete formulas available: 5-10-5, 15-30-15, 20-20-20, 8-7-6, 19-24-18, and so on. You can also find formulas that do not contain a complete meal for your plant. For example, 0-20-0 indicates 0 percent nitrogen, 20 percent available phosphorus, and 0 percent available potassium. There are many different single-element fertilizers on the shelf.

The sources of nutrients in fertilizer are either chemical or organic. With few exceptions, a plant cannot distinguish sources, because a nutrient must be broken down to ion elements before it is ingested by the plant. There are many sources of nutrients. Nitrogen is available from both inorganic and organic forms. Some inorganic forms of nitrogen are nitrate of soda, calcium nitrite, ammonium sulfate, urea, ammonium phosphate, and urea-form fertilizers. Urea-form fertilizers are a more recent advance in the field of chemical fertilizers, providing an extremely slow-releasing form of nitrogen that eliminates the danger of "burning." Some

Plant Nutrients

organic sources of nitrogen in fertilizer are dried blood, bat and bird guano, fish emulsion, cocoa shells, cottonseed meal, linseed, soy bean meal, and unflavored gelatin. Recent research shows unflavored gelatin provides 16 percent nitrogen in the amino-acid form. This means it is readily available for plant use.

Phosphorus is essential to all functions of plant growth. Some sources of phosphorus are superphosphate, basic slag, bone meal, and rock phosphate, as well as bat and bird guano. Phosphorus is fixed in the soil soon after application, and it does not leach out. Adding phosphorus to the soil mix, or thoroughly stirring it into the bottom of the hole before planting, is therefore advantageous. I add a handful of bone meal, 22 percent to 27 percent available phosphorus, to the bottom of the hole for all my bulbs and other flowering perennials.

Potassium is valuable in promoting general vigor and helps to increase resistance of plants to certain diseases. Potassium is found in potassium chloride, muriate of potash, potassium sulfate, wood ashes, and kelp or seaweed.

THE COMPOST PILE— MAKING THE GARDENER'S "BLACK GOLD"

Of any single source of organic matter, the compost pile has the greatest value. A compost pile can be the cheapest source of organic matter, and the best. Instead of taking them to a dump, save your grass clippings, sod, leaves, refuse from the vegetable garden, and many types of animal manure for your compost pile. In fact, many communities today forbid garden refuse to join the solid-waste stream.

To construct a compost pile, find an area in the garden that is out of the way but exposed to the weather. I learned from experience not to place a compost pile next to actively growing plants. One year I built my pile next to a berry patch. The roots from the plants quickly grew into my pile and made it almost impossible to use. With your garden spade, dig a dishlike area approximately six inches deep and the size the compost pile will cover. The size of the pile directly relates to the amount of garden waste generated during the year. Save the soil from the dished-out area by neatly piling it next to the compost area. The "dish area" will help collect moisture during wintertime. It is not absolutely necessary to make a cage around your compost pile, but it will keep the layers of decaying organic matter much neater. Once your cage is in place, you can start adding clippings, leaves, weeds, and refuse from the garden. After adding a layer of organic matter approximately one foot thick, spread two to three inches from the soil pile over it. Always be sure the center of the pile is dished inward, so that it can collect rainfall. If it hasn't rained by the time you are ready to add the next layer, thoroughly wet the pile with water. You can continue adding layers as the season progresses. With each new layer, remember to add two or three inches of soil to cover it. This soil will provide bacteria necessary to properly break down organic matter. I do not add lime to my compost pile, because I do not know which plants will be using it. Some plants like acid mixes and some do not. I simply add lime at the time of planting. When the season ends, I wet my completed compost pile thoroughly. If winter brings no snow or rain, I make certain to wet my pile about midwinter. To hasten the composting process, you can spade the compost pile into another big pile, though I do not do this. When spring arrives, the center of my compost pile is ready to use. It has become the black liquid called humic acid, or the gardener's "Black Gold." Since I did not turn my pile, the outer shell has not completely decayed. I rake off the outer layer into my dirt pile. This partly decayed material is loaded with bacteria eager to act, making a perfect base for my next compost pile.

The only plant material or garden waste that I don't add to my compost is from tomatoes, eggplants, peppers, squash, melons, and cucumbers. The upper parts of these plants can contain potential diseases that I don't want to entertain. Don't add meat scraps to your compost pile, either. They will inevitably attract rodents, an unhealthy risk to take; and dog feces are not recommended, since they can contain parasites harmful to humans. A good, actively working compost pile gives a giant boost to your garden.

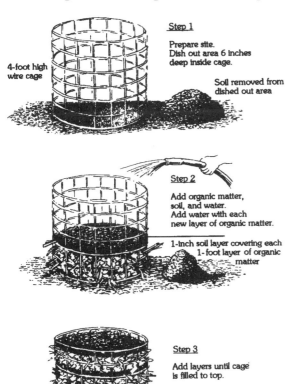

Step 1

Prepare site.
Dish out area 6 inches deep inside cage.

4-foot high wire cage

Soil removed from dished out area

Step 2

Add organic matter, soil, and water.
Add water with each new layer of organic matter.

1-inch soil layer covering each 1-foot layer of organic matter

Step 3

Add layers until cage is filled to top.

Composting

POTTING SOILS AND POTTING MIXES

For centuries, soils have been experimentally mixed, mixed, and remixed. Each gardener has his best mix, his "secret" mix. His *is* the best and he will swear to it.

It is good to have a basic potting mix that can be altered to fit the needs of almost any plant. If you go to a garden shop today, you will find a multitude of bagged soils, potting soils, and potting mixes from which to choose. I counted fourteen different kinds at one garden center. They included two different brands of sterilized soil; two all-purpose potting soils; three all-purpose potting mixes; one professional-mix potting soil; one professional-grower potting mix; one professional potting mix; one professional all-purpose potting mix; one cactus potting mix; and two African violet potting mixes.

If we understand the differences among the various bags' contents, we can select the right consistency for our plants, or we can amend a mix to fit our plants' needs. You must read the list of ingredients. Different components include topsoil, sand, perlite, sphagnum peat moss, vermiculite, compost, lime, nutrient blends, and even a wetting agent.

If we know the purpose of each ingredient, we can determine which blend or mix will best suit our plants. Bagged sterilized soil is generally treated to eliminate weed seeds, pests, and some soil-borne plant pathogens. Sand, silt, and clay contents of soil will vary due to origin. Most come from stripping soil from the field. I use bagged soil as one ingredient in my standard potting mix.

Sand is usually a coarse, clean builder's grade, also know as horticultural grade. As we've discussed, sand is used to improve drainage and aeration in the soil or mix. You will find substantial sand quantities in a standard cactus mix.

Perlite is a transformed type of volcanic rock, heat-treated to 1,800 degrees Fahrenheit, which produces the white, gritty granules often found in a potting mix. Horticultural grade perlite is often used as a sand substitute because it is lightweight (dry weight equals six to nine pounds per cubic foot). By using perlite instead of sand in a standard 1:1:1 mix (one part soil, one part peat moss, one part sand or perlite), overall weight can be reduced by as much as one third. Perlite's ability to hold moisture and air in the soil makes it a primary ingredient in many light-weight potting mixes.

Sphagnum peat moss is stripped from decaying peat bogs, created over centuries by nature. Peat moss is decidedly acid, with a pH range between 3.5 and 5.0. Peat moss is valuable to the gardener as a soil additive. We mix peat moss into garden soil to improve soil structure, and as peat moss deteriorates, it improves aeration, drainage, and moisture-holding capacity. Sphagnum peat moss is the primary ingredient in professional propagation mixes because of its disease-inhibiting properties. It is also a standard ingredient in many potting mixes, adding organic bulk.

Vermiculite, the "gold-looking" flakes often found in potting mixes and professional propagation mixes, is a sterile, heat-treated mica-type rock. Its value in horticulture resides in its moisture-holding properties. Vermiculite is often used in soil mixes for plants that like to be slightly moist at all times. I have found it very advantageous to use as much as 20 percent by volume in my standard potting mix for container plants like impatiens and coleus. If you tend to over-water plants, use vermiculite very sparingly, if at all.

Compost might be nothing more than what you obtain from your own compost pile. It is screened and milled into a fine-textured blend of decaying organic matter. It is the bulk organic matter often used instead of peat moss in a mix.

Lime is added to a peat moss potting mix to adjust the pH, increasing its nutrient availability. Without lime, plant nutrients may be needed in amounts exceeding their recommended rate.

Nutrients are often added to get plants off to a good start. They may include one, a few, or all of the primary and secondary elements needed by your plant. Just because the bag advertised nutrients in the soil, your responsibility for feeding your plants in the future is not relieved.

A wetting agent is added to some mixes particularly high in peat moss so moisture can be absorbed more readily. The wetting agent increases the moisture penetration of moisture into the organic fibers of the mix. If you have ever tried to wet some dry peat moss, you know the value of the wetting agent.

From the ingredients listed above, you can make your own potting mix to suit your plants' needs. My standard potting mix is rather simple to prepare. It is by volume one part soil, one part peat moss or compost, and one part sharp builder's sand or perlite; that makes it a 1:1:1 ratio. It is the mix I use for nearly all my house plants. For those plants requiring better drainage and aeration for their roots, I add as much as two parts sharp builder's sand or perlite. Very few plants fail to grow in this mixture.

With the increasing popularity of window-sill and rooftop gardening, horticultural experts have developed many lightweight growing mixes. Original work done at Cornell University gave rise to the "Cornell soilless mix." This artificial soilless mix contains two bushels of shredded peat, one bushel of horticultural vermiculite, ten tablespoons of limestone, five tablespoons of superphosphate-20 percent, two tablespoons of potassium nitrate, 14-0-44, and one teaspoon of chelated iron. This mixture is thoroughly stirred to incorporate all ingredients evenly, and results in two bushels of artificial soilless mix. You will find many variations of this mix on the market today. Over the years, I have altered the Cornell mix to increase its air-holding capacity by adding perlite in place of vermiculite. An obvious advantage of the soilless mix for the indoor gardener is its light weight.

All ingredients used to make the soilless mixes are available through your local garden center or plant shop: Regular potting soil may be purchased in small and large quantities; peat moss may be purchased in cubic-foot to six-cubic-foot bales; perlite and vermiculite in the three-cubic-foot bags or smaller; and ground limestone, superphosphate and additional fertilizers may be added at recommended rates.

As you become a connoisseur of gardening, you will learn soil characteristics and how to make a plant grow in each type. You will learn watering and fertilizing requirements of an individual soil or soil mix. Odds are, you will kill a few plants as you learn, but don't give up.

QUESTIONS AND ANSWERS

1. **Q. Is it worthwhile to start a compost pile?**
   A. It sure is. Composting is one of the most environmentally sound procedures we can use in today's garden. Some communities are demanding organic recycling to save space in landfills. With the pressure on sanitary landfill operations, it is a must for the gardener to recycle as much garden waste as possible. If you have the space and a good location, waste materials can be transformed into a valuable organic mixture to incorporate in the soil of vegetable gardens and flower beds, or it can be used as the organic component in backfill for planting trees and shrubs.

2. **Q. Is it true that limestone added to a lawn makes fertilizer more effective?**
   A. Yes! Generally, if the soil is acid, you lose much of the value of applied fertilizer. At a pH of 5.0, as much as 40 percent of the fertilizer value is lost when compared to fertilizer applied to a soil with a pH of 6.0.

3. **Q. My soil is very alkaline. What should I do so I can grow azaleas and rhododendrons?**
   A. Composted organic matter and sulfur can be added to the soil in the planting area and mixed to a depth of two feet. Both compost and sulfur can be used to lower the pH to a range acceptable to rhododendrons and azaleas. Another alternative would be to replace the soil in question with acid-rich humus.

4. **Q. Do rhododendrons, azaleas, and mountain laurel require special soil?**
   A. They prefer an acid soil condition. You should have twelve to eighteen inches of topsoil containing up to 50 percent acid humus, above a well-drained subsoil. To

create an acid humus, use peat moss, spruce, pine, hemlock, or oak leaf mold. Peat moss mixed with a small quantity of well-rotted manure makes a good soil for these plants.

5. **Q. Can aluminum sulfate be used to acidify and condition alkaline soil around rhododendrons?**

    A. If soil is rich in humus matter, yes, but sulfur is safer. To maintain a properly acid condition, it will be necessary to apply it periodically. Do not expect to be successful with aluminum sulfate where the soils are poor in humus. Acidity is only one consideration in preparing soils.

6. **Q. Do coffee and tea grounds help acidify the soil?**

    A. No, not to any marked degree. Coffee grounds can supply limited quantities of organic matter and potassium. Both tea and coffee grounds can be added to the compost pile.

7. **Q. I have very sandy soil and my trees and shrubs do not grow well. What can I do?**

    A. Incorporate a liberal quantity of peat moss, leaf mold or humus, and some well-rotted manure to the backfill at planting time. Organic matter improves the structure of sandy soils by increasing nutrient and moisture-holding capacity. It is preferable to plan before you plant by selecting varieties of trees and shrubs that are especially suited for light, very sandy soil.

8. **Q. Why do we need to fertilize plants?**

    A. Fertilizers are used to supply the essential elements required by normal plant growth.

9. **Q. A soil test indicated there is a need for phosphorus and potash in my flower and vegetable garden. How can I correct this deficiency?**

    A. Apply commercial fertilizers, such as 0-10-10 or 0-20-20. Superphosphate and muriate of potash can be used separately to supply phosphorus and potassium, respectively.

10. **Q. Can I spade or till clay soil when it is wet?**

    A. Absolutely not. Handling wet clay soil will create a compacted condition, making a poor growing environment for roots of plants. If dug too soon in the spring, you may make soil practically useless for the whole season.

11. **Q. What is an inorganic fertilizer?**

    A. Inorganic fertilizer is derived from mineral or chemical substances, such as phosphate rock, potash salts, and nitrate salts (nitrate of soda).

12. **Q. I prefer not to use chemical fertilizers in my city garden. What alternatives can I use to provide nutrients?**

    A. To add nitrogen use blood meal, soybean meal, cottonseed meal, or dried manures. To add phosphorus use bone meal or rock phosphate. To add potash, use kelp meal or greensand.

13. **Q. How is humus important to soil fertility?**

    A. Humus supplies negative ions to the soil particles, which increases the nutrient-holding capacity of essential elements, especially nitrogen.

14. **Q. Why is sulfur recommended for use in some soils?**

    A. Sulfur is used to increase the acidity of soil. If a soil pH test indicates the soil is alkaline, sulfur may be added to lower the pH.

15. **Q. Will wood ashes be beneficial if used in heavy clay soil?**

A. Wood ashes will supply calcium and potash, and raise the pH of clay soil. Use at least ten pounds per hundred square feet.

16. **Q. My soil is high in organic content and drains well. Can I use wood ashes or the ashes from burning leaves for my garden?**
A. Yes. Wood and leaf ashes contain potash and lime, which are of value to organic soils. I prefer to compost leaves and *then* add them to the soil.

17. **Q. I think the humus in my potting soil keeps it too moist. What can I do?**
A. Incorporate sand or perlite to improve aeration and drainage.

18. **Q. What nutrients are in cottonseed meal?**
A. Cottonseed meal is primarily a source of nitrogen at approximately 7 percent, but also supplies 2.5 percent phosphoric acid, and 1.5 percent potash.

19. **Q. Kitchen garbage: Should it, or shouldn't it, be added to the compost heap?**
A. Most kitchen garbage is a great source of compost. However, do not add meat scraps or meat drippings, as they tend to encourage rodents and neighbors' dogs to dig in the pile. Cover the garbage with soil to prevent odors. You could place garbage in a pit that is some distance from the house and sprinkle it with soil and raw ground limestone. Then, when the contents are decomposed, it could be added in layers to a new compost heap. By doing this, the garbage is decomposed underground (no odor) and the rodents are kept out of the compost heap.

20. **Q. How fast do grass clippings decay if I add them to the compost pile?**
A. If a two-inch layer of grass clippings are added to the compost pile, mixed with a four-inch layer of soil, it will be ready for use the next spring.

21. **Q. A bag of fertilizer stated on the front label, "Contains trace elements," and I noticed it was much more expensive than those that didn't have such content. What are "trace" elements?**
A. They are micronutrients, such as magnesium, boron, manganese, and cooper, which are present in most soils, in addition to the major elements of nitrogen, phosphorus, and potassium. They are needed in such small quantities for plant nutrition that they are referred to as trace elements.

22. **Q. I am starting a vegetable garden. What is the best fertilizer to use?**
A. In general, I recommend a 5-10-5 fertilizer, or its equivalent, for most vegetables. If you plan to grow tuber crops (potatoes) or root crops (beets), I would say a 0-10-10 fertilizer, or its equivalent.

23. **Q. Can I incorporate sawdust in my soil?**
A. Sawdust, as it breaks down in the soil, will produce an acid condition and may cause nitrogen-deficiency symptoms. Rather than apply raw sawdust to the soil, compost it first.

24. **Q. How often should I apply lime? What time of the year? How much?**
A. The only way to tell if lime is needed in soil is to perform a soil pH test and test for calcium content. For general soil maintenance of a flower or vegetable garden, apply lime about once every three or four years. Apply it during late fall or early spring, so it will leach down deeply into the soil. Use about ten to twenty lbs of limestone per one hundred square feet. Limestone takes up to six months to begin to provide benefits. Heavy applications of ground limestone may be applied without doing harm, but they do little more good than a light application.

25. **Q. What is the value of lime, besides its use to sweeten a sour soil? My soil is not sour and is a heavy clay.**

A. Lime not only neutralizes, or sweetens, a sour soil, it renders other plant foods available. It is of value on a clay soil because it flocculates clay, making it more porous and granular. On a sandy soil, it has the opposite value, in that it cements particles of sand together. It increases the growth of pea- and beanlike plants, in other words, legumes, by favoring growth of beneficial bacteria that change organic matter into nitrates that can be used by plants. Lime acts upon the poisonous iron compounds and other toxic substances formed in soil. Lime is not a fertilizer in the true sense, but is indirectly of value.

26.   Q. **I would like to grow a collection of rhododendrons, azaleas, mountain laurel, trailing arbutus, and andromeda but I have a limy soil. Can it be made acid enough to grow members of the heath family?**
      A. Members of the heath family prefer an acid soil. If these plants are to be grown in a limestone region, the soil must be treated to produce an acid condition. Dig out the beds to a good depth and fill with silica sand mixed with acid-producing organic matter, like oak leaf or sawdust compost. Further acidification can be accomplished by applying aluminum sulphate; about one half pound to the square yard is needed. Cottonseed meal should be used as a fertilizer.

27.   Q. **I have a weed called sorrel that is growing in my perennial border and vegetable garden. I have been told that if this weed grows in a particular soil, that means the soil is sour. How can I test it?**
      A. If sorrel is a weed in your garden, there is reason to believe the soil is acid. Sorrel loves acid-type soils. An easy and quick test is with litmus paper. Litmus paper is blue, pink or neutral. Apply a piece of it to moist, acid soil, and the blue or neutral litmus paper will turn red or pink; if the soil is alkaline, pink or neutral paper will turn blue. Do not touch the litmus paper with your fingers, as the paper will react with the acid in your skin. Litmus paper may be purchased from your local druggist. Commercial soil pH test kits are also available.

28.   Q. **What value are nitrate fertilizers?**
      A. Nitrate fertilizers are used to encourage leaf growth, to cause a greener appearance of foliage plants, and to increase the size of flowers when applied to plants in bud. In the vegetable patch, nitrates produce fast leaf growth on spinach, lettuce, and Swiss chard. Excessive use of nitrogen keeps the plant growing vegetatively and delays flowering and fruiting. The result is an overgrown plant that needs staking.

29.   Q. **What is the value of bone meal?**
      A. Bone meal contains phosphorus which is a primary element used in making good flowers and stiff stems. If used too freely, it merely stays in the soil until used by the plants. Enough bone meal should be applied to whiten the soil, and then it should be cultivated into the upper layer.

30.   Q. **Is manure tea or liquid manure a good source of nutrients?**
      A. An excellent source of nitrogen, liquid manure is made by suspending a sack of manure into a barrel of water. It is used for flowers that are just coming into bud, leaf crops, and for all purposes where plants are not doing well. To prevent possible burn from liquid manure, water the plants thoroughly before application of the manure tea, or use it only in a greatly diluted solution.

31.   Q. **How can I prevent an odor from developing in a compost pile?**
      A. Cover the decaying vegetation with garden soil to absorb the moisture. The soil will suppress any objectionable odors.

32.   Q. **Will salt adhering to seaweed cause problems with garden soil?**
      A. Salty coated seaweed is useful to chlorine-tolerant, sodium-loving plants such as

cabbage, spinach, potatoes, beets and most other root crops. The salt may cause injuries to some tender young plants. If there is any doubt, wash the weed well before spreading it.

33. Q. **Should a bluegrass lawn be limed each spring?**
    A. Bluegrass prefers a pH range of 6.2 to 7.0. If a soil pH test indicates the need to correct acidity, apply lime. Keeping the proper pH range will make existing soil nutrients available to the grass plants. Lime will also increase bacterial action in the soil, important in controlling thatch.

34. Q. **I was told moss growing in my lawn is an indication of a highly acid soil. I had the soil tested and the results indicated a pH of 6.8—just slightly acid. So how could acid be the cause?**
    A. A pH of 6.8 would not likely be the only cause. Moss and algae growth can be due to a combination of too much shade, poor drainage and dampness, compacted soil, nutrient deficiency, and/or soil acidity. I doubt that the soil acidity is the major cause. Check for other contributing factors. Moss seldom invades a dense, vigorously growing lawn.

35. Q. **Is it necessary to put lime on the garden every year?**
    A. In most garden soils, no. Test the soil pH to determine the need for lime. Lime is the adjustment valve in the soil. It releases nutrients and increases bacterial action. If needed, apply agricultural lime in the fall, so it has time to react with the soil particles before spring.

36. Q. **I live in an area where the soil is made up largely of stones. It seems as though my soil is growing stones. Every spring, I "harvest" bushels of them before I plant my crops. Do they continually work to the surface? If so, why?**
    A. In areas where soil alternately freezes and thaws during winter, stones do seem to "grow." The expansion of ice crystals between the soil particles or stones causes them to be forced to the surface. This is the direction of least resistance. During winters with deep freezing of soil, the stone crop may be larger.

37. Q. **What depth of topsoil should be added to a sandy ground? I intend to put in a bluegrass lawn.**
    A. Add three to four inches of loam to the surface and till or spade it into the sandy ground to a depth of six inches. Additional organic matter, in the form of peat moss or compost incorporated into the mix, will prevent the soil from being washed down into the sand.

38. Q. **I purchased several truckloads of topsoil from a farm to enrich my soil, but results were poor. What is wrong? I thought topsoil was a good investment.**
    A. Topsoil is soil from the top. It could have been taken from a worn-out, abandoned field having little nutrient value. Before purchasing topsoil in quantity, submit a soil sample to a soils testing lab for complete soil analysis. Your Cooperative Extension Agent can give direction in submitting a soil sample.

39. Q. **What is gypsum?**
    A. Gypsum is calcium sulfate. It can be used to provide calcium when it is not necessary to decrease acidity. In compact clay soils, gypsum is used to improve drainage and soil aeration.

40. Q. **My local farm supply store has raw ground limestone available. Will it work in my garden soil? It is substantially cheaper than the pulverized or pelletized lime.**
    A. Yes, it will work. Raw ground limestone is calcium carbonate and is the material most commonly used for counteracting acidity. It is also known as agricultural lime.

41. Q. Can I raise the pH of soil with something other than lime.?

A. Wood ashes, pulverized eggshells and ground sea shells will all reduce soil acidity to varying degrees. Keep track of changes in acidity by performing a soil pH test on an annual basis.

42. Q. My peonies are growing in a sunny perennial garden and produce large green leaves with little or no blossom. What fertilizer do they need?

A. Since the peonies are producing large green leaves, stay away from fertilizers containing nitrogen for a year or two. Peonies need phosphorus and potash for flower production. Select a 0-10-10 fertilizer to provide phosphorus and potassium. Feed them just as the new shoots emerge in the spring and again as they start to bud. Bone meal and wood ashes can supply phosphorus and potassium as well.

43. Q. I purchased "giant" dahlias last year so I would have exhibition flowers for a local flower show. When it came time for flowering, all I had were large, green-leafed plants with few blossoms. What went wrong? Did they sell me the wrong plants?

A. The plants were probably the right variety. Either you used a fertilizer that contained too much nitrogen or your soil is too high in nitrogen content. Excess nitrogen will keep dahlias growing vegetatively, but with fewer flowers as a consequence.

44. Q. I have access to unlimited quantities of fresh chicken manure from a local poultry farm. Is there any danger of overmanuring with fresh chicken manure?

A. Chicken manure contains a quickly available nitrogen. Fresh chicken manure, if applied in excess, will "burn" the roots of sensitive plants. Compost the manure to reduce the potential of burn, and use it sparingly, no more than five pounds per one hundred square feet around new seedlings or transplants.

45. Q. Muriate of potash is available in five-pound bags at my garden center. How should it be used as a separate fertilizer?

A. Muriate of potash supplies potassium, a water-soluble nutrient easily leached from soil. Potassium is an essential element for root, stem and flower development. Potassium deficiencies often occur as stunted growth, particularly in sandy soils. Follow the label directions for side-dressing. Response will often be spectacular.

46. Q. What is meant by "side-dressing"?

A. Side-dressing is the application of supplemental nutrients over the root system of the plant. It is a term used when scattering a little fertilizer along rows in a vegetable garden. The fertilizer is usually applied as a light dusting and then cultivated or watered into the soil.

47. Q. Do newly planted trees and shrubs benefit from fertilizers added to the backfill?

A. Yes, slow-release fertilizers are a particularly valuable addition to backfill at planting time. It is the one time you can ensure proper placement of nutrients in relation to developing roots.

48. Q. Can fertilizer be applied to a bluegrass lawn in late fall instead of early spring?

A. Of any single application of fertilizer to a bluegrass lawn, one applied in late fall provides the most benefit. A slow-release nitrogen turf fertilizer in the form of IBDU (isobutylidene diurea) or sulfur-coated urea will feed the grass gradually, all winter long. When applied in the spring, slow-release nitrogen fertilizers do not green up the lawn as quickly because soil bacteria, which convert the nitrogen nutrients for plant use, do not become active until the soil warms.

49. Q. Is cottonseed meal a good fertilizer for rhododendrons, azaleas, and other acid-loving plants? If so, when should it be applied?

A. Yes, cottonseed meal is a recommended fertilizer for acid-loving plants. It is an

organic product, slow to break down, so should be applied during spring when the soil is moist. As with other organic sources of nutrients, it does not become available to the plant until the spring soil temperatures begin to warm. Follow the package directions for rates of application for acid-loving plants.

50. **Q. When preparing a new garden should fertilizer be tilled into soil?**

A. Absolutely yes. This is the time that nutrients can be added, by spading or tilling, to a depth where they will benefit the root systems of the plant. A preplanting fertilizer should be particularly high in phosphorus and potash, as these chemicals do not move readily downward through the soil. Work the soil and fertilizer as deep as practicable, six to ten inches down. Do not forget other improvements, such as adding composted organic matter or peat moss.

51. **Q. My neighbor uses one formula of fertilizer for root vegetables (beets, carrots) and another formula for leafy vegetables (lettuce, Swiss chard). Why?**

A. In general, leafy vegetables require more nitrogen than phosphorus and potash. Root crops—beets, radish, onions, and carrots—use more potash. If nutrients are available, plants are able to discriminate fairly well and take up what they need, so a general all-purpose vegetable garden fertilizer, 5-10-5, will do.

If the garden is divided, root crops on one side, leafy vegetables on another, it might pay to use a low-nitrogen fertilizer on the root-crop side and a higher-nitrogen fertilizer on the leafy vegetables. If you are growing by the acre, the money saved is worthwhile; in the home garden, the question is academic.

52. **Q. Can I substitute homemade compost for fertilizer?**

A. Homemade compost is an excellent source of organic matter for soil improvement, but usually too low in actual nutrition to serve as fertilizer. Compost does supply trace elements, made available from the decaying organic matter.

53. **Q. Can "overliming" cause injury to plants?**

A. Too much lime causes soil to become alkaline and, in some plants, creates deficiency symptoms of some elements, such as boron, manganese, iron, and zinc. These elements are not soluble in an alkaline solution. Usually growth is chlorotic (yellow). Depending on the extent of overliming, the condition can be corrected by applying sulfur to the soil. More than one application may be necessary to bring about the desired acidity.

54. **Q. How can I improve moisture-holding capacity and improve drainage of a dry, acid, heavy clay soil?**

A. Both moisture-holding capacity and drainage can be improved by adding organic matter in the form of compost or peat moss. Each time you work the soil, incorporate four to six inches of the organic matter to a depth of eight to ten inches. Pulverized limestone can be added at the same time to improve the acid condition. Test for pH improvement before and after each treatment.

55. **Q. Why is it not recommended to mix and apply lime and chemical fertilizer at the same time?**

A. The abrasive contact of lime particles and certain fertilizers such as superphosphate can chemically reduce the solubility and availability of the fertilizer. It is not a problem if the two products are applied separately, even on the same day.

56. **Q. What is the best way to counteract a highly alkaline soil condition?**

A. Sulfur or ammonium sulfate is used to alter alkalinity. The amount required of either material is dependent on the soil pH. Acid compost or peat moss is also a benefit in lowering soil alkalinity.

57. **Q. How can I recognize phosphorus deficiency?**

A. Phosphorus deficiency often results in dwarfed growth. The foliage is a dull, dark green having purplish leaf petioles. The cells between veins in the leaf sometimes turn purple, and the leaf margins often turn yellow. Following the onset of phosphorus deficiency, loss of lower foliage may occur.

58. **Q. We garden in a delta region and the soil is a heavy, black gumbo that bakes badly during the summer. Is there any hope for improving this type of soil?**

A. Add organic matter and coarse sand every time you work the soil. A well-rotted compost of sawdust and manure will provide fiber, hold moisture, and separate the soil particles.

59. **Q. What is a "well-drained soil" and what is "waterlogged soil"?**

A. A well-drained soil allows water to penetrate quickly after heavy watering or heavy rainfall. It reestablishes the water/air balance between the soil particles in a short time. A waterlogged soil is the opposite, holding too much water and little air for long periods of time. A waterlogged soil develops anaerobic conditions promoting root rot.

60. **Q. A white clay soil becomes hard and compacted after a rain. Will peat moss improve this condition?**

A. Peat moss will help, but the best improvement would be to add decomposed organic matter, in the form of humic acid, the black liquid which is the end product of compost.

61. **Q. Our vegetable garden soil is very sandy and acid. We have to water too much, and our plants look chlorotic. What should we do to sweeten the soil and improve its moisture-holding capacity?**

A. Each year, after finishing the harvest and cleaning up the garden, increase the organic content by growing and incorporating a green-manure crop. A green-manure crop for a vegetable patch could be annual winter rye. Plant the winter rye during late fall and till the rye plants into the soil when preparing the garden during spring. The roots of the green-manure crop will grow deep into the sand and they will gradually build an organic base for holding moisture. Apply lime as needed to modify the acidity.

62. **Q. Does the American Holly prefer a light, sandy soil?**

A. Yes, the fibrous root system of American holly prefers a light, sandy soil, containing some decaying leaf mold. Heavy clay soils should be avoided or improved when planting hollies.

63. **Q. I purchased dried cow manure for feeding my tomatoes, eggplants, and peppers in the vegetable garden? Should I use any other nutrients?**

A. To ensure maximum production, add superphosphate and muriate of potash to provide a balanced fertilizer mix for your fruiting vegetables. Cow manure by itself may stimulate only vegetative growth.

64. **Q. Is snow really called "poor man's manure"?**

A. Snow sure is the poor man's fertilizer because it absorbs the ammonia from the air, and prevents nitrogen loss from soil below. Small quantities of nitric acid are also contained in snow. These elements, combined with the sun's rays, provide nutrition much like a light top-dressing of manure.

65. **Q. Is superphosphate needed in the garden?**

A. Superphosphate provides phosphorus in one of its most economical forms. It is a commercial fertilizer which has the same use as bone meal. Phosphorus is essential in flower and fruit development.

66. **Q. What can be added to the compost pile to speed decomposition?**
A. Decomposition of organic matter depends on bacteria, water, and air. Add garden soil to each layer of organic matter to provide the bacteria; wet the pile to provide moisture, particularly during dry seasons; and stir or turn the pile to add oxygen. Some impatient gardeners add lime and nitrogen fertilizer to promote decay. Commercially prepared compost starters can be substituted for garden soil.

67. **Q. How is well-rotted compost used in gardening?**
A. A well-rotted compost is the gardener's black gold. Add it to soil in place of peat moss. To make it easy to handle, work the compost through a coarse (one inch) sieve. Compost can be used as the source of organic matter in preparing backfill for planting trees and shrubs, as a soil amendment in the flower and vegetable garden, and as the organic component in homemade potting mixes.

68. **Q. Is it necessary to use a compost starter to activate the decay process in my compost pile?**
A. Compost starters contain lime, fertilizer, and/or bacterial enzymes. If you build your pile using a fertile garden soil as the bacterial source, the additional compost starter will not be necessary. Compost starters are of value to the rooftop or patio gardener without access to soil.

69. **Q. Are clover and buckwheat good soil builders?**
A. There are many species and varieties of clover that will greatly benefit garden soil. They fix nutrients in the soil and can be grown as a living ground cover between taller garden plants. Buckwheat accumulates phosphorus that will become available when the crop is spaded or tilled into the soil.

70. **Q. What is humic acid?**
A. Humic acid is the end product of decayed organic matter. It is the black, sticky liquid which acts like cement, holding soil particles together as well as apart. Humic acid increases the nutrient-holding capacity of soil and provides the dark, rich color.

71. **Q. What relationship do humic acid and humus have with each other? Are they the same?**
A. Humus is the resultant brown or dark-brown substance that develops following the breakdown of organic materials by various soil organisms, but is not technically humic acid, the liquid. A soil rich in humus is high in decomposing organic matter and likely contains humic acid as a coating on the soil particles.

72. **Q. What is the function of humus in the soil?**
A. Humus improves the nutrient-holding capacity of soil particles, increases beneficial microbial and bacterial action in the soil, and enhances granulation of the soil, thereby improving drainage and aeration.

73. **Q. What refuse from our lawns, vegetables, and flower gardens can go into our compost pile?**
A. You can add most all the garden refuse to the pile for recycling. I *do not* knowingly add diseased plants, such as verticillium and fusarium wilt-infected tomato, eggplant, or peppers. I *do not* add grass clippings that have been treated with a chemical broad-leafed weed killer until after at least the third mowing. And, I *do not* add flower seed heads that I know can become a weedy pest in the garden. I once threw spent flowers from shasta daisy into a pile only to have billions of shasta daisy seedlings emerge in about three weeks.

74. **Q. After each winter, we have buckets of oak-wood ashes from our wood stove. Are they of any value as fertilizer for flowers or vegetables?**

A. Yes. They can be incorporated into the soil, as they contain potash and calcium and are always safe to use.

75. Q. **One end of my property has a hard-packed, black alkali soil. Can it be made friable and productive?**
A. Apply sulfur to neutralize the alkali and, if the soil drains poorly, consider an underground drainage system. Add well-decomposed compost to improve the soil structure.

76. Q. **Our soil is mostly made of a sand and gravel mix. Can I improve it for growing flowers and vegetables?**
A. Sand and gravel make for great drainage. Add a mixture of garden loam, rotted manure, and compost to a depth of three inches and spade to a depth of six inches. You will need to repeat these additions on an annual basis for a few years.

77. Q. **I succeed with most flowers but not with gladiolus. The bulbs rot. What is the reason?**
A. Check the drainage, particularly in the gladiolus section of the garden. They require soil with moisture-holding capacity, but must have good aeration in addition. No wet feet. Also check the soil pH. Gladiolus plants do best in slightly acid soil—acidify it with sulfur and use acid-forming fertilizer.

78. Q. **How much topsoil is needed to cover an area of fill in order to grow flowers and vegetables?**
A. At least twelve inches; preferably more.

79. Q. **After the first killing frost in the fall, can I cut off the annuals and leave their roots in the soil to decompose?**
A. Yes. The roots provide a source of humic acid to the soil.

80. Q. **Last year, I had magnificent marigold plants, lush geranium foliage, and tons of green leaves on petunias. I had very few flowers though. What went wrong?**
A. Your soil had too much nitrogen and probably not enough phosphorus and potassium. This spring, add a 0-10-10 fertilizer (or equivalent) at a rate of three to five pounds per one hundred square feet. *Do not* use a nitrogen-based fertilizer.

81. Q. **Will a phosphate fertilizer help produce more flowers on my perennials?**
A. Since phosphorus does not migrate in the soil very well, best results will be obtained by applying phosphate when the flower beds are first prepared. Spade or till it into the upper four to six inches of soil. If your perennials are already in the bed, apply phosphate between the plants and cultivate it into the soil as deep as possible without disturbing or injuring the roots.

82. Q. **Why is clay so sticky when it is wet?**
A. Clay is composed of extremely minute particles (.002 millimeters in diameter) with large surfaces for absorbing water. Water causes the stickiness.

83. Q. **What amendments should be added to sandy soil so we can grow roses?**
A. By volume, add at least 50 percent compost and rotted manure to the soil used for planting. Peat moss can be substituted for the compost. Organic matter is a must, or the roses will do poorly. Water will be essential as well.

84. Q. **Do organic fertilizers supply humus?**
A. Some organic fertilizers are used for their humus content as well as their nutrient content. Soybean and cottonseed meals supply a very small amount of humus, while dried manures, alfalfa meal, and worm castings provide more.

85. **Q. How do I maintain an acid-soil garden in a limestone country?**
A. Incorporate acid peat moss or oak leaf mold into the soil at planting time. Sulfur and ammonium sulfate can be cultivated into the soil around existing plants.

86. **Q. Are eggshells valuable as fertilizer?**
A. Eggshells contain calcium and a very small amount of nitrogen. Many African violet growers soak eggshells in water and then use the water to supply calcium.

87. **Q. I have been told the earthworms in my soil benefit from the use of lime. Is that right?**
A. Acid soil conditions greatly reduce and, in extreme cases, almost entirely eliminate the earthworm population. Lime adjusts the bacterial action in the soil and encourages better root growth of plants. The organic matter in the soil is the food of earthworms.

88. **Q. I used sawdust and wood shavings as organic matter when I constructed my new lawn. The grass germinated, but now looks pale in color. Did the wood products make my soil too acid?**
A. Sawdust and shavings will cause acidity as they decompose, but I doubt if this is the main problem. The pale color is most likely due to nitrogen deficiency. The nitrifying bacteria—microorganisms that effect the decay of organic material—often need more nitrogen than the materials supply. As a result, the microorganisms compete for the nitrogen in the soil. The remedy: Use extra nitrogen in fertilizer form.

89. **Q. Is sea kelp or kelp meal valuable as a fertilizer?**
A. Kelp is high in potash and provides trace elements. Kelp compares favorably with farm manure in nitrogen, but is low in phosphorus.

90. **Q. At what rate can I apply wood ashes to my garden soil? My soil is sightly acid.**
A. Wood ashes supply potash and calcium to the soil. Their use will adjust soil pH. Apply at least ten pounds of dry wood ashes per one hundred square feet.

91. **Q. What causes toadstools to grow in my lawn? I rake them away, but they show up again the next day. Can I get rid of them?**
A. Toadstools grow from decaying organic matter. They are most likely originating from decaying roots of nearby trees and shrubs. There is no chemical control. Test the soil pH. The addition of lime or sulfur as needed may reduce the toadstool growth.

92. **Q. How is dried blood used as a fertilizer?**
A. Dried blood, a by-product of slaughter houses and available at garden-supply stores, is an excellent source of quickly available nitrogen, about 15 percent, for use as a side-dressing around leafy vegetables, but must be cultivated into the soil to eliminate the pungent odor, which attracts dogs. Do not use dried blood for crops grown for flower or fruit, as the nitrogen may keep the plant in a vegetative state, not allowing flowering or fruiting.

III

PLANT
PROPAGATION

PROPAGATION TAKES TIME

ONE LATE SPRING Monday morning, when the azaleas, forsythia, and flowering cherries were in full bloom, at exactly nine A.M. an attorney and his client arrived at my office with a bagful of soil and seed. They wanted to know whether the seed was "any good." The attorney's client had purchased and planted several pounds of expensive bluegrass seed from a local nursery. Not one grass seed had germinated. Consequently, they were planning to sue the local garden center for selling bad grass seed, and to be compensated for their effort and loss of time.

The attorney spilled the grass seed onto my desktop and asked me please to test the seed for its viability. He showed me the box in which the seed had been sold. The label indicated the seed had been tested for that current growing season. I carefully separated one hundred seeds from the soil and placed them on a damp paper towel. I folded the damp paper towel containing the seeds and placed it in a plastic bag, noting the date, the variety of seed, and the client's name. I then laid the plastic bag on a shelf and said I would call them in eight to ten days to let them know what number of seeds had begun to sprout. I would have a pretty good idea of the percent of germination by then. If eighty out of one hundred seeds showed signs of sprouting (a tiny little rootlet coming from the seed), then the seed would have approximately an 80 percent germination rate.

The client immediately said, "What do you mean, eight to ten days?"

I explained this was the time this particular variety of bluegrass took to show signs of germination. The attorney, puzzled,

turned to his client and asked, "When was it planted?" The client replied, "Last Friday." Since this was Monday morning, the seed planted the preceding Friday had been given only three days. There was no way anything could have happened in that short a period of time. I suggested they plant sod if they wanted an instant lawn.

A footnote to this growing experience: After eight days, I opened the bag and ninety-two of the one hundred seeds had started to grow, a 92 percent germination rate. It simply takes time for plants to grow.

One of the greatest joys of gardening is the inner gratification derived from propagating your own plants. Watching a plant grow from the emergence of its first two little leaves to flowering and fruiting as a mature specimen is a real reward. Plant propagation is any method used to perpetuate a species: seed, division, layering, cutting, grafting, budding, or tissue culture. Starting plants from seed is sexual propagation. Growing plants from vegetative parts is asexual propagation.

SEXUAL VERSUS ASEXUAL PROPAGATION

There are reasons for using sexual propagation instead of asexual propagation, and vice versa. Sexual propagation can give great variation to the offspring. Asexual propagation produces an exact likeness of the parent. Let me explain this further.

Go to your local produce stand, buy a Jonathan apple, eat it, and collect all of the seeds. Dry them and plant them properly. You will obtain as many new, different types of

Jonathan apples as you have seeds. Not one would be exactly like another. And you would probably get apples that were inferior to the ones you planted.

If you select seeds from an F-1 hybrid, such as the beautiful large-blossomed petunias or some varieties of tomato plants, you would most likely get new plants that had characteristics similar to one of the parents. Again, you would probably have an inferior variety.

Asexual propagation produces an exact likeness of the parent. The Bartlett pear, first propagated in England in the 1700's from seed, is identical to the Bartlett pear that we eat today. It is, cell for cell, the exact same pear produced in the eighteenth century. From the original Bartlett seedling, new plants were propagated vegetatively. These first-generation plants taken from the seedling or "mother" are clones. Each clone bears an exact likeness to each other clone and to the parent. Granted, the original Bartlett pear tree has long since expired but, cell for cell, because each generation has been propagated asexually, modern pears are identical. In other words, asexual propagation allows no change in genetic makeup.

Environmental factors, however, such as climate, type of soil, and disease, may modify the appearance of a plant, flower, or fruit. In some years, the Bartlett pear grown in California produces a round, apple-shaped fruit; those grown in Washington and Oregon produce a fruit that is long and narrow, typically pear-shaped. These differences are asserted to be due to environmental and climatic factors. If you have ever grown tomatoes in your garden, you know the type of soil and weather definitely have an effect on the quality and quantity of fruit. If you have poor soil and do nothing about it, there sure will be a difference in your crop compared to those grown in fertile soil.

ASEXUAL REPRODUCTION— VEGETATIVE PROPAGATION

Asexual propagation, we repeat, provides an exact likeness of the parent. Normal cell division makes this possible. By starting new plants from stem, leaf, or root parts, whether you use cuttings, division, layering, grafting, or tissue culture, cells retain their exact chromosomal structure. Your new plant is a perpetuation of the mother plant.

In order to understand asexual reproduction of a woody stem, we must discuss some of the physiology. Examining a cross section of a woody stem, from the outside to the center, we first see the bark, then the phloem layer (the layer of cells that carries manufactured food parts to the root system). Inside the phloem is a microscopic layer called the cambium layer which contains meristem, the growing tissue. The inner portion of the plant is the pith and xylem which carry water and mineral elements to the stems, leaves, flowers and fruits. Adventitious roots develop from the meristematic tissue, and so does wound tissue, or callus growth.

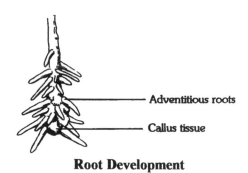

Adventitious roots

Callus tissue

Root Development

KNOW YOUR CUTTINGS

Cuttings are taken from the vegetative portions of a plant, and are classified according to their origin: stem, leaf, leaf bud, and root. Most plants can be propagated by one or more types of cutting. If you know what part of the plant to take and take it at the right time of year, success is yours.

Stem Cuttings

Stem cuttings are divided into four categories: hardwood, semi-hardwood, softwood, and herbaceous.

Hardwood Hardwood cuttings are further divided into two more groups: deciduous and narrow-leaved evergreen.

Deciduous hardwood cuttings are taken during the dormant season (from late fall to early spring) from growth developed during the previous growing season. Some of our deciduous ornamental shrubs, trees, and fruit species are propagated by hardwood cuttings. Some common examples are wisteria, forsythia, privet, honeysuckle, spirea, pussy willow, lilac, willow, poplar, fig, grape, gooseberry, and some plums.

Narrow-leafed evergreen cuttings are best taken from the tips of the past season's growth, during late fall to late winter. It is essential to keep the cutting material moist at all times, and in a humid environment like a greenhouse or propagation chamber. Bottom heat, temperature 75 to 80 degrees Fahrenheit, gives best results. Some species take longer to root than others, but will root in time. Juniper cuttings, for example, should be four to eight inches long with the lower one half of the leaves removed.

Semihardwood Semi-hardwood cuttings are usually made from broad-leafed evergreens such as camellia, pittosporum, rhododendrons, evergreen azaleas, laurel, leucothoe, holly, euonymus and andromeda. The best time is mid to late summer as the new growth begins to harden. Before taking the semihardwood cutting, test to see if the cutting has hardened sufficiently. Apply pressure to the growing tip of the stem, usually the top three to four inches, by bending the tip with one hand while holding the main stem with the other hand. Release the pressure all at once. If the tip springs back immediately to a rigid position, the stem is ready. If the stem remains bent, wait a week or so and test again. Remove all but two or three leaves from the very tip of the evergreen cutting. If the leaves are extra-large, as with a rhododendron, the leaves may be cut back by as much as two thirds to reduce the rate of transpiration and to enable you to get more cuttings into the propagation space. Keep the broad-leafed evergreen cuttings moist at all times and away from the full sun. Bottom heat and rooting hormones both are beneficial, substantially reducing

rooting time and increasing the number of cuttings that take root.

Softwood Softwood cuttings are used to propagate many of our ornamental shrubs such as forsythia, weigela, and spirea. Cuttings, usually three to five inches long, from the soft, succulent, new spring growth tips, develop roots in four to five weeks if kept in a highly humid environment with gentle bottom heat of 75 to 80 degrees Fahrenheit. Rooting hormones also stimulate root development.

Stem Cutting: Geranium

Herbaceous Herbaceous cuttings are taken from many of our garden and house plants. Herbaceous plants, such as chrysanthemums, geraniums, and coleus propagate easily from tip cuttings treated in the same way as the softwood cutting. It is not absolutely necessary to use rooting hormones on herbaceous cuttings, but if you do, they will stimulate a more even development of roots.

Leaf Cuttings

Leaf cuttings, as the house-plant connoisseur knows, present one of the easiest methods for propagating African violets, begonias, peperomia, and snake plants. This type of cutting requires the leaf blade, or leaf blade and petiole. The new plant emerges from adventitious roots at the base of the leaf or petiole. The original leaf is shed after the new plant forms.

To propagate the sansevieria, commonly known as the snake plant, by leaf cutting, remove one of the parent's long-leaf blades and cut it into segments approximately two to three inches long. Each segment will produce a new plant. Take care that the base of the leaf segment is not too deep in the propagating medium, and make sure the right end is up. If the cuttings are upside down, they may never root. African violet petiole leaf cuttings should be inserted no deeper than one-quarter inch into the medium. From the lower basal point, a new plant will arise.

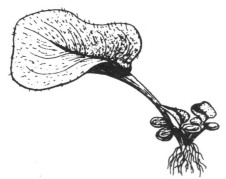

Leaf and Petiole Cutting: New African Violet Plant Arising from Base of Petiole

Rex begonias may be propagated by placing an entire leaf flat on the propagating medium and wounding the veins with a sharp knife, making sure the wounds are in contact with the propagating medium. New plantlets will arise from the cut areas.

Leaf Cutting: Begonia Leaf with New Plants Arising from Cuts in Veins

Leaf-bud cuttings are used to propagate numerous plants from one individual plant. The procedure produces plants that require a bud to be present to develop a new plant. The *Crassula*, commonly called the jade plant, is one plant that requires both a bud and the leaf.

Horticulturally, stem cuttings are probably the most important. Huge numbers of our hardwood, semihardwood, softwood, and herbaceous plants are propagated stem cuttings. For outdoor propagation of stem cuttings, select the cutting *only* at the proper time of year for that particular plant. Timing is critical. Any good gardening encyclopedia provides the proper information for the correct time for propagating a specific variety.

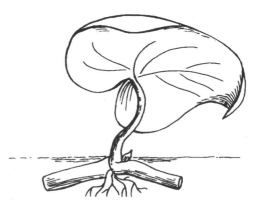

Leaf Bud Cutting: Philodendron

Leaf-bud Cuttings

Leaf-bud cuttings consist of a leaf blade, petiole, and a small portion of stem containing the axillary bud. The axillary bud develops into the stem and roots forming the new plant. Insert the cuttings into the propagation mix with the bud no deeper than one half to one inch below the surface. This method is valuable where a limited amount of cutting material is available, and where new shoots will not develop from the leaf or petiole alone, as with the jade plant. Many of our tropical philodendron house plants are propagated by leaf-bud cuttings.

Root Cuttings

Root cuttings are sections of the root system that develop adventitious buds from root tissue. It is important to maintain the correct polarity of the root when planting. I cut the top or upper part straight across and the lower, or distal, end at an angle. In the case of horseradish, the root sections may be placed horizontally about one inch below the soil surface. Both adventitious shoots and roots will develop from the root section.

TYPES OF WOUNDS

Before taking cuttings from a plant, know the plant's degree of difficulty for rooting. The angle of the wound at the base of the cutting will increase the possibility of rooting for hard-to-root plants. The angle of the cut is dictated by the length of time required for rooting. The object is to expose the maximum amount of the cambium layer which contains meristematic tissue.

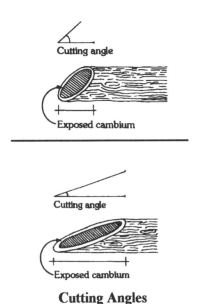

Cutting Angles

The Procedure

Though there are exceptions to the rule, a general procedure for taking cuttings is as follows: Take the cuttings just below a node. A node is the point at which a leaf is or has been attached. The highest concentration of natural rooting hormones exists in this area. Take cuttings from the plant early in the morning. Plants are generally most filled with moisture early in the morning before photosynthesis and transpiration begin for the day. Timing is important to the new cuttings because after they are removed from the parent plant, they have little ability to take in additional moisture; they have no roots.

Now, prepare the cuttings for the propagation bench or for your little plastic greenhouse.

Remove some of the leaves but retain enough on each cutting to allow photosynthesis, the food-manufacturing process.

1. Snip off semi-firm 3-to 4-inch long shoots.

2. Trim cutting at 45° angle just below a leaf node.

3. Place cuttings, dipped in rooting hormone, in holes in propagation mixture.

4. Cover with clear plastic to make a greenhouse.

Removing some of the foliage will reduce the need for water and slow the rate of transpiration.

Apply a rooting hormone to the base of each cutting by either dipping the wounded stem base into a liquid rooting hormone solution or by rolling the stem base into the rooting hormone powder. Insert the cuttings into the propagation medium. I generally figure one third of the stem should be inserted into the mix. Increase the humidity by providing filtered shade, covering the cuttings with a single sheet of newsprint, or placing the cuttings in a greenhouse environment, easily made from a clear plastic bag.

For cuttings not being propagated in the greenhouse, take care to ensure the cuttings are not in a draft. Place the cuttings in a propagating medium which is slightly warmer than the air temperature. Bottom heat comes from warming the propagation medium, and can be accomplished by using a heating cable or coil with a carefully controlled thermostat. Keep the propagation chamber in filtered bright light and keep the medium slightly moist at all times.

Now, the question: How do you know when the cuttings have rooted? First, you should already know the expected length of time for your specific plant to root under normal conditions. Don't confuse new growth as a sign that the cuttings have rooted. Open the bag and carefully lift out one of the cuttings to see if it has rooted. If it has, check additional cuttings to see if they have rooted, too. If they have, you are ready to pot them in your growing mix and watch them grow. If they haven't, return the cuttings to the rooting mix and check again in a few days. Remember, patience is a virtue when propagating plants.

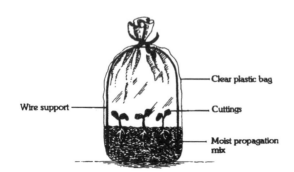

Plastic Bag Greenhouse

Wire support — Clear plastic bag — Cuttings — Moist propagation mix

THE ROOTING MEDIA — THE MIX

A plant propagator uses one of many rooting media or combinations thereof. The most popular ingredients are sand, peat moss, shredded sphagnum moss, perlite, and vermiculite. Develop a rooting mix to suit your needs, and stick with it. Remember, sanitation is a must; never reuse a propagation mix. Chances are it will be contaminated with undesirable bacteria and fungi. The mix is probably the cheapest part of propagation, so don't be "penny-wise and pound-foolish."

My favorite medium for easy-to-root plants like coleus, begonias, and impatiens is a coarse builders' or sharp plaster sand (not the fine masons' finishing sand). This is inexpensive and readily available from most building-supply houses. For harder-to-root cuttings like junipers, taxus, and rhododendron, I add by volume as much as 20 percent vermiculite or peat moss to sand to increase its moisture-tension capacity. A mixture of perlite and vermiculite can do just as well. For leaf cuttings of African violets and snake plants, I use perlite alone, because it holds just enough moisture and allows excellent drainage and aeration.

Water, though not my recommendation for rooting cuttings, is probably the most universally available medium. What do you see on your windowsill above the kitchen sink? A glass of water filled with roots from the philodendron cutting you never got around to potting. Water as a propagation mix makes for a sorry type of root development. Water loses its free oxygen after sitting for more than twenty-four hours. Roots developed in this environment suffer when transplanted into a growing medium. I have had many plants, transplanted from their glass of water, collapse and die before their roots could adapt to their new medium. If you choose to root cuttings in water, it would be wise to add oxygen or air to the water with an air pump.

USE OF
ROOTING HORMONES
FOR CUTTINGS

With few exceptions, the use of rooting hormones pays a substantial dividend. Rooting hormones generally increase the number of cuttings that take root. They hasten rooting and increase the number of roots per cutting. I use rooting hormones on all cuttings except coleus, begonias, and Swedish ivy. These three plants root easily, no matter what. It should be pointed out that using a rooting hormone does not substitute for good cultural practices. The procedure I use to apply a powdered rooting hormone to a cutting is as follows:

1. Place a small quantity of rooting hormone on a piece of paper.
2. Roll the base of the cutting, approximately one inch of the stem, into the hormone. A white dust adheres to the treated portion of the stem. In some cases, it is necessary to wet the cutting to encourage powder to stick to the tissue.
3. Place the cutting into the rooting medium; generally one third of the cutting will be below the surface.
4. Press the mix around the cutting to ensure the moist medium contacts plant tissue.
5. Water thoroughly.

Since pathogens from your cuttings have probably invaded it, do not try to salvage any rooting hormone from the paper. If you were to pour any hormone remnants into the original rooting hormone supply, you would infect your supply with possible diseases.

Powder-type rooting hormones come in several strengths or concentrations and must be mixed with additional talc if dilution is necessary. And never dip a cutting into the container itself. A diseased cutting could spread its disease to future cuttings.

Liquid rooting hormones, whether indolebutyric acid (IBA) or naphthaleneacetic acid (NAA), used separately or in combination, should be used sparingly. Pour only enough diluted solution into a sterile container, such as a glass jar, to cover the base of the cutting. Cover it to the same depth that you would with powders. After the cuttings have been dipped, do not try to save the unused portion,

for the same reasons we discussed for powders. Advantages of the liquid versus the powder are that the liquid completely coats the desired stem portion with hormone without its having to be moistened, and several cuttings can be dipped at the same time. Liquid concentrates can be diluted to the strength recommended for a particular species. You will, therefore, need only one container of rooting hormone for vegetative propagation.

No matter which formulation you use, whether powder or liquid, it is not a substitute for good cultural practices. You must start with healthy, clean stock, use sanitary practices, and know the degree of rooting difficulty for the particular species, or even variety, being propagated.

The rooting hormone IAA (indoleacetic acid) was discovered to be a naturally occurring auxin in plant tissue that stimulated root growth on stem cuttings. Shortly after this revelation, synthetic auxins of IBA and NAA were proved to be even more effective as rooting hormones. In today's market, rooting supplies include both powder and liquid rooting hormone concentrates containing both IBA and NAA.

Division

Division is propagation by dividing into pieces. I often think of a plant-propagation lecture I once attended. The lecturer placed an overgrown Boston Fern on a large chopping block, picked up a double-bitted axe, stepped up and—wham!—split the plant right down the middle. He backed away, laid down the axe, looked at the audience and said, "Now that's division."

Multiple-stemmed plants, such as Boston ferns, *Asparagus springeri*, chrysanthemums,

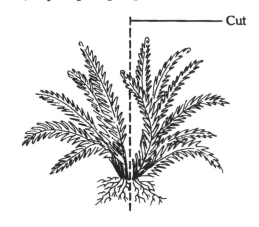

Division: Fern Division

lilacs, and others, can be propagated by division. Indoor plants usually can be divided at any time of year, whereas outdoor plants require division only at specific times for the best results.

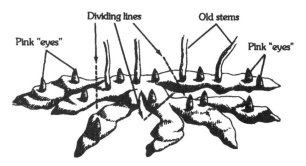

**Peony Division:
Minimum 3 eyes per Division**

The potato tuber also propagates by division. Purchase seed potatoes in early spring, cut them into sections, and allow three eyes or buds per division to provide new potato plants. Daffodils and other bulbs are propagated by division by removing the side bulbs and allowing them to reach maturity.

Deciduous shrubs (those that drop their foliage during winter) are best divided after their foliage falls and prior to their new spring foliage: their dormant period. Herbaceous perennials (plants that die to the ground each year, such as peonies) should be divided every few years to avoid overcrowded root systems. I find that dividing peonies every five to seven years provides a luxuriant plant the following year. Leave a minimum of three eyes per set of toes (roots) when dividing peonies. The eyes will be little pink buds attached to the top side of the toes.

Layering

Layering is the process of rooting a stem while it is still attached to the parent plant. Some plants layer naturally. Forsythia may bend over, touch the ground and, at that point, produce a new plant. Roots and shoots develop at the point where the stem touches the soil. You can help this procedure by bending a stem to the ground, anchoring it with soil, and allowing the tip to show. By the following growing season, you can expect a new plant ready for transplanting. This procedure is also followed for propagating grapevines.

Another type of propagation used on house plants is air layering, a simple procedure that requires only shredded sphagnum moss, rooting hormone, string, a polyethylene bag, and several months of patience. If you have a dieffenbachia, or dumb cane, which is about to hit the ceiling, you have three alternatives: air layer the top, cut off the top for a stem cutting, or give the plant away. The point at which you air layer the plant will provide good roots and make a good conversation piece.

Grafting

A graft is the joining of parts of two plants in such a way that they will unite and grow together as one plant. The new plant consists of the *understock* (roots of one plant) and the *scion* (the branches, leaves, flowers, and fruit of another plant).

One reason for grafting as a method of propagation is that some plants cannot be successfully raised by other means. Many years ago, the American grape industry decided to grow the European grape in America, but found the European grape plant often succumbed to a root disease found in our soils. To get around this problem, the European grape plant is grafted to the

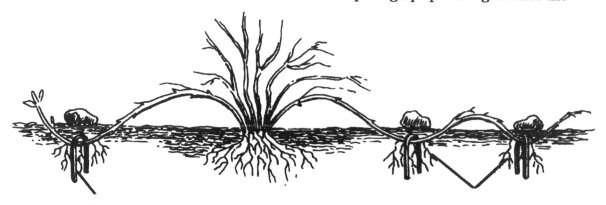

Simple Layering   **Multiple Layering**

American rootstock for grapes. By growing the above-ground parts of the European grape on the American grape rootstock, we can enjoy European grapes "made in America." Grafting is a form of asexual propagation.

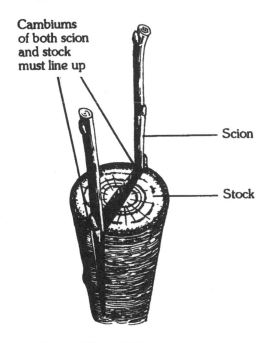

Grafting: Scion and Stock

Rose cuttings often fail to develop a hardy rootstock on their own stems that will overwinter in our northern climates. To solve this problem, we graft the desired rose onto a hardy rose rootstock. Grafting is also used to increase the numbers of a plant within a very short time frame.

From a single rose plant you may be able to produce twenty or more new plants in one season.

Another benefit of grafting can be seen by browsing through any fruit grower's catalog. You'll find many fruit trees that produce more than one variety of fruit on the same plant. This is accomplished by grafting buds from the different fruit varieties to a single rootstock or producing plant. This procedure can eliminate the need for more than one fruit tree, since the grafted plant can contain both desired varieties and their pollinators.

As with most other methods of asexual propagation, success with grafting depends on its being performed at the appropriate time of year, usually the dormant season. In addition, the two plants to be grafted into one must be compatible. The stock, also called rootstock or understock, is the lower portion of the graft which produces the desired root system. The scion, the upper portion of the desired variety, often comprises the entire aboveground portion of the plant. The scion and stock of the compatible varieties are matched so the cambium tissues of both scion and stock make direct contact. The graft union is the site where two tissues grow together; massive callus growth develops around the wounded plant tissue.

Tissue Culture

A major step forward for the plant propagator came in the 1970s with the development of micropropagation. Better known as tissue culture, micropropagation is the growth of new plants, called explants, from small pieces of plant tissue and in some cases, from single cells. In a glass container and under aseptic conditions, the plant tissue is cultured on a sterile nutrient medium. The advantage of tissue culture is production of exponentially large numbers of identical plants in a very short time. Micropropagation has been used to produce many herbaceous plants such as chrysanthemums, asparagus, carnations, gerberas, ferns, and orchids, and thanks to development of new nutrient media, also many woody plants such as roses, rhododendrons, azaleas, and apples. The tissue can derive from virtually any part of the plant: from shoot tips, roots, and even from seed embryos.

SEXUAL PROPAGATION — SEED PROPAGATION

To understand seed propagation, we need to know the life cycle of a seed-bearing plant. The cycle divides into two phases: one, the vegetative or growth cycle; and two, the reproductive cycle, or production of seeds. Let's follow the growth cycle from seed to seed.

First, if conditions are right, the seed germinates, juvenile growth of vegetative plant parts (roots and shoots) follows, and, finally, we see flower-bud induction—the plant knows it is time to flower. The induction signal could be triggered by day length (photoperiodism), as with many annuals, or by a certain amount of chilling (vernalization), as with many biennials, or by age or maturation of growing tissue, as with many woody deciduous and evergreen plants. Bud initiation and development follow the bud-induction signal. Buds are visible at this point of the flowering cycle. If pollination occurs, we have fruit and seed development, followed by the ripening and dissemination of seeds. We have come full circle in the plant life cycle.

THE SEED

If we look closely at a seed, we will find three basic parts: the embryo, the living portion of the seed and the point from which all living parts develop; the cotyledons, the food-storage tissue which provides the living parts with their initial nutrients; and the testa or seed covering, the outer protection of food-storage tissue and the embryo. The embryo contains the radicle, which grows downward to form the root, and the hypocotyl and epicotyl, which grow upward to produce the visible parts of the stem. These living parts are usually tucked neatly inside the protective cotyledon, the meaty part of the seed. The seed coat protects and holds everything together. Mother Nature has performed wonders in protecting her new plants.

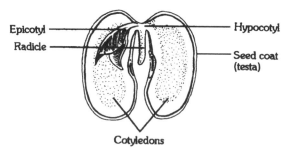

Seed Parts: Dicot Bean Sead

SEEDLESSNESS

Some plants grow and flower, but produce no seeds, for three basic reasons. One, fruit without fertilization produces a fruit without seeds. Embryo abortion or death to the embryo is the second reason, often causing fruit drop or an abnormally small fruit. The third reason is the inability of the embryo to accumulate food reserves, due, perhaps, to physiological problems in the plant or climatic conditions.

To get seed production, you must have pollination. Plants such as grasses, peas, wheat, oats, and tomatoes can self-pollinate; other plants need cross-pollination. These include many of the fruit trees such as Bing cherry, beach plum, dwarfed hybrid red Anjou pear, as well as the sweet corn you might be growing in your garden. Pollination simply is the transfer of pollen, from the pollen-producing part of the flower (the anthers), to the pollen-receiving part of the flower (the stigma). Pollination by wind is common, and so is pollination by insects that visit the pollen-producing part of the flower. When pollen makes contact with the stigma, a pollen tube grows down the style into the ovule, where fertilization proceeds. Pollen received from the same flower, from different flowers on the same plant, or from different plants of the same variety, shows us a self-pollinating plant. If pollen is used from a different variety, we have a cross-pollinating plant.

SELECTING SEEDS

Have you ever stood in front of the seed rack at a garden center and wondered where all those seeds came from? How did we get so many varieties to choose from? Will they really grow? The production of seeds for our gardens didn't just happen. Breeding new varieties is a long and arduous task. Breeders plant thousands of seeds and select only those which show growth superiority. They often try to combine into one plant several different characteristics taken from specific plants. They might find a plant resistant to a certain disease, cross it with a plant not resistant to that disease, and come up with a new disease-resistant variety. Many years may pass before a single new variety is born. Right now, some experiments focus on insect-resistant plants.

In selecting seeds for my garden, I make sure to plant some tried-and-true varieties each year, but I will also try a few new varieties. In other words, I do my own testing. This is definitely one activity of gardening to record in your garden diary. Keep good records of growth and fruiting capabilities so you will know whether to plant the same variety again next year or switch to another. Some helpful information includes how long it took seeds to germinate, the number of weeks to grow into transplants, transplanting date, plant's ability to harden-off in preparation for outside planting, plant's condition after transplanting to the garden, and length of harvesttime. Also record which nutrients were used at planting time and fed to the plants as the season progressed, severity and control of any pest problems, and number of fruits or pounds of harvest. It's quite a joy to record picking the first tomato of the season, especially when it's the first on your block. Seeds purchased from a mail-order seed catalog or from your local garden center are in their dormant stage.

DORMANCY

A dormant seed is in a state of reduced activity; there is little or no respiration, and nutrients stored in the cotyledons stay there. Dormancy is induced by external and/or internal factors. A seed packet may be nothing more than a paper envelope, or it might be foil-lined. The kind of packaging depends on what conditions will keep seeds in their dormant state. Directions on the seed packet suggest length of time for germination. Most seed producers provide this information: "Takes three to four days" or "Takes ten to twelve weeks," depending on the species and variety of plant. Read the directions and be patient. Some seeds can germinate immediately after removal from the parent plant. And some seeds require "after-ripening", an additional treatment necessary for them to germinate.

FAILURE TO GERMINATE

Understanding some of the causes of failure to germinate will help you grow plants from seeds. Both external and internal factors can influence failure. External factors include the lack of moisture, lack of favorable temperature, and lack of oxygen.

External Factors

Moisture softens the seed coat and allows oxygen to enter the cotyledons where the seed food is stored. Even though we water our seeds, they will fail if we forget to keep them moist. A seed must be kept moist throughout the entire germination cycle, or embryo death is a near certainty. Remember, some seeds like to be quite wet and some seeds like to be only slightly moist. You must know the germination requirements of any seeds you want to grow.

Temperature also plays a dominant role in germination. Garden seeds fall into two groups: cool season and warm season. All seeds have minimum, maximum and optimum temperature ranges for germination. Some of our cool-season crops are lettuce, celery, endive, and peas. They germinate best when soil temperatures are relatively cool; 40 degrees Fahrenheit and above. Warm-season crops include beans, eggplant, peppers, and the cucurbits, as well as sweet corn and tomatoes. If you plant warm-season crops when the soil is too cool, you may get nothing more than rotting before rooting.

Oxygen must be present in the soil; it is absorbed through the seed coat to start the respiration process within the seed and to complete germination. In poorly drained soils after heavy rains, there is little oxygen left between soil particles. Whether starting seeds indoors in a seed-starting mix or starting them in garden soil, moisture content should not be so great that all pore spaces in the soil are filled. A too-wet condition drives out available oxygen and provides little or no oxygen for the seeds.

Internal Factors

Internal factors which affect germination are the seed coat's impermeability to water, degree of embryo restriction, and chemical inhibitors within the seed.

Some seed coats are virtually impermeable to water, due to the membrane on the inner layer of the seed coat or to the structural or chemical makeup of the seed coat itself. Impermeability can be overcome by external forces. An extremely tough and hard seed coat can restrict the embryo by not allowing it to expand.

Chemical inhibitors also play a role in seed germination. Some inhibitors, like ammonia, break down and become inactive when the seed makes contact with soil particles. Other chemicals in seeds prohibit germination unless they are converted into another chemical or until they are removed completely. If the combination of all external and internal factors is favorable, you should get good seed germination.

BREAKING DORMANCY

Two procedures often used to break seed dormancy are stratification and scarification.

Stratification—Winter Elements

In nature, seeds are automatically stratified. This happens during winter when seeds are exposed to the elements. Alternating freezing and thawing break down the fibers of the seed coat. Conditions required for stratification are reduced temperatures, absorption of moisture by the seed, good aeration for chemical changes within the seed, and time. If you have seeds that must be stratified so the "after-ripening" process can occur, you can use your refrigerator. Temperatures of between 32 and 50 degrees Fahrenheit should be adequate to accomplish most stratification.

Dry seeds should be soaked in water for twelve to twenty-four hours, drained and mixed with a moisture-retaining medium, and then refrigerated for the required period of time. The length of time may vary from one to four months, depending on the variety of seeds being stratified. Media for stratification are well-washed sand, peat moss, milled sphagnum moss, or vermiculite. I use a mixture of one part sand to one part peat moss, slightly moistened and allowed to stand for some twenty-four hours before use so the moisture is evenly distributed. The medium should be moist, not wet. If you can squeeze water from a handful of the medium, it is too wet.

Cans or glass jars with perforated lids make good containers for stratifying seeds. Place a layer of moist medium in the bottom of the container, then a layer of seeds, then a layer of medium, then a layer of seeds, and so on. If plastic bags are used instead of cans or jars, be sure to use a polyethylene bag, because it is permeable to air. Seeds must receive oxygen.

Out-of-doors stratification may be accomplished by preparing the container as previously discussed, and burying the can, jar, or bag about six inches under the soil surface. Freezing and thawing cycles along with temperature fluctuations will yield the same results as the refrigerator treatment. The secret to this procedure is to place a marker in the garden where the bag, can, or jar has been buried. You've heard that squirrels can bury a nut in the fall, and find it the next spring. We humans are less likely to find our "nut"—container —unless it is well marked.

Scarification—The Scratching Process

Scarification occurs by scratching the seed coat or causing some mechanical damage to the outer membrane. Simple scarification is accomplished by soaking seeds in water. This modifies hard seed coats and removes chemical inhibitors. Some seeds are soaked in hot water and some in cold water. Soil organisms, insects, and wildlife perform a natural scarification. They all damage the outer seed coat. Birds and four-legged animals not only scarify the seeds they eat but, if they are incompletely digested, pass them on with prepackaged fertilizer. Acid scarification is used to modify hard or impermeable seed coverings. Seeds are placed in a sulfuric acid bath, soaked for a specific time, and then rinsed. The acid eats away a certain amount of the outer seed coat, making it permeable to moisture and oxygen. Acid scarification is an exacting art. Time is critical! One second too long in an acid bath destroys the embryo.

STORING SEEDS FROM LAST YEAR—THE SEED SAVER

Never has a year passed that I haven't had some seeds left over; either I didn't get a chance to plant them or I didn't need as many as the seed packet held. I sure don't throw them out. My experience with broccoli seeds leads me to believe that many seeds can be saved from year to year, in fact for many years, with little drop in the germination percentage. A few years ago, I ordered hybrid broccoli seeds from a mail-order seed catalog. My order requested one packet, approximately 125 seeds. Much to my surprise, I received a one-ounce packet of broccoli seeds counting over nine thousand seeds. I plant only thirty-six broccoli plants each growing season. I planted forty seeds that first year, leaving me with some 8,960 seeds. I stored the remaining seeds, sealing them in their original package in a moisture-tight glass jar. A sealed jar keeps moisture from the seeds. I placed the jar in a cool area, 40 to 50 degrees Fahrenheit, and the next spring counted out another forty seeds. After eleven years, I believe I am now down to 8,520 seeds. At this rate, I will be planting broccoli from this packet well into the twenty-first century, if their viability continues to hold.

Many seeds can be saved in the same manner. Tomato, eggplant, cucumber, and radish from the vegetable patch and marigold, zinnia, and impatiens from the flower garden can be saved for two to three years with little reduction in the germination percentage. Just remember, seal the seeds in their original package so you always have the necessary seed-starting information, and store them in a moisture-tight container in a cool location.

GERMINATION TEST

Perhaps you have noticed a stamp on the packet or box of seeds you have purchased that says, "Tested for the current year." This means that the viability or germination percentage should be accurate for the year printed on the container. Often seeds, as they age, lose their optimal percent of germination. There is no hard-and-fast rule to predict the percent of germination that may be lost with each succeeding year. You may have old seeds on hand that still have a high germination rate. And again, you may have seeds from last year that won't germinate at all, whose viability is lost. When I save seeds from year to year, I always test them against possible disaster: "no germination." For most of my regular garden seeds, such as annuals and vegetables, I count out ten seeds, place them on a moist paper towel, roll them up and place them in a plastic bag, label them with the date and variety, and lay them in a warm environment. Room temperature is

quite adequate.

By reading the directions on the seed packet you will know the average time for germination. After half to three fourths of the time has elapsed, take them from the bag and count those seeds which have begun to germinate. If eight out of ten seeds have started to grow, you have, approximately 80 percent germination. If the seeds show no sign of germination whatsoever, discard the remaining seeds and buy fresh ones for the current season. Don't be penny-wise and pound-foolish when starting seeds.

1. Place 10 Seeds on damp paper towel.

2. Roll up towel with seeds.

3. Place in plastic bag. Label and date.

4. After germination time as stated on seed packet, open and count seeds that have sprouted.

STARTING SEEDS INDOORS

Starting seeds indoors has become a relatively simple procedure. There are many different types of containers and soilless mixes, or artificial mixes as they are known to the trade, that are sterile and ready for use. I highly recommend you use a commercially prepared, sterile seed-starting mix, as opposed to trying to make your own.

Over the past two years, another important advancement in commercially prepared mixes has been found in those containing a wetting agent. The wetting agent makes watering the mix a much easier job and, therefore, less disturbance to the seeds or damage to the seedlings.

Containers for starting seeds vary from wooden flats to plastic trays. You can even use egg cartons, margarine trays, and paper or plastic cups, as long as you provide adequate drainage holes. The only qualifications I look for in a seed-starting container are its rigidity and drainage capability. A rigid container, one that does not bend or twist when picked up, can be moved from one location to another without damaging the new seedlings. The drainage capability is tantamount. Drainage holes not only let excess moisture escape, but also admit life-giving oxygen. The seed germination medium should be sterile, capable of holding moisture, and provide good aeration.

For years, soil mixes with equal parts of sand, soil, and peat moss have been the old standbys. With the introduction of new artificial seed-starting mixes, starting seeds indoors has become very simple. Completely fill the container with the propagating mix. Rake off excess medium and tamp the material so the surface of the mix is approximately one-half inch below the top of the container. Now, water the propagating medium thoroughly and you are ready to plant the seeds.

Rather than scattering seeds over the surface of the soil, plant them in rows. With the edge of a ruler or other sharp instrument make a narrow, shallow trench across the surface of the mix. Space the rows one inch apart. After planting the seeds in the individual trenches, cover the entire flat with a very fine shredded sphagnum moss. Sphagnum moss inhibits or prevents damping-off, a common soil-borne fungal

1. Fill and firm container with moist, sterile see-starting mix.

2. Create straight, shallow planting rows.

3. Space seeds evenly in planting rows.

4. Cover seeds with thin layer of mix, moisten mix and seeds, and cover container with clear glass or plastic.

disease that often appears during seed germination and causes growing seeds to simply fold over and collapse. The rapid development of the damping-off organism could be due to excess moisture or to the lack of air circulation. Slightly moisten the sphagnum moss and cover the container with a piece of clear plastic or a sheet of glass. This cover will help prevent the seed flat from drying, so much less frequent watering is required.

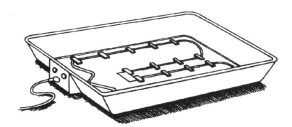

Bottom Heat for Propagation

Remember, as we discussed earlier, seeds once moistened must be kept moist to complete the germination cycle. Small containers may be placed in clear plastic bags and sealed. This provides a humid, green-house environment perfect for germination. Once seeds have sprouted, remove the plastic immediately or remove the container from the plastic bag. This allows for proper air movement around the tender seedlings and helps reduce the possibility of damping-off.

Don't forget that new seedlings need to be watered, and must receive the proper amount of light. In containers where several rows of seeds of different varieties are being germinated simultaneously, make sure they are all compatible in their moisture requirements and time it takes for germination. Seeds that start to grow in a short period of time should not be planted in the same container as those with extended germination time. The differential would create a handling problem.

Don't forget to label your seeds with the planting date and the variety. To plant seeds directly in the outdoor garden, follow the directions on the packet. Pay particular attention to the planting instructions for your area.

QUESTIONS AND ANSWERS

1. **Q. When is the best time to start a California privet hedge from cuttings?**
   A. During late winter, bury cuttings, six to seven inches long, in a box of sand placed in a cool area such as a cellar. By spring, the cuttings should have callus at the base and some of them will even have rooted. Plant cuttings as soon as the soil can be worked, cultivating them for a year or so before you transplant them for a hedge.

2. **Q. When should seeds from hardy, herbaceous perennials be sown?**
   A. Midsummer is the best time to start most hardy perennials from seed so the plants will be mature enough to produce blooms the following year. Yarrow, delphinium, heliopsis, candytuft, and coneflower are herbaceous perennials that germinate in two to four weeks. Stokes aster and verbena are hardy perennials that bloom the first year is sown in spring.

3. **Q. Can I grow roses from seed?**
   A. Shore rose, *Rosa rugosa*, can be grown from seed gathered in the fall. Sow the seeds in a shallow container of sandy soil placed in a cold frame, or any protected spot outdoors, so the winter freezes will crack their seed coats. They will germinate in the spring. Hybrid roses can be propagated from seed using the same method, but they do not come true from seed. A thousand seeds from hybrid roses would produce a thousand new varieties.

4.   Q. **What are the basic ways to propagate perennials?**
      A. Perennials are propagated by seed, division, root cuttings, and stem cuttings.

5.   Q. **My perennial phlox is becoming crowded. How often should phlox be divided?**
      A. Every three years, divide and transplant phlox to overcome the clumpy growth habit and to renew the soil. The outside pieces of the divided clumps make the best transplants.

6.   Q. **When should one take hardy phlox cuttings?**
      A. The cuttings should be taken in the late summer. Protect the cuttings over winter by rooting them in a cold frame. If you take cuttings in the spring, do so when the plants are about six inches tall.

7.   Q. **Will the individual "potatoes" of the dahlia roots produce plants?**
      A. Dahlias can be propagated by "potatoes," tuberous roots, if you take a sliver of the stem with each tuber. It is from this point, where the tuber and stem meet, that the new plant develops. To ensure that you have active growth points, wait until the plants begin to sprout before dividing.

8.   Q. **Is it hard to grow cannas from seed?**
      A. Canna propagated from seed will not produce the same beautiful blooms of the parent plant, as the canna is very hybrid in nature. Plants from seed will exhibit many of the qualities of its primitive lineage. To grow cannas from seed, scarify the seed by carefully nicking the seed coat with a knife. This cut allows water to enter the seed to begin germination. Place the scarified seeds in sterile sand and maintain a steady warmth until they germinate. Plant them immediately and you should have good plants within the year.

9.   Q. **How can I propagate viburnum by layering?**
      A. Carefully bend a long branch to the ground. Where the stem touches the soil, wound the bark by making a long incision or several short ones. Apply rooting hormone to the wounded area of the stem and anchor it to the soil. Cover the wounded portion of the stem with sandy soil, allowing the free end of the branch to protrude. To induce rooting, and to reduce loss of water from the leaves, cut off the tip of the layered branch.

10.   Q. **What are some examples of shrubs that can be propagated by layering?**
      A. Magnolias, roses, rhododendron, laurel, hydrangea, raspberries, grapes, wisteria, *Clematis*, climbing *Euonymus*, *Forsythia*, holly, *Viburnum*, and various honey-suckles.

11.   Q. **How can I know what sort of graft to use?**
      A. Use the size of the stem as a general guide. Use the whip or tongue graft if the branches are small. Use the cleft graft on branches which are bigger than an inch in diameter.

12.   Q. **When should apple trees be grafted?**
      A. Graft apples in early spring, just as the buds begin to swell (when the sap begins to flow). The scions must be gathered earlier and placed in damp sand or moss in a cool storage area (cellar).

13.   Q. **Can an apple bud be grafted onto peach stock?**
      A. No—it won't work. Plants from different families cannot be grafted on each other. You may graft core fruit upon each other, with varying degrees of success, but you cannot graft core fruit (apples) upon stone fruits (peaches). A peach and an apricot could be grafted on a plum, but the peaches wouldn't bud very well on the apricot.

14. **Q. Can iris be grown from seed?**
    A. Yes. Iris come true from seed. Sow the seed at a depth of about a quarter-inch in a light, well-drained soil in a cold frame in spring or fall. The plants should bloom in two or three years.

15. **Q. How can I propagate *Vinca minor*?**
    A. Take cuttings of young shoots in late summer and root them in moist sand, or divide the crowns in spring.

16. **Q. When is the best time to divide perennials?**
    A. Generally, the best time to divide perennials is immediately after they have finished blooming. If you divide them at this time, they will have the maximum amount of time to root in before winter. For perennials that flower in the fall, it is best to divide them in early spring.

17. **Q. How can I layer climbing roses?**
    A. Bend a cane of the current season's growth (shiny green cane) to the ground. Wound the cane by cutting into the bark at the point where it comes into contact with the soil, and dust the wound with rooting hormone. Anchor the cane at the point of the wound and cover it with soil. When the cane becomes rooted, sever it from the main plant, but wait to transplant the new plant until the following year.

18. **Q. When should I plant seeds from an evergreen tree? Does it matter how old the seeds are?**
    A. Collect the seeds in the fall and sow them in the spring. If you have older seeds that were kept under proper conditions, they will probably germinate, but vitality diminishes with each year that passes.

19. **Q. How do I grow evergreens from seed?**
    A. Collect the seeds in the fall. In the spring, sow the seeds in a flat filled with a light, well-drained soil, covering the seed with a light sifting of soil (to about the diameter of the seed). Place the flat in a cool, shaded cold frame and keep it evenly moist, but avoid disturbing the surface soil when watering. Transplant seedlings when they are large enough to handle.

20. **Q. Can I propagate the clippings from my evergreens?**
    A. Yes. Most of the junipers, boxwood, yews, hollies, arborvitaes, cypresses (*Chamaecyparis*), and some of the spruces may be propagated by means of cuttings. If you have a greenhouse, you can take cuttings in November or December. If not, you may take cuttings in late August, but as a rule, many of them will not form roots before winter.

21. **Q. How can I store the seeds of evergreens until it is time to plant them?**
    A. Store them in a jar or paper bag that is nearly airtight, in a cool, dry location.

22. **Q. How can I root cuttings from a boxwood?**
    A. When the current season's growth has hardened-off in July or August, take cuttings three to four inches in length from the new growth tips, apply rooting hormone for "difficult to root" plants, and insert the cuttings two inches deep in a flat of sharp sand. Maintain them in a cold frame until there is danger that the sand will freeze. Then remove them to a frostproof shelter for the winter months, keeping the sand moist, but not wet.

23. **Q. How can I tell the sex of a holly tree? I have one tree and want to buy another, but I don't know the sex needed.**

A. Observe the flowers, which appear in June. In the male flowers the pistil is small and undeveloped and the stamens bear pollen. In the female flowers the pistillate or fruiting flowers have a well-developed pistil in the center, and undeveloped stamens.

24. **Q. How is American holly propagated from cuttings?**

A. Cuttings should be about four or five inches long, taken from the tips of the current year's growth in August or September. Wound the bark on the lower one inch of the cuttings by scraping with the edge of a knife. Do not remove the bark entirely. Dip the wounded portion of each stem cutting in rooting hormone for hard-to-root plants, and place them in a propagation container of moist sand or a mixture of sand and peat moss. Provide humidity by covering the container with clear glass or clear plastic. Place the covered container in a cool (40 to 50 degrees Fahrenheit), filtered-light location. The cuttings callus and root in ninety to one hundred and twenty days.

25. **Q. How is English holly propagated from cuttings?**

A. English holly is propagated in the same manner as American holly. (See preceding question.) Cuttings should be about four or five inches long, taken in August or September. If being propagated in a greenhouse or cold frame, shade the cuttings with cheesecloth to reduce transpiration.

26. **Q. Are azaleas propagated by seed?**

A. Any of the native or wild forms may be grown from seeds, because the seedlings will reproduce the characteristics of the parent. Hybrid forms and "sports," which cannot be reproduced from seeds, are propagated from cuttings and/or by grafting, depending upon the kind and the purpose for which they are needed.

27. **Q. I would like to have more of the bright-red azaleas that are part of my landscape planting. Can I propagate them by cuttings?**

A. Some of the more familiar garden and landscape varieties can be propagated by cuttings taken in late July and early August. Tip cuttings should be about three inches long, taken just after the new growth is completed. Apply rooting hormone to the base of the stems before placing the cuttings in a rooting mixture of sand and peat moss in a cold frame. It is difficult to root cuttings from the native azaleas.

28. **Q. How do you start ornamental gourds from seed?**

A. In colder growing regions, gourds are usually raised in pots from seed started in April or May and then transplanted into the garden in June, after the soil has warmed. Gourds are members of the cucumber family, which requires warm soil to root and grow. Start the seeds in preformed pressed-peat pots, which disintegrate quickly in the ground, to avoid root damage at transplanting time. Damaged roots will greatly reduce the productivity of the gourd plant. Seed can also be sown directly into the garden when all danger of frost is past.

29. **Q. How and when do I plant rhododendron and azalea seeds?**

A. As soon as the seeds are ripe, sow them thinly in a flat of peat, leafmold, and sand, or a light potting mix and cover them lightly with shredded peat moss or chopped sphagnum. Water from below and cover with glass or clear plastic. Once the seedlings are large enough to handle, carefully remove them and transplant one to two inches apart in the same type of mixture. Feed them with a liquid plant food, as needed.

30. **Q. Can I divide peony roots in the spring?**

A. The best time is *early* in the fall. Spring-divided peonies often do not bloom for two or more years.

31. **Q. What do I need in the way of supplies to start seeds for tomatoes, peppers, and eggplants indoors?**

A. You need a sterile seed-starting mix, a container for germinating the seeds, (preferably a windowsill greenhouse), water, nutrients, and fresh seeds. Read the back of the seed packet for specific germinating tips for each variety.

32. Q. **What is a windowsill greenhouse?**
A. A windowsill greenhouse is a watertight tray with a clear plastic cover as a top. There are several commercially made versions available, varying in width and length, some with solid tops and some with adjustable vents for moisture control.

33. Q. **What does it mean to "harden-off" a plant?**
A. Plants are very sensitive to a change in environment. Seedlings grown in a greenhouse, for example, must be exposed gradually to new growing conditions. Before planting them in open soil, move the plants to a cold frame or, if they have been growing in a hotbed, leave the sash open at night. The plants will become a darker green as they harden-off.

34. Q. **How do I harden-off transplants which have to be moved from a windowsill greenhouse to the garden?**
A. Set the windowsill greenhouse, without its top, outside for a week to ten days, in an area with partial sun protected from wind exposure. Return the growing tray indoors each night during this period. Water as needed and feed according to the directions on the fertilizer label. After the ten-day period, the growing tray with the seedlings can be moved to a sunny exposure and remain outside, both day and night, until planting time.

35. Q. **Must I harden-off plants before I move them from the greenhouse to the garden?**
A. Yes. They could be injured by a sudden exposure to wind, a lower humidity, or more intense sunlight, which they would receive once they are in the garden.

36. Q. **What is the difference between a cold frame and a hotbed?**
A. A hotbed is heated by electricity, steam, hot water, or by fermenting material. A cold frame has only the heat of the sun.

37. Q. **Is it necessary to use a commercially prepared "sterile" seed starting mix, or can I make my own?**
A. I highly recommend the use of a prepared "sterile" mix in place of a homemade mix, because its use reduces the potential onset of one of the most dreaded plagues of seed starting, damping-off. This disease causes the seedlings to collapse when they are just a few days old.

38. Q. **What is a good material in which to root cuttings?**
A. A half-and-half mixture of peat moss and sand is a good mixture for almost all cuttings. Sand, sphagnum moss, vermiculite, and perlite are other media used for special purposes.

39. Q. **How do I propagate leucothoe?**
A. If the plant is a large clump, you can divide it with a spade or an ax. Do this in the early spring. If propagating by cuttings, place them in a flat of sterile mix and cover it with clear plastic, or root them in a greenhouse bench with bottom heat. You can take both hardwood and softwood cuttings.

40. Q. **Using slips, can shrubs be propagated in the summer?**
A. Yes, many can. The cuttings are taken throughout the summer, according to the species of plant. Use cuttings from wood that is not too soft and juicy nor too hard and woody, and about three to five inches long. It is best to take them with a heel, that is, with the base of the shoot left on. Insert the cuttings in a flat of sand, or in a

cold frame, and cover them with plastic or an old window sash. Shade the propagating area with muslin or a canvas.

41. **Q. I would like to try my hand at propagating shrubs by cuttings. Can you give me a list of those that root easily?**

A. Provided you have prepared the right conditions, privet, honeysuckle, mock orange, forsythia, euonymus, spirea, hydrangea, butterfly bush, and weigela are easily propagated by cuttings. Use a rooting hormone of medium strength.

42. **Q. How can I make hardwood cuttings during the winter?**

A. Cut the whiplike branches into six-to-eight-inch lengths and bury them in a sandy place during the winter. They should root nicely and provide a ready means of propagating. Take the cuttings anytime during the winter. They are referred to as dormant, deciduous cuttings.

43. **Q. What can I do about sour soil in my seed boxes?**

A. Seed flats *must* have adequate air circulation and proper drainage to correct or prevent the sour soil condition. Bore a few holes in the bottom and raise the flats on bricks or wood strips. This type of *"sourness"* generally does not mean that your soil is acid.

44. **Q. How do I propagate slips from oleanders?**

A. Cuttings from oleander should be taken from the current season's growth in July and August. Treat the base of the cuttings with rooting hormone and place them in sand in a close, humid environment such as a cold frame or a glass-covered box. You may also keep shoots in water until rooted and then pot them in soil.

45. **Q. I received a flower arrangement in early March that contained both pussywillow and forsythia stems. Can I root them?**

A. Both forsythia and pussywillow stems root if kept in water. Change the water every three to four days and keep them out of direct sun. While the stems are rooting, foliage will emerge. Reduce the rate of transpiration by making a greenhouse environment. Humidity can be trapped around the stems by covering them with a clear-plastic-dry-cleaning bag.

46. **Q. Can I propagate a camellia by layering?**

A. Yes. Bend a branch, which has been scored with a knife, to the ground and cover it in a shallow trench with sandy soil. The tip of the branch will protrude from the trench. Anchor it with some heavy object to prevent motion and be sure the layer of sandy soil is kept constantly moist. You can start this in June or July.

47. **Q. When and how can one start camellias from cuttings?**

A. In July, take firm, young growths, three or four inches long; prune away the lower leaves and cut the stems horizontally below a joint with a sharp knife. Apply rooting hormone to the base of the cutting and insert it in a sand and peat moss medium, or just in sand. To speed the rooting process, provide a humid environment and bottom heat.

48. **Q. How do I grow a Japanese yew from seeds?**

A. First, you must clean the fleshy pulp from the seeds. Then, stratify by alternating layers of moist peat moss and seeds in a flat which is kept at a temperature of 30 to 40 degrees Fahrenheit. Sow the seeds in early spring. Don't be discouraged if all the seeds do not emerge within a few months, because some may not germinate for a full year.

49. **Q. How can I grow seedlings from the berries of a Hicks yew?**

A. The same way as for the Japanese yew (see preceding question). However, the Hicks yew is a hybrid and the new plants will not have the upright shape that is characteristic of the Hicks yew. To grow an exact likeness, propagate the Hicks yew by stem cuttings taken in early summer.

50. **Q. What is the easiest way to start cuttings of junipers and arborvitaes?**
   A. Cuttings taken in the latter part of August, treated with rooting hormone of medium strength, should be set out, about one and a half inches apart, in flats containing sand that has been made firm before the cuttings are placed in it. Maintain them in a cold frame until there is danger of the sand freezing; then move the flats to a place that is cool and frostproof for the winter.

51. **Q. How can I make a propagation chamber?**
   A. Use a wooden box, ten to twelve inches high, covered snugly with a pane of glass or clear sheet of plastic. Provide drainage holes in the bottom; cover with one inch of peat moss and put in four inches of sterile rooting medium and pack down firmly.

52. **Q. I was told to remove all but a few leaves from a rhododendron cutting before putting it in the propagation chamber. Why?**
   A. Removing foliage from a cutting reduces moisture loss from plant tissue during the rooting process. In addition to pulling off excess foliage, clip the remaining leaves back by one half to reduce transpiration even further. This technique conserves internal moisture for use during rooting.

53. **Q. Can I use a clear plastic sandwich bag as a greenhouse for propagating a Swedish ivy houseplant?**
   A. Yes. Any clear plastic bag that does not have holes can be used to make a greenhouse. Place moist propagating mix in the bottom of the bag to a depth of at least two inches. Take a two- to three-inch cutting from the growing tip of the stem with at least three nodes (points where leaves are attached), strip off the lowest leaf, and insert the cutting into the propagating mix to a depth of one inch. Seal the bag and place it in filtered bright light. Mark the starting date in your garden records, as Swedish ivy develops roots in five to seven days.

54. **Q. How can I tell if a cutting has developed roots when it is inside of the propagation chamber? I cannot see the base of the cutting.**
   A. The *only* way to tell is to carefully lift the cutting from the propagating mix and look. If you have researched the species being propagated, you will have a clue as to the length of time it takes. Do not confuse the presence of new growth on a cutting as a sign of rooting.

55. **Q. What is meant by hardwood cuttings?**
   A. Hardwood cuttings are from fully mature shoots, generally taken from the current year's growth after a few frosts. They are packed in moist peat moss or sand and stored at 35 to 40 degrees Fahrenheit until they can be planted in the spring. During the cold-storage period, callus tissue grows over the basal end of the cutting. Roots may grow from the callus tissue.

56. **Q. What is meant by half-ripe wood cuttings?**
   A. Half-ripe wood cuttings are taken in July and August when the shoots have finished growth but are not yet mature.

57. **Q. What are softwood cuttings?**
   A. These are cuttings from hardy shrubs taken during May and early June, from shoots that are still actively growing.

58. **Q. How can one hurry the germination process for hard-shell seeds?**
A. Soften the shells by soaking them overnight in warm water, or nick the hard shell of larger seeds with a knife. Professionals sometimes treat seeds with acid, but this is not recommended for the amateur.

59. **Q. What are the main conditions in seed germination?**
A. Seeds must have moisture, proper temperature, and free oxygen for germination. Once the seed has been moistened, do not let it dry out, as this will stop the germination process and kill the seed. Some seeds require light as an additional condition for germination.

60. **Q. What are various methods of plant propagation?**
A. Bulbils, cormels, cuttings, division, grafting, layers, offsets, rhizomes, runners, seeds, spores, stolons, suckers, and tubers.

61. **Q. How can I set up a system for mist propagation?**
A. Choose a site, with an area of about one square yard, located in full sun, and protect it with a windbreak if the area is windy. Drainage is very important; the rooting medium should be coarse sand and the pots must be placed on a platform of galvanized wire mesh, raised an inch or so above the ground. Finally, you need a water source to deliver one and a half gallons of water per hour at thirty to fifty pounds of pressure, and an adjustable mist nozzle.

62. **Q. What are the advantages and disadvantages of rooting cuttings by constant mist?**
A. It allows you to root larger cuttings than you could under normal means, and it is an easier method for cuttings that are usually considered hard to root. A disadvantage is the high mortality rate of transplants.

63. **Q. When rooting cuttings by constant mist, is it necessary to keep the spray on all the time?**
A. An intermittent mist is considered to be the most desirable schedule. The installation of an automated electronic leaf will shut the water off when it is wet and turn it on when it is dry. It should do no real harm, however, to run the mist night and day.

64. **Q. When air layering, how does one know when to remove the layer?**
A. If you have used a clear plastic wrap as the outer covering of the layer, remove the layer when roots are visible. Because the time at which the layer is removed is probably the most critical period, the layer should be treated as though it were an unrooted cutting. Remove the plastic wrap and pot the cutting; keep it in an environment protected from wind and direct sun.

65. **Q. What plants can be raised by root cuttings?**
A. Many plants can be propagated from root cuttings, including rose, daphne, phlox, raspberry, lilac, sumac, locust, sweet fern, breadfruit, pear, and apple. However, if root cuttings are made of grafted or budded plants, you must remember that it will be the understock that is propagated.

66. **Q. What should I do with the cuttings once they are rooted?**
A. What you do with a cutting after rooting depends on the time of year. Cuttings root in July or August should be potted up and the pots plugged into sand or peat moss in a cold frame, to be planted the following spring. Cuttings that root later than this can be left in their rooting medium until it's time to plant in the spring. Under both circumstances, they should be protected after the first severe frost by covering them lightly with a scattering of salt hay.

67. **Q. Can any sort of root be used to graft on an ornamental tree?**

A. No. An ornamental tree must be grafted on a root stock very closely related to it, botanically. Not even all oaks can be grafted on just one kind of oak stock, and elms cannot be grafted on ash, nor ash on beech.

68. **Q. Why is budding sometimes preferred to grafting?**
    A. Only one bud is needed to produce a new plant, and less time is consumed in budding. A given amount of scion wood will give you more buds than scions. When dealing with the stone fruits, budding ensures better results than grafting.

69. **Q. What is a scion?**
    A. It is a short portion of stem of the plant that is to be duplicated, usually containing several dormant buds. The base is cut in such a way that the cambium will come in direct contact with the cambium layer of the understock, which is cut to fit the scion. When united with the understock, the scion becomes the stem and/or branches of the graft.

70. **Q. What is the understock of a grafted plant?**
    A. Understock (rootstock) is the lower part, which develops into the root system of the grafted plant, to which the scion or bud is attached. Rooted cuttings, a layered plant, or seedlings are generally used as understocks.

71. **Q. What is a bud stick?**
    A. A bud stick is a shoot from which buds are cut for budding, usually taken from the current year's growth.

72. **Q. Can any plant be grafted on any other plant?**
    A. No. Only those plants that are closely related botanically can form a successful graft union.

73. **Q. What is double grafting?**
    A. Double grafting has one graft between the rootstock and the interstock and another graft between the interstock and the scion. Double grafting is done to overcome graft incompatibility, to obtain dwarfing capability of an intermediate stock, to obtain a strong trunk, or to obtain a disease-resistant trunk.

74. **Q. How are plants propagated by runners?**
    A. It's easy. Dig up the runners when they are rooted, and replant. If you want to avoid disturbing the roots, fill a pot with earth and secure the runner to the soil. Sever the runner from the main plant as soon as it has rooted.

75. **Q. How are plants propagated by suckers?**
    A. Rooted suckers (sprouts emerging from the root system) can be severed and dug up during the dormant season. They can be potted, pruned back if necessary, and treated much as you would cuttings.

76. **Q. Can I make new plants from leaves, if I treat them in the same way as stem cuttings?**
    A. Yes, *in some cases.* Many succulents such as sedum are propagated from leaves. Other common examples are African violets and Rex begonias.

77. **Q. How should I propagate new plants from my old lilac bush?**
    A. If your lilac bush is not a grafted plant, you can propagate from suckers by digging them up, cutting the tops back by one half, and planting. If you have a grafted variety, the best method would be to propagate from dormant, deciduous cuttings.

78. **Q. When I use vermiculite for rooting cuttings, it gets too wet. What am I doing wrong?**

A. You are adding too much water. Vermiculite absorbs three or four times its volume in water; after that, it can't hold anymore. Use a flat that provides better drainage, or try using a mixture of sand and peat moss.

79. **Q. Can I use plastic or fiberglass as a cover for a cold frame?**

A. They both will work and the light weight is nice when it comes to lifting and storing the sash. Plastic may only last a year or two, but the low cost of replacement will be offsetting. You may have problems in high winds unless you can anchor them down properly.

80. **Q. How is milled or ground sphagnum moss used?**

A. It is valued highly for its use in propagation, due to its ability to inhibit damping-off of seedlings which are germinated in it. This medium must be supplemented with nutrients in order to sustain plants for an extended period of time but, because of its tremendous water-holding capacity (ten to twenty times its weight), germinating seeds can be exposed to light without drying out.

81. **Q. When I try to root an avocado seed, it gets slimy and rots. What should I do?**

A. After removing the seed from the fruit, wash it under water until it no longer feels slick. Insert three toothpicks into the seed at the middle to act as supports and suspend the flattened end in water. After filling the glass with enough water to cover the base of the seed, set it in a bright, warm place, replacing water as it evaporates. Change the water and wash the glass and seed once a week to remove any slime that accumulates. Since there is no way to tell the ripeness of the seed, it may take a few days to several weeks for the taproot to appear.

82. **Q. When should layering be done?**

A. Spring is best because, in most cases, there will be plenty of time for a good root system to develop before winter. In colder parts of the country, the roots may be disturbed by winter heaving if the plants are layered too late.

83. **Q. Why is it recommended to use bottom heat when rooting cuttings indoors?**

A. Bottom heat stimulates the hormone balance and callus formation in the cutting tissue. Nearly all cuttings will benefit from keeping the tops of the plants cool at 55 to 65 degrees Fahrenheit and the bottom warm at 70 to 75 degrees Fahrenheit. Keeping the tops cool also reduces the rate of transpiration.

84. **Q. How can I provide bottom heat for rooting cuttings and germinating seeds?**

A. You need only a few degrees difference from the temperature at the top of the propagation chamber to the bottom. Set the seed or cutting flat on top of the refrigerator or on the top of the gas dryer (the pilot light provides the bottom heat). Thermostatically controlled, electric heating mats and heating cables are also available.

85. **Q. I broke a leaf from a jade plant and put it in a sterile cactus propagation mix, but it did not grow. What happened?**

A. You did not take a portion of the node with the leaf cutting. To propagate *Crassula*, use a leaf with a small portion of stem attached. It is from the node that the new plant will arise.

86. **Q. My dieffenbachia has grown to where it has reached the ceiling. It has only two leaves at the top and a "telephone pole" for a stem. What to do?**

A. Major surgery is in order. Remove an eighteen-inch cutting from the very top, apply rooting hormone, and place the cutting in moist sand in a greenhouse environment.

The leaves must be in a humid environment while the stem is rooting. The "telephone pole" can be cut into logs six to eight inches in length and rooted in moist sand. When cutting the "logs" from the mother plant, mark the base of each in order to know which end is up. An eight-foot-tall dieffenbachia plant will yield as many as fourteen new plants. Leave a stump in the original pot and it will grow at least two more new shoots.

IV

———

PLANTING

I'M SURE YOU'VE SEEN SHOPPERS in the supermarket with luxuriant, fat-budded gardenia plants sticking up from their grocery carts. The plants may even have shown off a few crispy white, fragrant flowers in wide open bloom. Did you know that the great majority of those gardenias die within a very short period of time? Fat, green buds drop off without opening, the leaves turn bright yellow and droop, and the stems dry up.

The problem is not with the gardenia; it is with the person who purchased the plant and placed it in an adverse environment. The demise of the gardenia could be caused by trying to grow it in poor light, in a room lacking humidity, with too much or too little water. The most important factor to discuss about growing plants is a proper environment for the plant you select.

The old adage or guiding principle of placing a fifty-cent plant in a five-dollar hole (environment) is what gardening is all about. Adhere to this principle and, before long, you will have a five-dollar plant. Don't ever be guilty of placing a five-dollar plant in a fifty-cent hole (environment) as it will be dead shortly. Whether you are gardening in a window box or on a one-acre site, it is a *must* to properly consider the entire environment including the type of plant, location (sun versus shade), soil conditions (drainage and soil type), preparation, and time of year you are planting.

Over the years, I have seen many mistakes in planting new trees and shrubs. One that comes to mind is the family that wanted to take a local garden center to court for selling bad plants. The family had purchased and planted an entire landscape planting, over three hundred plants—all of which died. They had no idea what might have gone wrong.

They requested my professional analysis of the situation. I made a house call to see the site first-hand, and to discuss the procedures they used for planting.

They had drawn a complete design to scale, mindful of the ultimate growth of each plant. They had tested the soil for both drainage and soil acidity, and prepared a top-quality backfill mixture for planting by adding a rich, decomposed organic matter to the parent soil. All seemed well until we walked to the side of the house. I noticed a pile of burlap strips mixed with hemp string, fresh soil and portions of severed roots. The soil in the pile didn't look anything like the natural soil in the planting bed or the backfill mix they had so carefully prepared. Upon further questioning, the owner said the plants had been purchased *after* the holes were dug. They believed that having the planting holes prepared in advance would speed up the planting process and reduce the chance of drying of the soil balls. They wanted to lessen the chance of anything going wrong with their new specimens. Finding the balled and burlapped portion of each plant too large to fit in the predug hole, they used a sharp garden spade to shave off some of the soil to make the ball smaller. In doing so, they had cut away a majority of the roots of each plant.

With this mistake in mind, let's review the thought process I use to plan my planting. I consider: one, the selection of the plant; two, the site selection; three, the site preparation; and four, the time of year for planting. By considering these points in advance, I hope to eliminate potential disasters. A cardinal rule of gardening is to *plan before you plant.*

SELECTION OF THE PLANT

Before I purchase any plant, I ask myself these questions:
1. What will the plant be used for?
2. How hardy is the plant?
3. What is the life span of the plant?
4. How fast does it grow?
5. Is the plant relatively pestfree?
6. Are there specific maintenance requirements?
7. How much will the plant cost?

Let's discuss each one of these questions as it relates to purchasing new plants for your home. If you spend some brainpower before you spend money, you will never buy a plant unsuitable to your environment, or you will be aware that changes are necessary to ensure success.

1. *What will the plant be used for?* Is it a tree to provide shade for a patio? If so, do you want filtered shade or deep shade? The *Gleditsia triacanthos inermis*, the Shademaster Thornless Honey Locust, would provide filtered shade, whereas a sugar or Norway maple would provide deep shade.

Are you looking for a living hedge to provide screening from your next-door neighbor? Do you want the hedge to provide a year-round screen? If yes to either, an evergreen plant (one which holds its foliage year round) must be selected for planting. Evergreens like hemlock, taxus, or arborvitae might be chosen as they can be maintained in height and width and, at the same time, provide a dense screen. If summer screening is all that is needed, a deciduous hedge (one that drops its foliage in the fall) may be planted. Forsythia, privet, lilac or spirea may fill the bill.

For the indoor environment, would you like to use living plants instead of drapes for privacy at the windows? If yes, you'll select a plant with a relatively dense growth habit such as *Cissus rhombifolia* (grape ivy) or *Plectranthus australis* (Swedish ivy). They both grow into lush, dense hanging baskets of dark-green leaves. An alternative to hanging plants might be large, potted upright-growing specimens. The large, banana-sized leaves of the Schefflera or umbrella tree, or the dense, dark-green leaves of a weeping fig, *Ficus benjamina*, each provide screening since they grow into sizeable specimens, holding foliage from top to bottom. Avoid the *Dracaena marginata* (Madagascar dragon tree) for screening purposes. Although the dragon tree has an architecturally interesting trunk and stem-growth characteristics, it loses its lower foliage and with it, its ability to screen.

2. *How hardy is the plant?* When we speak of plant hardiness, we primarily speak of the plant's ability to survive given winter temperatures. Study the *USDA Plant Hardiness Map of the United States* to determine the zone (range of average annual minimum temperatures) in which you live. Knowing the zone allows you to better determine whether a specific variety of plant has a chance to overwinter in your garden. If you live on the line between two zones, or have any doubt about your zone, you may want to order the colorful four-by four-foot hardiness map, item #1417, from the Government Printing Office.

Many mail-order plant companies that distribute perennials, fruit trees, berries, and ornamental trees and shrubs list the growing zones for their plants. Hardiness is often listed as a range. For example: in the *Spring 1999 Wayside Gardens Catalog*, page 35, "Hybrid *Rhododendron* 'Jericho': Hardy to at least -20 degrees F. Zones 4-8." Or on page 29: "*Gillardia grandiflora* 'Goblin' Blanket flower: Zones 3-10." This zone rating tells you this plant adapts to almost anywhere in the continental United States.

When we speak of hardiness as it relates to growing regions, the zone rating tells us the plant may "burn up" in a given location, or there is not enough cold to set the flowering and fruiting mechanism properly. A fruit tree and landscape catalog such as the *Gurney's Seed & Nursery Co.*, Spring 1999 edition gives additional information in the description, page 55 of Belle of Georgia Peach: "Ripens in August: For Zones 5-8. Self-pollinating."

Because it is not technically tied to cold temperature, we often overlook one more aspect of hardiness: the hardiness of plants in the indoor environment. The indoor environment could be so adverse to the plant's growing needs that the plant has little chance of survival. During winter months, heating in many homes creates an environment as dry as the Sahara Desert, 5 percent humidity or less. This lack of moisture in the air creates a dehydrating effect on plant tissue. Ferns present a good example. If you live in an extremely dry home, you will have enormous difficulty keeping Boston fern foliage from turning crisp and drying up. The drying back of the foliage tips on all varieties of *Dracaena* corn plants, spider plants, and peace lilies is also common during winter. The gardenia plant suffers in a hot, dry environment. Earlier, we discussed purchasing a gardenia and watching it die. It could have been insufficiently hardy for its environment.

3. *What is the life span of the plant?* Simply put, how long will the plant live? Compare the Lombardy poplar to the tall white oak. The Lombardy poplar matures in twenty-five to thirty years, whereas the white oak may survive for centuries. Most landscape plants have a knowable and measurable life span. Depending on the general, overall growing environment and the care you give your plants, it is easy to expand a plant's useful life.

Indoors, much enjoyment can be derived from growing morning glories in hanging baskets. They last for only a few months but give colorful blossoms during this short period. The ivy geranium, on the other hand, will continuously bloom for years in the proper environment.

4. *How fast does it grow?* A classic example is the willow versus the oak. A ten-year-old willow tree can be a monster, forty, fifty, or even sixty feet tall and equally broad, but a ten-year-old oak may only double in size and still be quite small. The quickness of growth is important to many landscape situa-tions. A hedge to block out a view must grow quickly, or you will need to start with much larger, more expensive plants. On the other hand, plants used to frame a picture window, such as taxus or juniper, must grow slowly enough with normal maintenance so they do not obstruct the view.

The indoor plant *aficionado* need only compare the *Dieffenbachia*, commonly called the dumb cane, with the *Ficus benjamina*, weeping fig. Dieffenbachia may grow two to three feet a year and produce weak, brittle stems, but the weeping fig may add only a few but rigid, strong inches of new growth during the same period of time.

5. *Is the plant relatively pestfree?* When it comes to picking an unpestered plant, that's a tough one. Somewhere along the line, most plants are susceptible to something. If you take the time to identify possible pest problems *before* you acquire a plant, you may choose a different species, or at least you will know what to expect and, hopefully, how to combat them.

The lilac is highly prone to borers that invade the main stems, scale that covers the bark, and powdery mildew that turns the foliage white. All these problems have solutions, but take time and effort to accomplish.

Many varieties of roses are susceptible to black spot and mildew leaf diseases, and to piercing and sucking pests like spider mites and aphids, as well as to chewing insects, including the Japanese beetle and rose chafer. Some of the new landscape or shrub roses appear to be somewhat resistant to many of these pest problems.

Coleus, an attractive bedding plant grown for its colorful foliage, is prone to mealy bugs, slugs and spider mites. And, as you may already know, something in the way of a pest attacks almost every fruit and vegetable.

I guess there is always an exception to every rule. One plant with no major pest problems is ginkgo, the maidenhair tree. It is the only surviving species of the ginkgo family, *Ginkgoaceae*, which included many species in ages past.

Indoors, too, all our plants seem to catch something. The gardenia is highly prone to invasions of spider mites; the fuschia is often infested with clouds of whitefly; and the dieffenbachia is laden with cottony blobs called mealybugs. Most all these pests can be controlled *if* you know what you're fighting.

6. *Are there specific maintenance requirements?* This is one category to be scrutinized very carefully. How much time do you have to prune regularly? A fast-growing plant like mint needs to be pruned back several times a year. If you don't keep it clipped, mint can crowd out neighboring plants very quickly.

I often think of the homeowner who planted a row of rhododendrons between the walkway and the house. The plants bloomed only for the first two years after planting. Shortly after planting they began to grow. To maintain their size, the plants need to be pruned back annually so people can use the walkway. The major problem was, the homeowner pruned the shrubs every fall to remove the summer's growth. In his effort to keep the plants compact, he pruned them at the wrong time of the year, guaranteeing nary a bloom. Rhododendrons bloom on last year's growth.

Have you ever tried to build a terrarium? Have you ever seen those tiny plants in small bottles? Have you ever purchased what you thought were dwarf plants only to find out later that they grew into enormous plants?

Remember, little plants often become big plants. If you want to construct a terrarium, you must know the varieties and the growing characteristics of all the plants to be used. Then, and only then, you'll have a terrarium that is basically maintenance free. You may have to clip a few plants now and then, but it should be a manageable job. We're lucky in this day and age, because many plants come in dwarf varieties, that is, plants that stay relatively small.

7. *How much will the plant cost?* Last but not least, for the average gardener, cost is a significant consideration. There are many factors that determine the price of a plant; one is size. If you select *Rhododendron 'Roseum elegans'*, a two-foot-tall plant will cost much less than a five-foot-fall plant of the same variety. But, if you select the one-foot tall, dwarf rhododendron "Shamrock", it will be many times more expensive than the five-foot-tall 'Roseum elegans'. The reason in this case is the variety. Slow-growing plants cost growers more in time and labor to ready them for market. So, for quick landscaping results, it just might pay to use fast-growing, more readily available varieties.

Of course, house plants vary in price according to size, too. The price of a twelve-inch *Dracaena marginata* in a six-inch pot will not compare to a six-foot-tall specimen of the same variety. Due to the cost of greenhouse space, house plants, no matter what the variety, get substantially more expensive as their size increases.

The time of year can add cost, too. In areas of the country where a particular time of year is the most popular for planting, plants generally will be more expensive during that busy season. As soon as the out-of-season planting time arrives, most nurseries and garden centers reduce their prices to make room for new merchandise, and to be rid of this year's plants. Being able to wait and have patience can save big bucks on plant-material costs.

If you consider all of the seven previously listed points under "Selection of the Plant," very seldom will you go wrong in gardening.

SELECTION OF SITE AND ENVIRONMENT

Now that we have considered the crucial points of plant selection, it is important to match that plant to the site and environment. As the environmental optimum decreases, so does growth. We are back to the adage of a fifty-cent plant in a five-dollar hole; the site and environment are part of the hole. So, start by doing a complete analysis of the growing conditions of your home and property, indoors and outdoors.

Indoor Plants

For indoor plant culture, you must consider light, temperature, and humidity. The light varies substantially in every part of the home. You might have a south-facing window with full sun all day long, or only an obstructed, partial bright light. An east or west window can, at the most, provide only a half day of direct sun. The balance of the day contributes only filtered bright light. As the seasons change, the amount of light available to your plants fluctuates, too. Where light is insufficient, you may need an artificial light source. To measure available light, use a standard light meter that measures foot-candles. The foot-candle reading can be matched to the plant and its light requirements.

In most cases, temperature in the home created by a forced-air furnace or a steam-heat boiler can be adjusted by turning the thermostat up or down. If you live in an apartment with central heat controlled by the landlord, changing the temperature may be much more difficult. Windowsill temperatures vary depending on the outside temperature and use of insulated glass. During the daytime, the windowsill may be a toasty warm environment for your African violets, but at night, the same windowsill could be too cool and cause collapse of the root systems. African violets love warm roots both day and night.

Knowing the amount of moisture in the air during winter heating months and during the air-conditioning summer months will help you determine what plants will grow best in your indoor environment. Tropical plants, such as philodendron, ficus, and croton, all appreciate high humidity. One solution for air lacking moisture is to grow more plants.

Each plant gives off moisture through its leaves (transpiration) and from the soil (evaporation). Cactus and other succulents, like jade and sedum, make great candidates for a dry or desertlike environment.

Outdoor Plants

In the outdoor garden, site and environment must be considered, too. Minimize winter temperature fluctuation around your plants. Marginally hardy plants can often be grown in areas called sun traps, small pockets for growing where the sun is captured and the cold winter temperature is held at bay. My crape myrtle, planted in an open part of the garden, always suffered from dieback each winter. This plant species is marginally hardy in my area, usually hardy only to Zone 7. I followed a suggestion of another gardener and moved the plant into a sunny location protected from cold winter winds. Now the plant flourishes, even though I garden in Zone 6.

Soil must also be considered as part of the site and environment. Check the soil conditions in relation to drainage, organic matter, pH, moisture-holding capacity, and nutrient content.

With few exceptions, drainage problems can be corrected. If you can discover a drainage problem before planting, the European-developed French drain, a drywell, perforated plastic pipe, or agricultural tile drains may solve the problem. Even simply adding sand to soil that drains poorly, may do it. In areas that cannot be conveniently drained, raised beds may be the solution. In wet areas where I use a raised bed to solve the drainage problem, it pays to start with small plants. The roots have a chance to acclimate to the wetter soil underneath. For the outdoor-container gardener, perlite and/or sand can be added to the potting mix to improve drainage.

Soil structures and textures vary throughout the world. In fact, they may vary substantially from one side of your property to the other. If you have a sandy soil, a clay soil, or any soil in between, the structure can always be changed and improved. Improvements may come from adding proper amounts of lime or sulfur, if needed, to stimulate beneficial soil organisms; by turning under crop residues to supply more organic matter and nutrients; and by never handling soil when it is too wet. Organic matter from the compost pile or from peat moss will help stabilize sandy soils and improve the drainage capacity of clay soils.

Generally, the darker the soil color, the higher its organic content.

As discussed earlier, the pH represents soil acidity or alkalinity. Just as you may find a difference in soils from one side of the property to the other, so may the pH of the soil also vary greatly. Before adjusting the pH, you must know which plants you plan to grow.

If you are growing azaleas, rhododendrons, laurels or other acid-loving plants, make sure the soil pH is in the acid range, 5.0 to 6.5 pH. If you are establishing turf, such as a beautiful bluegrass lawn, you'll want the pH to tend toward the neutral, 6.2 to 7.0 pH.

Adding either sulphur or lime adjusts the pH of the soil. The addition of lime makes an acid soil more alkaline. Alkaline soil can be adjusted toward the acid level simply by adding sulphur. Adding well-decomposed organic matter also lowers the soil pH. At your florist and garden shop there are many kits available for testing pH or soil acidity. If you do not have this test kit in your arsenal of gardening products, it's time to buy one and learn how to use it.

For gardeners in a sandy region, such as along the seashore or in the desert, the soil's moisture-holding capacity may be critical. Adding organic matter to a sandy soil will increase its moisture-holding capacity. If you have a poorly draining soil, its capacity to hold water is probably high. Add sand and organic matter to alleviate the drainage problem. In claytype soils, incorporate gypsum to improve drainage over a period of time.

Last but not least when considering soil, it pays to do a complete analysis of the nutrient content so you have an inventory of what elements were present when the planting project began. Tests are done for nitrogen, phosphorus, and potassium, the three major elements for plant growth. If you are considering intensive gardening, it will pay to have a complete analysis done, including one for the minor elements. The minor elements include zinc, boron, magnesium, molybdenum, sulphur, iron, and so on. Testing for them is extremely valuable in flower and vegetable gardening where crops have grown in the same area, year after year after year. By cultivating the same crops year after year, you probably have depleted the soil of some minor elements, despite your annual applications of nitrogen, phosphorus, and potassium, such as 5-10-5 or 5-10-10.

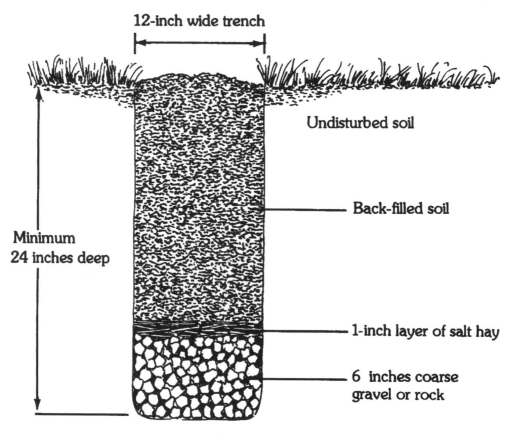

French Drain

Raised Bed Gardening

Another question concerning the site and environment has to do with exposure. How much wind and sun is the plant exposed to? In the northern garden, a typical example of exposure is rhododendron winter burn. If a rhododendron or azalea lives on the northwest side of the house and if during March and April much of the foliage seems burned, you are seeing desiccation caused by winter winds and sun. When the ground freezes, the root system of a shallow-rooted plant also freezes; consequently, the plant cannot take up adequate moisture to fulfill its needs for photosynthesis and transpiration during the winter. With sun and wind striking the foliage, the plant especially requires moisture; but with moisture frozen in the ground, the root system cannot absorb it. Without a constant source of water, the cells in the leaves and stems dehydrate.

For winter protection we can apply an anti-desiccant, or we can put up a burlap screen to break the cold, dehydrating winter wind. To me, there is nothing more dissatisfying than driving up to a home surrounded by landscape plants wrapped in brown burlap all winter. (Of course, you can now buy green burlap.) What I'm saying is: Select the right plant for the right place!

Mulch protects as it insulates the soil's microclimate. Soil temperatures can be influenced by a "blanket" over the surface of the soil. Some mulches are used to keep the soil cool and some are used to retain heat. Mulches and their uses will be discussed in a later chapter.

Another site-and-environment-related consideration is competition. We know that plants compete for nutrients and water, particularly if they grow in close proximity to one another. A good example: planting a ground cover, such as pachysandra or vinca, under a big, Norway maple tree. The maple tree's surface roots will compete with the shallow root systems of the ground cover. By identifying competition on the site, you can simply adjust your watering and feeding procedures.

Consider, also, the likelihood of insect and disease problems due to growing conditions of the site and environment. Specific growing conditions can and will encourage pathogenic problems. Classic examples: Roses grown in a protected environment with little air movement often succumb to heavy infections of black spot and mildew, and infestations of aphids and spider mites. Lilac shrubs grown without adequate air circulation are beset with powdery mildew on their foliage, and scale insects on their stems.

SITE PREPARATION

If you have selected the proper plant and correctly matched it to the environment, you are now ready for the next step—digging and preparing the hole for that fifty-cent plant.

Until recently, it was recommended to dig a hole one to one and one-half times the depth of the container, bare-root system, or ball and two or more times the diameter of the ball or spread of the root system. I still subscribe to this system, particularly if you are planting in "suburbia" or "urban" America, areas where the builder may have disturbed the soil.

Start with the soil. The same procedure for soil preparation applies whether you are planting a bare-root plant, a balled and burlapped plant, or a container-grown plant. Both deciduous and evergreen plants come in all three types. A general rule of thumb for planting any of them is to dig a hole at least two times the diameter of the container, the ball and burlap, or the spread of the bare-root system. This seems like extra work, but you will be rewarded with a healthy growing environment for the new root system. Dig the hole half again as deep. This depth will allow you to explore the soil's subsurface, an absolute necessity for planting in soil which has previously been disturbed. While exploring the depths of your new planting hole, you may find construction debris, rusty beer cans, or any variety of refuse.

If there is any question about your soil draining properly, stop after digging the hole and fill it with water. If water remains visible for more than twenty-four hours, you must correct the drainage; otherwise, you'll be planting your investment in a "bucket of water,"—sure death for the plant. Before amending the soil to prepare the backfill, return enough of the original, unamended soil to the hole to establish the planting depth. Compact this soil to reduce settling.

I know some horticulturists recommend discarding the soil taken from the hole and replacing it with fresh topsoil. But, as I mentioned in Chapter II, "Soils," you *can* make a "silk purse out of a sow's ear" by amending the soil. For sandy soils, mix the soil taken from the hole, by volume, with as much as 30 to 50 percent organic matter, in the form of well-rotted compost or peat moss to prepare "backfill". For amending claytype soils, I add organic matter to improve the clay structure. Organic matter breaks down into humic acid which coats the clay soil particles, thus improving aeration and drainage. Adding bone meal to this mixture will provide a slow-release source of phosphorus. In general, for balled and burlapped plants and container-grown plants, the planting depth is determined by the top of the soil ball or the level of soil in the container. If the flair of the root system is buried with excessive potting mix (a very common problem with container culture), scrape away as much of the surface mix as needed to expose the flair. This may mean that you are removing as much as two to three inches of the soil surface. Bare-root plants with woody stems will show a difference in coloration of the stems, indicating the soil line.

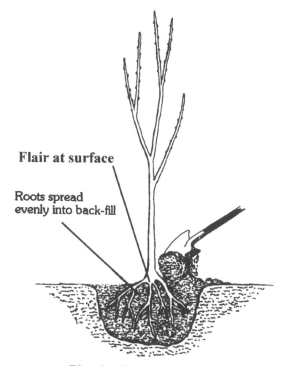

Flair at surface

Roots spread evenly into back-fill

Planting Bare Root Tree

When planting bare-root plants, always read and follow the planting instructions that come with them. In most cases, the directions will instruct you to soak the roots in water for a given period of time, usually overnight. This soaking helps rehydrate the root

system. To figure the planting depth for bare-root plants, pile backfill into the center of the hole to make an inverted cone. Then spread the roots around the cone and fill the balance of the hole, gently packing the soil down to remove any air spaces.

Balled and burlapped plants should be set into the hole by grasping the burlap or string, never by lifting plants by the stem. Check the planting depth by placing a straight edge (shovel handle will do) across the hole to determine that the ball is not below the proper planting level. Then, add backfill to the hole to one-half full and pack firmly. Next, cut the strings used to secure the burlap; peel the burlap back from the top of the soil ball and let it lay in the hole. Generally, we do not remove natural fiber burlap from the balled and burlapped plant. However, if the "burlap" is really nylon or plastic, remove it after the plant is placed in the hole and before the first backfill is placed around the ball. These nylon or plastic materials do not deteriorate and will inhibit normal root penetration. Then, fill the hole to the top with backfill, leaving a dishlike impression around the outside edge to retain water.

If the specimen is a container-grown plant, remember to remove the container unless the directions specifically say it is "biodegradable". I still prefer to remove biodegradable containers because of potential watering and root-development problems that will lurk around for months to come. If a plantable container dries out before the new plant is established, roots will not grow through the container walls into the backfill, and water flow from the backfill to the root mass is inhibited.

Now, don't forget to thoroughly "water in" your new plant. Watering in means giving the plant a thorough soaking of water with two waterings. The initial watering should be done immediately after planting to settle the soil around the roots and to remove air pockets between the soil particles. Air pockets (not the normal spaces between the soil particles) cause dehydration of roots, inhibit hair root development and show up as a slow death to the plant. The second watering-in should be done the following day. This second watering, or the lack thereof, is the one, I believe, that is the killer of many plants. The first watering saturates the backfill, but often does not thoroughly wet the ball of soil or root system. The second watering

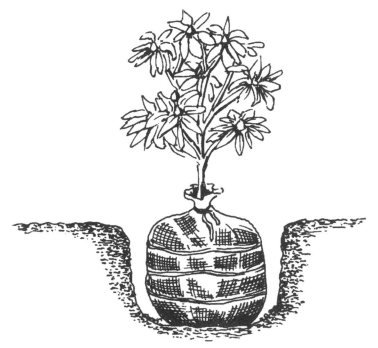

Planting: Balled and Burlapped (B & B)

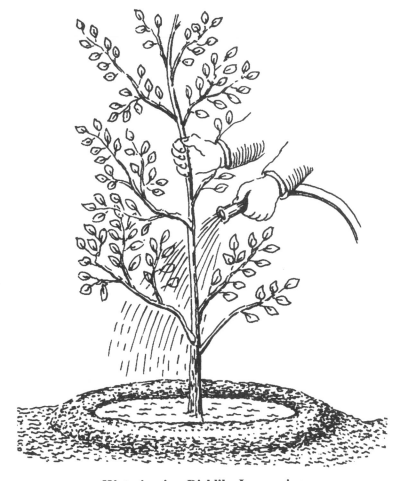

Watering-in: Dishlike Impression

ensures penetration of moisture to the entire planting area, including the root mass and backfill.

If you are eager to feed your plants to give them a boost, consider the fertilizer you are using: organic or slow-release versus water-soluble inorganic. There is little chance of burning the plant's root system when using commercially prepared organic or slow-release forms of fertilizer. Water-soluble inorganic forms of fertilizer, which have readily available nitrogen, may cause damage if used excessively. In any case, no matter what fertilizer you use, *read the label!*

Root Stimulators

Recently, several commercially prepared root-stimulator products have been intro-duced to the consumer market. They include, but are not limited to, Roots, Help, BioPak, and Organica Plant Growth Activator and, in my experience, are beneficial when used according to the label directions at planting time. These products contain natural plant extracts, vitamins, amino acids, enzymes, naturally-occurring beneficial bacteria, humic acid and microbes. These ingredients stimulate growth of, and activation of, beneficial bacteria in the soil, resulting in faster and increased root growth. I have used all of the above-mentioned root stimulators for planting balled and burlapped, container, and bare root plants, by incorporating the product in the initial watering immediately after planting. In all cases, when compared to identical plants in similar planting conditions, those

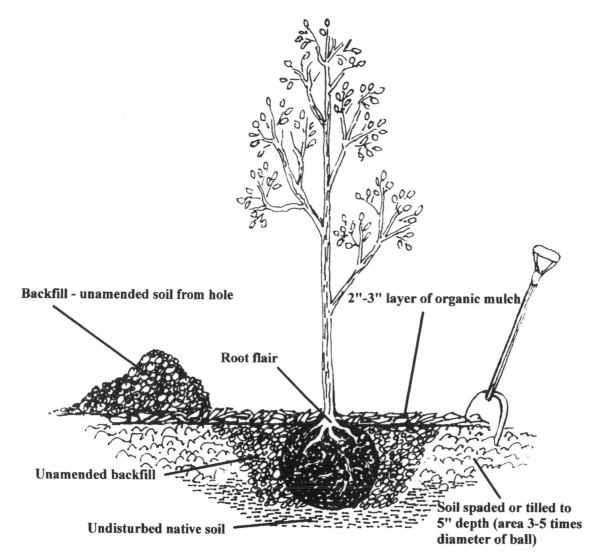

Backfill - unamended soil from hole

2"-3" layer of organic mulch

Root flair

Unamended backfill

Undisturbed native soil

Soil spaded or tilled to 5" depth (area 3-5 times diameter of ball)

Balled & Burlapped: Recommended Planting Procedure
American Forestry Association

treated with root stimulator showed little or no symptoms of transplant shock (wilting and/or desiccation). This treatment was particularly an advantage when planting mail-order, bare-root rose plants. The bare-root plants had already sprouted by the time they were set out in late May.

Latest Planting Procedures

The latest recommendations for planting procedures come from The American Forestry Association, the National Urban Forest Council, Cooperative Extension agents, and other horticulturists. These new recommendations have resulted from planting and plant problems resulting when gardening in the hard and compacted soils of suburban and urban environs.

The problem: compacted soil from construction, peat moss amendments to the backfill which act like a sponge, and poor drainage. The result is a "pot" or pit, which soon fills with water and eventually drowns the roots.

The solution: Ensure that the new tree or shrub can produce healthy, vigorous branches, foliage, and roots. Instead of making a planting hole, make a large planting area that is wide, but not excessively deep. The soil should be loosened to accommodate root development. Mark out an area five times the diameter of the root ball, container, or spread of the bare root system. For a general landscape bed, such as a foundation planting, it may be easiest to use a power tiller to work the entire planting area to an approximate depth of twelve inches. For small planting areas, turning the soil with a spading fork, round-pointed shovel, or nursery spade is sufficient. If organic matter is to be added in the form of well-rotted compost or peat moss, it may be added to the loosened soil as long as it is uniformly incorporated throughout the planting area. This loosening of the soil encourages an even development of the root system in all directions from the plant.

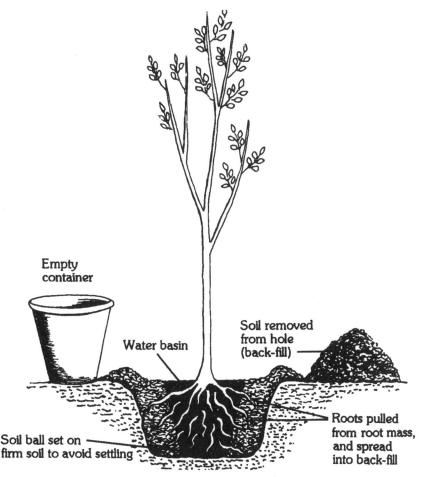

Empty container

Water basin

Soil removed from hole (back-fill)

Soil ball set on firm soil to avoid settling

Roots pulled from root mass, and spread into back-fill

Planting Container-Grown Tree

STEP BY STEP PLANTING

To install a tree or shrub, dig a planting hole no deeper than the depth of the ball or container, and three to four times its width. Set the plant in the hole to check the planting depth. If too deep, remove the plant and pack unamended, native soil in the bottom of the hole to establish a proper depth. If too shallow, remove more soil from the bottom of the hole, making it deeper for planting. To prevent sinking or shifting of the root system, the plant ball or root mass must be set on solid, undisturbed soil, rather than loosened soil. Once the root ball is set in the hole, the top of the root ball should be level with the surrounding soil. For soils that drain poorly, particularly claytype soils, it is recommended to plant the root ball at a somewhat shallower depth, exposing the top of the root ball by as much as two to three inches. This portion of the soil ball that is still exposed is backfilled and top-dressed with soil as the planting process is finished. Do not leave the soil ball exposed.

If planting container-grown stock, remove the container after a thorough watering. Gently loosen roots which may be encircling the root ball and spread them out onto the loosened soil.

If balled and burlapped, set the plant into the hole before removing or loosening the burlap. The burlap may be laid back into the hole as long as it does not obstruct the root zone.

Backfill around the ball to create a level planting bed and gently compact the soil. This compacting can be done at the time of watering in. Cover the entire area with a two- to three-inch layer of mulch such as bark, wood chips, or pine needles. A mulch reduces compaction, runoff, and evaporation, and increases the opportunity for a better penetration of moisture into the soil. If the planting area is relatively level, it is not necessary to create a water dish but, on sloping ground, I have found that the water reservoir, created by a "dam" or dished out area, is beneficial, ensuring that the root ball receives adequate moisture while the plant is becoming established.

It is estimated that a properly planted tree or shrub will grow twice as fast when planted correctly and will live twice as long as one that was not properly planted or maintained.

TIME OF YEAR

There is a best time of year for planting almost any plant. But, any plant can be planted at almost any time of year *if* certain factors are considered. These factors are: temperature, water, and general care. In the northeast, where I live, it used to be that many contracts specified planting in early spring to mid-June and no planting after that until a short period of time in the fall. Now, with improvements in both planting and maintenance technology, most plants can be planted, with outstanding success, through-out the entire growing season, though some plants do establish themselves better at specific times of the year, though. For specific plants and their preferred planting times in your area, I suggest you contact your local Cooperative Extension Agent. As a general rule in the northern garden, plants set in early spring have a longer growing period and are better established by the onset of winter. For planting in warmer climates, fall and early winter is preferred to enable plants to be better established before the hot, dry months of summer.

For mid-season planting of both deciduous and evergreen trees and shrubs that are actively growing, I find an application of an antidesiccant spray (called an antitranspirant when used during the summer) adds insurance. There are many brands of commercial antidesiccants available. Follow the manufacturer's recommended rates and directions relating to "summer" applications. The summer rate may be listed as an antitranspirant application. The sprayed material plugs up some of the stomata in the leaves, thus reducing moisture loss from the foliage. This reduction in the loss of water allows the moisture in the plant to be used for photosynthesis, the manufacture of building blocks.

Care should always be taken not to crack the ball or disturb the soil in which the plant presently grows. If the soil is disturbed, the hair roots are destroyed and must be totally repaired before the plant can be established. If hair roots are destroyed, severe leaf drop —or even death—may occur! Never handle the plant by its stem, but always by its ball or soil mass. Picking up a plant and/or carrying it by the stem will damage the roots, because the weight of the soil ball pulls against the roots. Each time you handle the plant by its stem, you guarantee the destruction of some of its hair roots.

As stated earlier, there are always exceptions to the rule when it comes to growing plants. "Butterfly" the root system of a container-grown plant, particularly if the root system shows signs of being rootbound (a solid mass of roots). The butterflying procedure is simple. After thoroughly watering the soil so you will be handling moist roots, slip the plant out of the container and physically cut into the root mass. I make three or four cuts about one inch deep with a sharp knife, evenly spaced, into the sides of the root mass from the top to the bottom of the root ball. Then I stick my fingers into the cuts and pull out roots. Butterflying the roots allows roots to be spread immediately into the backfill. I have seen many cases, particularly in growing regions where soil freezing and thawing occurs, where root systems were not butterflied and never grew into the backfill. The plants died.

Another point to remember in purchasing and handling plants is to keep them watered until they're planted. Plants sitting above ground have no source of water other than sporadic rainfall or what you supply from the watering can.

THE LAWN

Planting time for lawns is a an entirely different kettle of fish, with plenty of red herrings. We know there are better times than others for establishing certain grasses by seed. If you must have an instant lawn, try sod, assuming warm enough ground to encourage good rooting and an adequate water supply. Seeded lawns fall prey to weather conditions. Hot, dry weather equals a definite need for additional moisture from unnatural sources like a sprinkler system. Remember, once lawn seed has become moistened, it must be kept moist until it germinates, starts to grow, and has developed a root system able to seek and obtain water on its own.

To install a new lawn from seed in the north, I prefer to plant in early fall for several reasons. The temperature of the soil is warm, which speeds germination and encourages root development. Annual weeds barely

compete because they die off in the fall. Fall's cooler air temperatures reduce the need for extra watering.

Planting a new lawn is a rather simple, step-by-step procedure, whether it be by seed or by sod. First, prepare the soil. Perform a pH test to see if lime or sulfur is needed, and make a nutrient analysis to determine the best fertilizer formula for your soil and grass variety. Check drainage to eliminate any wet spots, and add organic matter in the form of peat moss or compost to improve the soil structure. All these ingredients are tilled or spaded in, to a depth of six to eight inches. The deeper the better. Rake out any debris, such as sticks and stones, and smooth the planting surface. This is the time for any contouring. If the lawn is to grow to the foundation of your home, create a slight pitch in the soil level away from the structure to keep water from becoming a potential basement problem.

Once raking and leveling is complete, seeding can begin. Select the seed appropriate for your particular planting area. There are many varieties of grass from which to choose. They include, but are not limited to, bluegrass, rye, and fescue. The grass variety you select will determine the quality of lawn you have later. I rely on information provided by my local Cooperative Extension Agent and State Turfgrass Research Facility to select the latest and best recommended varieties. I want to know as much as possible about the growth conditions for a given variety: need for sun or shade, disease and insect resistance, and drought tolerance. Some new grass varieties have been developed and introduced that require less nutrition and water.

If the area to be planted with grass has both sunny and shady conditions, select a sun-shade mix, a blend of grass varieties for both sun and shade. It is better to let Mother Nature figure out which one will grow where.

Once I have selected the seed, I read the back of the seed package. This will tell me the number of pounds of grass seed per thousand square feet. Don't be penny-wise and pound-foolish at this point. You have spent a lot of time and effort preparing the seedbed, so complete the job with the best seed and put it down at the recommended rate.

Now, rake the seed into the top layer of soil—gently. Information on the seed package includes the depth for covering the seed. One step—not absolutely necessary but helpful to the overall smoothness of the lawn and to increase the percentage of germination by putting the grass seed in good contact with the soil—is to roll the seeded area. A roller may be rented for a nominal fee from most equipment rental shops. Don't waste your money purchasing one. Once the seed has been rolled, a light covering of mulch can be spread over the surface of the seeded area. A mulch helps the seed stay evenly moist by slowing evaporation and reducing possible erosion of loosened soil. I prefer salt hay or bedding straw as the mulch.

Water is essential for the newly seeded lawn. Once the seedbed has been moistened, either by rain or irrigation, you must not let it dry. Keep the seed bed slightly moist, not wet. You may need to water several times a day if there is sunshine and wind. Or, if there are clouds and rain, you may not need to water at all. When watering, you are providing moisture only for the seed. If water runs down the curb into the street, you are watering too much.

THE VEGETABLE PATCH

In vegetable garden planting, certain times of the year are most critical for certain crops, depending on where you garden. For the northern garden, cool-season crops, those that like cool soils, must be planted in the early spring. Examples are broccoli, Brussels sprouts, cabbage, peas, spinach, lettuce, radish, and carrots. After the heat of summer passes, I have success planting these in autumn for fall and early-winter harvest. Other plants in the vegetable garden such as tomato, eggplant, pepper, squash, melon, and cucumber, establish themselves better in a warmer soil; assume these plants are susceptible to even the lightest frost. If soil is too cool for root development, your plants will show little or no growth for a considerable length of time.

The southern gardener can take advantage of the cooler winter months to enjoy the cool-season crops, and early spring and late fall for the warmer-season crops. In the South, when it is too warm or downright hot, even the warm-season lovers may fail.

PERENNIALS

Perennials have become a very popular addition to gardens worldwide. Perennials are plants that come up year after year, but don't be fooled into thinking there are no planting or care procedures that must be followed. They all need food, water, and a proper site and environment.

When I design a perennial garden, I try to imagine a symphony orchestra. As the violin section softens, the tympani reverberate, then the flutes flutter, and so on. I want my perennial garden to fade and crescendo like a symphony orchestra, with variations of plant groups performing a concert of blooms during the entire growing season.

Two groups of perennials I have come to love are bulbs, both spring-flowering and summer-flowering species, and roses. Both groups can provide many months of brilliant blossom and years of continual joy.

Spring Flowers

Spring-flowering bulbs, such as the tulip, daffodil, and crocus, must be planted in the fall, from September to December. The later in the fall you wait to plant—but before the ground freezes—the less chance there is of premature sprouting. During the fall and early winter months, the bulbs develop roots and change chemically, so the flower will emerge at the proper time in spring. The change is caused by cool soil conditions. To obtain spring bloom in growing regions where cooling is inadequate, precooled bulbs are planted. Precool by refrigerating the bulbs at approximately 40 degrees Fahrenheit for a period of nine to twelve weeks, depending on the species. Spring-flowering bulbs can be planted in any well-drained soil, and a general rule for depth-of-planting should be two times the height of the bulb. Spacing for daffodil, fritillaria, and the giant, ornamental onion may be five or more inches, whereas minor bulbs like grape hyacinth, snowdrops, and crocus, exhibit well when spaced four inches apart, or less. There are exceptions to planting directions depending on bulb species, so check the package for specific instructions.

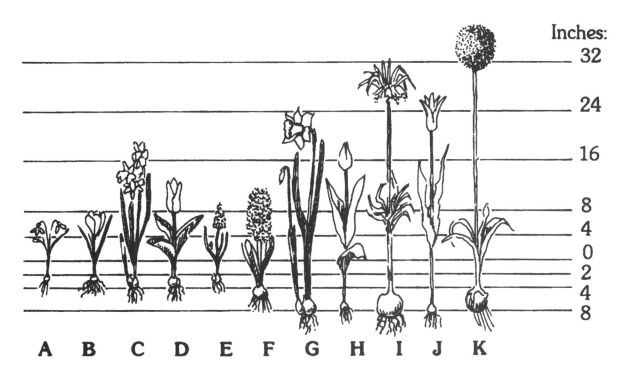

A. Snowdrops
B. Crocus
C. Botanical Narcissus
D. Botanical Tulip
E. Grape Hyacinth
F. Hyacinth

G. Trumpet Daffodil
H. Darwin Hybrid Tulip
I. Imperial
J. Lily-flowering Tulip
K. Ornamental Onion

Bulb Planting Guide

Summer Flowers

Summer-flowering "bulbs" are planted in the spring for blooms July through September, depending upon the species. The phrase, "summer-flowering bulb" is a misnomer. The industry has grouped many bulb and *non*bulb summer flowers into the "summer-flowering bulb" classification. They include: tubers of dahlia, nonstop tuberous begonia, and cannas; gladioli and cyclamen corms; bulbous Spanish, English, and Dutch iris; and lilytype bulbs. All the summer-flowering "bulbs" can be grown in well-drained, sandy to rich, humus soil, but they all have varying light requirements. The tuberous begonia thrives in the shade, whereas the cannas and gladioli need a half day or more of sun.

Depending on your growing zone, some of the summer-flowering "bulbs" are hardy and can remain in the ground over winter, but some must be dug up and stored in a frost-proof environment, generally at 45 degrees to 50 degrees Fahrenheit. Hardy species include bulbous iris, hardy gladioli corms, and corms of autumn crocus and meadow saffron. Cannas, dahlia, tuberous begonias, and caladium are among those that must be dug and stored over winter.

Roses

According to a recent Gallup Organization survey, I am not alone in my desire to have roses in my garden. There are over twenty-three million rose-growing households in the United States. That's a lot of roses. Why so many? The answer is simple. Accumulated knowledge has made the culture of roses easier, even in the hottest summers and coldest winters. Roses can be grown in almost any climate if they are given five to six hours of direct sun, good air circulation, water, and proper nutrition.

The most popular of all roses is the hybrid tea, often grown as single blossoms on a single stem as a specimen plant. Floribundas flower in clusters. The low-growth habit of the floribunda, usually no more than four to five feet in height, makes them perfect for edging a walkway or creating a low hedge.

Grandifloras combine the traits of both floribundas and hybrid teas. Most are tall plants exhibiting multiple blossoms on single stems, making them strong candidates for background plantings.

Climbing roses produce long, arching canes that can be attached to trellises, arbors, fences, or posts. Their versatility in landscape use is limited only by your imagination. I have used them to hide an ugly fence and to accent a covered entrance to the house.

The reintroduction of heritage or old-fashioned roses has brought the fragrance back to rose culture. Many of these roses are vigorous growing, disease-resistant plants that produce a multitude of double or semi-double blossoms throughout the growing season.

Landscape roses include both ground-cover and shrub types. Many of them are low-maintenance roses with few pest problems.

Miniature roses, thanks to improvements in varieties and cultural practices, have become an extremely versatile plant. They grow to a height of one to two feet with miniaturized leaves and flowers, a real conversation piece in the small garden, in a container on a sunny patio, or indoors on a sunny windowsill. They can be grown indoors and flower year round, even under artificial light.

Success in rose gardening begins with and depends on proper planning and planting. Start with site selection. Roses must have at least six hours of direct sunlight each day. Morning sunshine is essential to reduce leaf diseases like black spot and mildew. If morning sunshine isn't available to remove moisture from the leaf surface, the resulting incubator action promotes diseases. Air movement through the foliage also reduces disease potential. Proper spacing of plants and pruning practices that allow for open growth encourage better air circulation.

One must also take into consideration soil condition. The soil must have proper drainage. Adequate moisture must be available to the roots at all times when roses are actively growing, but they cannot stand wet feet. Any doubt about the drainage capabilities of your soil can be tested by digging a hole twenty-four inches deep and filling it with water. Check the hole after twenty-four hours. If water remains in the hole, drainage must be improved. Solutions include digging a deep pit below the planting site and filling it with coarse gravel or rock, installing a drain system of pipe and gravel pitched away from the planting area, or construction of raised beds.

If you are preparing a planting bed for a rose collection, not just an individual rose, dig a planting trench at least two feet deep and incorporate, by volume, one part organic matter in the form of well-rotted compost with one part soil removed from the trench. To improve drainage and aeration of the soil mix add, by volume, 20 percent sand or coarse perlite. Superphosphate blended with the planting soil at the rate of three to four pounds per hundred square feet of planting area encourages stronger root development. To plant single or individual plants, dig a hole fourteen to sixteen inches deep and the same width. Check drainage, and improve it if necessary. Mix, by volume, equal parts of organic matter and soil removed from the hole.

Roses prefer a slightly acid soil with a pH of 6.0 to 6.5. Since you are taking the trouble to prepare a five-dollar hole for your rose plant, take time to do a soil pH test for each planting area. Alkaline soils can be adjusted by mixing sulfur into the planting soil.

The techniques used for planting a rose differ depending on whether it is a bare root or containerized. Follow the directions provided with the bare-root rose to prepare it for planting. Carry the bare-root plant in a bucket of water to the planting site and do not remove it from the water until the hole is dug and ready for planting. You *do not* want the roots to dry out. At that time, you can finish the recommended pruning instructions that came with your particular variety of rose.

Build a cone of mixed soil in the center of the bottom of the hole so that when the bare roots are spread out, the bud union, the point at which the root stock and the upper part of the rose plant are joined or grafted together, is even with the proper planting level. In severely cold climates, this union may be planted as much as two inches below the soil surface. In warmer climates, the swollen bud union is planted at or slightly above the soil surface. Before adding more backfill to the hole, check the planting level by laying a straight shovel handle or stick across the hole to represent planting depth. Hold the plant in position and begin filling the hole with more planting mix. When the hole is about three-quarters filled with soil, fill the hole with water to thoroughly soak the backfill and roots. Work the wet backfill into the mass of bare roots to ensure there are no air pockets adjacent to the roots. Add enough more backfill to the hole to reach the proper planting depth, and water thoroughly once again.

To establish bare-root plants, cover the stems with either a loose soil mix or mulch to at least two thirds of the plant's height. Keep this mulch cover moist to prevent drying of stems and to encourage better bud break. Carefully remove the mulch or soil after the new growth on the stem reaches one to two inches long.

For containerized rose plants, the hole's width should be at least two times the diameter of the container, and one-and-one-half times deeper. Soil-mix preparation is the same as for bare-root roses. Place prepared backfill into the bottom of the hole to the proper planting depth determined by winter climate. Water the rose plant while it is in the container to thoroughly moisten the roots and soil. Moisture will also act as a lubricant and make it much easier to remove the soil and root mass from the container. Slip the plant from the container to its position in the hole, checking for proper planting depth once again. Backfill around the soil ball until the hole is one-half filled. Compact the soil mix to eliminate air pockets and continue adding backfill until the hole is filled. Water the plant thoroughly to settle the backfill and to moisten the roots again. Since the container rose is already growing, it is not necessary to add mulch to cover the stems. Mulch the soil to prevent rapid drying and keep the plant well watered until it becomes established.

I could go on and on talking about individual plants and how best to plant them. Just remember the general rule for planting your trees, shrubs, or house plants: Place a fifty-cent plant in a five-dollar hole and very shortly—behold!—you have a five-dollar plant.

QUESTIONS AND ANSWERS

1. Q. **Last fall I saw a sign at a local garden center that read FALL IS FOR PLANTING. I have always heard that spring is the best time. Which statement is accurate?**
    A. Fall is for planting of spring flowering bulbs, cool-season grasses, and many evergreen and deciduous trees and shrubs. Cooler air temperature and warm soil makes possible the establishment of many plants without much in the way of supplemental moisture. Check with your local Cooperative Extension Agent for a list of plants recommended for fall planting.

2. Q. **What time of year is best for transplanting house plants?**
    A. A general rule of thumb is to transplant house plants during the spring, when active root growth begins and the heating season ends. The end of the heating season brings with it a return of moisture in the air.

3. Q. **How can one tell when a house plant needs to be transplanted?**
    A. The need for transplanting depends on the growth habit of an individual plant. Moisten the root system and carefully slip the plant from the pot. Examine the roots. If the outer surface of the root ball is a solid mass of thick, dry roots, repot using a soil mix of the same consistency. If the roots are actively growing and have a healthy look, return the plant to its original pot. Some plants love to be potbound, and some need space for root development.

4. Q. **My *Ficus benjamina* house plant has roots growing through the holes in the bottom of the pot. Does this mean it is rootbound and it is time to transplant it into a larger pot?**

A. No. It only indicates that roots found the holes in the bottom of the pot. They may be reaching for air or moisture in the saucer below. Cut them off at the point where they emerge from the pot.

5. Q. **I found a bag of daffodil bulbs in the unheated part of my garage. They have been there for at least three months. Can I plant them when the ground thaws this spring?**
A. Daffodil bulbs which have been stored in cool temperatures are probably in good condition. If the bulbs are solid, not powdered out, plant them at the first sign of spring and they will bloom, although probably later than normal for your area. The same rule applies to other spring flowering bulbs that need a cold treatment to release their bloom.

6. Q. **Can tulip bulbs that have been forced for indoor bloom be saved and planted in the garden?**
A. They can, but they may not bloom until they complete another year's growth cycle. When bulbs are forced in containers, they generally do not have a long enough growing cycle and sufficient nutrients available to them to manufacture next year's bloom.

7. Q. **I want to move lilies to a new location. When should they be transplanted?**
A. Transplant and divide lilies when the tops begin to die back.

8. Q. **A two-year-old hanging basket of Swedish ivy is producing smaller and smaller leaves. I am feeding it but it does not seem to help. What is the problem?**
A. Swedish ivy is one house plant that becomes massively root bound as it reaches eighteen to twenty-four months of age if not transplanted. The roots become so crowded and dense that they cannot hold water or nutrients. To restore healthy growth, moisten the root ball and cut away the outer inch or so of root mass. Repot the plant in a fresh soil mix, pinch back the smaller foliage, and continue watering and feeding. The new foliage will resume its normal growth pattern.

9. Q. **My begonias, planted in a specially prepared raised bed, get stem rot about a month after they start to bloom. What could be the cause?**
A. Begonias need a soil with excellent aeration and drainage. If the raised bed is comprised mostly of organic material such as peat moss or compost, add sand or perlite to improve the air and moisture balance. Also, check the spacing of the transplants. As they get larger, they may be growing into one another, not allowing good air circulation around the upper parts of the plants.

10. Q. **What should I do when my roses arrive from the mail-order nursery for spring planting?**
A. First, read the planting instructions that come with your order. Unpack the box in a shady, protected location; trim off broken roots or canes and then put them in a bucket of water to soak the roots before planting.

11. Q. **How often should bearded iris be transplanted?**
A. Every three years you may transplant irises shortly after they bloom, or up until about the middle of September. If you plant them on a slightly mounded ridge, it will help ensure good drainage in the winter.

12. Q. **When is the best time to plant a forsythia hedge from bare-root transplants?**
A. Bare-root transplants, available during the dormant season, must be planted before active leaf or flower growth. This is the time when little moisture is needed for establishment of the roots.

13. **Q. Can I plant a privet hedge and expect it to do well even though it is midsummer?**
A. Yes. If you can supply water to the newly planted shrubs, there should be no reason not to plant them. Privet plants are available as balled and burlapped specimens and as container stock during the summer. An antitranspirant sprayed on the foliage will reduce transplant shock.

14. **Q. When should peonies be divided and transplanted?**
A. Transplant peonies from mid-September to mid-October. It is bad to transplant in the spring, because that is when peonies produce their feeding roots.

15. **Q. How deep should I plant peonies?**
A. Plant peonies two to three inches below the surface, with the eyes (pink growth buds) no deeper than an inch and a half below the surface. If you plant them too deep, the roots may rot or the plant might not produce any flowers, or produce very small flowers. If you plant peonies too shallow, they can be heaved out in winter.

16. **Q. What should I do with daffodils that push up foliage each year but have not produced blooms for the past three years?**
A. After the foliage has begun to yellow (an indicator that the bulbs are going into their summer dormancy), dig them up, separate them, add nutrients to the soil, and replant at the proper planting depth.

17. **Q. When should hardy phlox be transplanted?**
A. Late August, just after flowering, is the best time to transplant hardy phlox. If done at this time, the plants should bloom normally the next year.

18. **Q. When should oriental poppies be transplanted?**
A. The only time is in late July or early August. Perennial poppies should not be transplanted unless they are completely dormant.

19. **Q. I want to use bulbs in some border areas. Can you give me some suggestions for arranging them?**
A. Many people plant bulbs singly and in rows. Around shrubs, a better method might be to set them in groups—small groups of five or six for the smaller areas, and larger groups for bigger areas. A back border of bulbs in the perennial garden adds a splash of color until the later blooming perennials assume their mature growth for the season.

20. **Q. How often should I transplant daffodils?**
A. Daffodils tend to pull themselves deeper into the soil as they grow from year to year, consequently affecting their bloom. A bulb initially planted eight to ten inches deep may be found twelve to fourteen inches deep when dug up in five to seven years. The bulb is not actually moving in the soil. New bulbs are produced at the base of the original bulb, causing the new bulb to be lower in the soil. Use lack of production and vigor as an indicator for transplanting.

21. **Q. When is the right time for planting dahlias?**
A. Mid-May to mid-June is recommended, when the soil is warm and mellow. However, dahlias may be planted as soon as the danger of frost is past.

22. **Q. When should pansy seeds be planted?**
A. Pansy seeds should be sown in the fall when there are cool nights and warm days, around late August or early September. In warmer regions, seedlings can be left in the ground over winter, but seedlings in northern areas should be sheltered in a cold frame. Pansy seeds may be planted in the very early spring, but they will bloom about a month later than the seeds sown last fall.

23. **Q. What type of soil do onions require?**
   A. Onions must have soil that is well cultivated and well fertilized. Organic, nutrient, and water content should be high. Onions are really at home in muck soil.

24. **Q. How should ground be prepared for perennials?**
   A. Cultivate to a depth of eighteen inches, preferably twenty-four inches, and ensure good drainage. Peat moss, compost, leafmold, or dried cow manure, with superphosphate, ten pounds to one hundred square feet, should be well mixed into the soil.

25. **Q. How should I prepare ground for rhododendrons?**
   A. Soil must be acid, pH 4.5 to 5.5, well-drained, and humus. Organic content can be improved by mixing in leafmold, peat moss, compost, or well-rotted cow manure. Incorporate the planting mixture and cultivate the area to a depth of twelve to fifteen inches.

26. **Q. What soil preparation is necessary for planting lilies?**
   A. In general, lilies thrive in good loam with an abundance of organic matter, such as leafmold, peat moss, or dehydrated cow manure incorporated into the soil. Good drainage is a must.

27. **Q. What kind of soil do I need for peonies, daphnes, and lilacs? When can they be transplanted?**
   A. Peonies and lilacs will do best in fertile soil rich in organic matter, but daphnes prefer soil that is coarse and gravelly. Lilacs and daphnes can be transplanted in the early spring or fall, but peonies should be moved in the fall.

28. **Q. Our soil is dry. Could pines and junipers be grown?**
   A. Yes, most pines and junipers tolerate dry soil.

29. **Q. Can I use a leaf-and-manure fertilizer for my evergreens?**
   A. When planting, depending upon the quality of the soil, you can mix leafmold and old manure with the soil. Use a top-dressing of old manure around yews and evergreens that are already established in a good soil.

30. **Q. When should I transplant evergreens?**
   A. In general, transplanting should be completed in the spring before new growth starts.

31. **Q. When I plant evergreens, should I remove the burlap instead of splitting it?**
   A. If the root ball is strong, you may remove the burlap. If the root ball appears weak, leave the burlap until the plant is in the hole. Then, cut the twine and spread the burlap away from the ball, or cut the burlap off close to the base of the ball.

32. **Q. How early in the spring can I transplant evergreens?**
   A. You may transplant evergreens before they have started into growth, and as soon as the soil is reasonably workable, when the frost is out of the ground and the soil has warmed and dried off.

33. **Q. How soon in the fall can I plant evergreens?**
   A. For pine and spruce you can plant as soon as the current year's growth has become hardened and terminal buds have firmly set.

34. **Q. What is the best time of the year to plant evergreen seedlings?**
   A. Plant in the spring before the evergreens have started their new growth, and as soon as the ground is warm and friable.

35. **Q. What is the recommended soil acidity for rhododendrons and azaleas?**
A. In general, a pH of 4.5 to 5.5.

36. **Q. I have a shallow soil over hardpan. Can I grow trees and shrubs?**
A. Hardpan is a layer of clay particles that are so tightly packed that water cannot drain through. Generally you need a foot of good soil for shrubs, and two feet for trees. To provide adequate drainage, you must attempt to break through the hardpan to a gravel layer underneath, or mound soil above the hardpan for planting. If you mound the soil, you should still attempt to break up the hardpan underneath.

37. **Q. I have soil often referred to as adobe clay. When it is wet, it is sticky and doesn't drain well. My neighbor said it is used for making bricks. Can I plant and grow iris in adobe soil?**
A. Since irises are especially easy to grow, the only precaution suggested is not to plant too deeply. When initially planting the iris bed, incorporate organic matter in the form of peat moss or compost to a depth of eight to ten inches to help improve the aeration and drainage. Feed them in the spring and be generous with the water, but don't overwater. About every three years, the clumps should be divided and only the new, strong rhizomes should be saved. This is best done in September in the hottest regions of the country.

38. **Q. How will the roots of trees affect my garden?**
A. The most serious problem is the amount of moisture and soluble plant food that trees take from the soil. If the roots are deep, such as oak, they are not likely to cause physical interference; but maple roots, which grow right near the surface, become a nuisance for tillers.

39. **Q. How do you fertilize vegetable plants that are growing in the garden?**
A. Apply the fertilizer in the row between the plants, where it can be worked into the first few inches of soil without injuring the roots of the plants. When you have done this, water if the soil is dry.

40. **Q. What materials do I need to construct raised beds?**
A. Use whatever material is on hand: redwood, pressure-treated lumber, concrete, bricks, or fieldstone. Keep in mind that you may wish to coordinate it with the site: deck, retaining wall, patio, sidewalk, foundation, or other structural features.

41. **Q. Will an acid soil make hydrangeas blue in color?**
A. The acidity of the soil will change the color of hydrangeas. An acid soil (pH 5.5 or lower) will produce blue flowers on pink varieties.

42. **Q. What is meant by the term *balled and burlapped*? I see the term used in many garden center ads when describing trees and shrubs.**
A. Nurseries and garden centers sell many plants, both deciduous and evergreen, with their root systems in a ball of earth that is wrapped in burlap. The ball contains much of the root system that developed as part of the plant when it was growing in the nursery field. Because trees and shrubs are difficult to transplant, it is prudent to move them with as large a ball of earth as possible.

43. **Q. Should I soak the balled and burlapped plants before planting them?**
A. Yes. The ball of earth can become very dry when held for long periods of time. A thorough soaking *before* planting reduces shattering of soil from the roots during the planting process. It is important to keep the soil in complete contact with the root system.

44. **Q. How is peat moss similar to compost and manure?**

A. Peat moss, compost, and manure are sources of organic matter that provide humic acid to the soil after they have totally decomposed. They are worked into soil to make a heavy soil lighter and to make a light soil hold more moisture.

45. **Q. Can shady soil that is damp and cold be fertilized in such a way to make up for lack of sun?**

A. No, and flowering plants and vegetables should not be planted in such a location.

46. **Q. When should I remove the straw mulch that was spread over my newly seeded ryegrass-and-fescue lawn? The grass seed has germinated and the plants are about two inches tall.**

A. I would remove the mulch when the seedlings are two to three inches tall. Allow the soil to dry slightly so you do not pull up the seedlings when you gently rake off the protective mulch.

47. **Q. I have a newly sown bluegrass lawn. How high should I let the grass grow before I cut it?**

A. Cutting the grass of a new lawn will encourage it to stool out rather than become tall and woody. Start mowing when the grass reaches about three inches in height. Set the mowing height at two inches, mowing about once a week, and allow the clippings to remain; they will make an excellent mulch to shade the soil and protect against loss of moisture.

48. **Q. Since I have no space for a compost pile, how can I use compost in my garden?**

A. Consider composting in large plastic bags (thirty-gallon capacity or more). With each bushel of leaves and lawn clippings, mix in a quart of good garden soil and a handful of good mixed fertilizer. Fresh grass clippings will not need additional moisture, but dried leaves should be sprayed enough to moisten, but not soak them. You can then stack the sealed bags in any convenient location, possibly the corner of your garage. At temperatures above 70 degrees Fahrenheit, you should have compost in three or four months. Compost is the only way to supply organic matter, unless you can afford to purchase large amounts of peat moss.

49. **Q. On the back of almost every seed packet, it says to "thin" the seedlings once they start to grow. Why? I feel as if I am reducing the potential harvest.**

A. If you do *not* thin seedlings at the recommended time, you reduce the harvest because they compete with one another for nutrients and space. Do it.

50. **Q. Can seedlings thinned from a row of lettuce be used as transplants?**

A. If carefully removed with their tiny roots, they make *fair* transplants. The ultimate consideration should be the condition of the plants that remain in the row. Try not to disturb their roots when thinning.

51. **Q. Is it better to plant my tomato, eggplant, and pepper transplants into the garden on a sunny or cloudy day?**

A. It is best to plant on a cloudy day, although this is not always possible. The reduced light exposure of a cloudy day reduces transpiration. In sunny conditions, provide shade or apply an antitranspirant.

52. **Q. Is it harmful to plant seedlings of marigolds, petunias, and coleus in the garden in the evening?**

A. No. Evening is an ideal time to plant, because there is less demand for water for transpiration. To reduce the potential of disease, avoid wetting the foliage when watering the transplants.

53. **Q. The soil my jade plant is potted in is very hard and difficult to wet. Can I use a different soil when I transplant it into a larger pot?**

   A. Soil can be changed during transplanting if the old soil, the soil in which the plant is presently growing, is completely removed from the root system. Adding a different soil mix without removing the old soil would change the drainage and aeration pattern, resulting in root problems.

54. **Q. I have begonia seeds which are the size of fine dust particles. How can I evenly scatter such small seeds?**

   A. To provide bulk to very fine seeds, mix them with powdered sugar or talc before scattering them on the seed-starting mix.

55. **Q. Why is there such a variation in the "days to germination" rating for starting seeds?**

   A. The variables in germinating seeds are both internal and external. They include ripeness of the seed at harvest, temperature, moisture, hardness of the seed coat, and depth of planting, to name a few.

56. **Q. I saved seeds from a new hybrid tomato that I grew last year. Can I expect success if I use them this year?**

   A. You most likely will have success if the seeds were stored properly over winter. The down side to the tomato seeds you saved is they were from a hybrid variety. The seeds will produce tomatoes, but will not be identical to those from which they came.

57. **Q. The last frost date in my area is May 20. Can I plant bush beans, corn, and cucumbers at that time?**

   A. The timing for planting of tender crops correlates not only with the frost date but also with the soil temperature. If there have been a few weeks of warm, sunny weather, such crops can be planted.

58. **Q. How far apart should I plant Japanese yews in order to grow a hedge?**

   A. The planting distance between plants initially depends on the size of the transplants. To obtain quick results plant two- to three-foot specimens eighteen to twenty-four inches apart. The further apart, the longer it will take for them to grow together as a hedge.

59. **Q. What considerations are there when planting a hedge as a divider between my property and my neighbors?**

   A. The first consideration, which has nothing to do with the planting process, is the location of the property line. Check local ordinances relating to planting distances from the property line. Then answer the following questions: Is the hedge for privacy? Do you need height to block a view? Is the hedge for year-round screening? Is it a barrier to keep out unwanted guests? Should it be evergreen and hold its foliage year round, or can it be deciduous and drop its leaves during winter?

60. **Q. Can I lay a sod lawn of bluegrass in the middle of summer when the weather is hot?**

   A. Bluegrass sod can be laid at any time during the year when soil is not frozen, provided it can be watered. During summer heat, water must be supplied to newly laid sod until the roots penetrate and knit into the parent soil. Hot weather fosters drying, which causes a shrinking of sod, thus severing new roots that are growing into the parent soil.

V

PRUNING

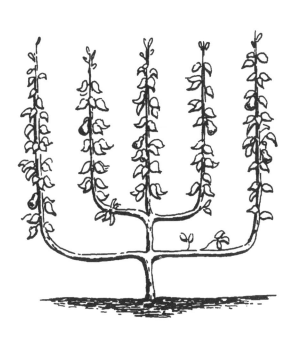

GARDENERS FROM ALL ACROSS America, amateur and professional alike, tell me that when it comes to pruning, they just close their eyes and do it. A drive through any suburban area would seem to confirm this statement. Azalea bushes, squared off at the corners, remind me of sugar cubes; forsythia shrubs have been butchered so severely that they have lost their natural cascading appearance and, even sadder, they have lost the growth that would have produced next year's beautiful yellow blossoms. Weeping cherry trees no longer "weep" because the graft has been removed by severe topping. To the other extreme are those plants that should have been thinned or clipped or pruned in some fashion, and weren't. The upright yew shrub and the American holly tree were originally intended to frame and balance the home landscape. Uncared-for and unattended, they have exploded, becoming unsightly and potentially damaging to the materials and structure of the very houses they were intended to enhance.

Pruning can be defined as the removal or reduction of plant parts that are no longer necessary or are injurious to plant growth. Pruning is performed in order to direct energy to particular parts of the plant. If you can understand the physiology of pruning and its effect on plant growth, you can become an expert pruning "artist." Pruning is an art, as well as a science, that can be learned.

You cannot attack your plants with a pair of pruning shears or loppers or a saw without a specific intention. Before you purchase any pruning equipment, study the reasons for pruning. We prune to:
- influence size
- increase quality and abundance of flowers and fruit
- modify form
- remove unwanted growth
- maintain attractiveness
- repair injury
- remove dead, diseased, or insect-infested material

INFLUENCING SIZE

Most people are aware of the first reason for pruning: influencing the size of a particular plant. Think of the shrubs, usually located below and in front of a picture window, typical to many foundation landscapes. If these shrubs are not pruned properly and in a timely fashion, before long the vista is obscured by plants that exceed their design. Many homeowners refer to these plantings as "builder's" shrubs—you know, the four, very small bushes that the builder planted before you first moved into your new home, so long ago. More initial attention to selecting plants according to their growth habits could preclude the later need to influence size by pruning. It is essential to remember: Little plants often become great big plants.

A perfect example of a plant that needs to be pruned properly is the California privet hedge. It is often used as a property divider and privacy screen between your neighbor and you. Untrimmed, the hedge will be devoid of foliage at the bottom and will stretch to a height of twenty to thirty feet. If pruned properly, the privet, and many other plants used as hedges, will provide a dense screen of foliage that can be maintained from top to bottom.

The spreading juniper is another landscape plant that must be pruned regularly to keep it in bounds. Often planted in a landscape that borders a walkway, its spreading growth habit, unless the plant is clipped intermittently, allows it to obstruct the walkway.

INCREASING QUALITY AND ABUNDANCE OF FLOWERS AND FRUIT

Our fruit industry is a prime example of pruning for this purpose. In mid- June, a peach grower might find that most, if not all, of the developing fruit has dropped from the tree. This phenomenon, called June drop, is the pruning practice of Mother Nature. In order for the grower to effectively reduce this June Drop, or to stop it completely, he must follow an appropriate routine of pruning practices.

But before we proceed, it's helpful to understand what causes June drop and why pruning is essential.

Spring-flowering trees depend on last year's growth. It was during last year's growing season that the peach tree developed the flower buds that would bear fruit the following spring. Come springtime, blossoms open and, if pollination occurs, fruit sets. Depending upon the age of the tree and the weather conditions at the time of blossom, hundreds or even thousands of fruits may set per tree. The opening of the flowers and the setting of fruit require plenty of moisture, usually quite adequate in springtime. The tiny fruits form and continue to grow under ideal conditions. Cool air and abundant moisture nurture the plant, stimulating its food supply and the cooling processes essential to the emerging fruits. But, later in the spring and in early summer, air temperatures rise and rains diminish at a time when the developing fruits and larger leaves require more and more moisture to be available to the tree's root system. Usually the plant, deprived of adequate moisture for its functions, has to yield something. This is when Mother Nature signals the plant that some of these fruits must go. The distress signal causes an abscission layer to form between fruit and tree, blocking the flow of moisture and nutrients into the fruit. The fruits dry up and fall off, or simply fall off still green. This is called June

drop. If only Mother Nature were able to instruct the tree to drop only 50 percent or even 20 percent of the total fruit, June drop could be a productive rather than a destructive event.

To prevent June drop, commercial growers will, at the proper time in May, spray the peach tree with a thinning agent. This type of pruning will cause a certain percentage of the fruit to drop off in May, thus preventing June drop. In general, thinning agents are not available to the home gardener because of the technical knowledge necessary to apply them properly. Effectiveness of thinning agents can be greatly enhanced or diminished by weather conditions such as air temperature, humidity, sunshine, time of day, number of fruit set, and stage of growth.

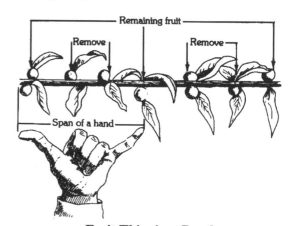

Fruit Thinning: Peach

The home gardener can reduce the drastic effects of June drop by hand-thinning when the fruits are about the size of your pinky fingernail. Hand pull all the developing fruits inside the span of a hand (the distance between your little finger and your thumb when the hand and fingers are spread apart). Pull off every fruit in this space. When pulling off the baby fruit, leave two peaches at the tip of your little finger and two at the tip of your thumb; notice that peaches tend to grow in pairs. Work your way up and down the branches, removing every peach inside the span of a hand, thus leaving pairs of fruit over the entire plant. As the season progresses, given normal growing conditions, the root system should be able to provide an adequate supply of moisture for the full development of the fruit.

In my garden I have had excellent results with this hand-thinning method; my peaches mature well and seem to be even larger than normal at harvesttime. The hand-thinning process is one method of pruning that affects not only the abundance of fruit, but quality too. This procedure works well for pears, apples, apricots, and many other fruiting plants.

Hand-thinning in the vegetable patch works great with tomatoes, eggplants, and peppers. Note that these plants often flower in three, four, five, even six or seven blossoms per cluster. If all the blossoms were allowed to develop into mature fruit, you could have three, four, five, even six or seven below-average, small-sized tomatoes, eggplants, or peppers. To achieve quality production from these plants, hand-thinning is advised. When the fruit have developed to the size of your little fingernail, probably a few days after they began to form, pinch out all but two fruits per cluster.

Now, I know that this can be a disturbing idea to those who have never tried it, but I suggest you do it. If you can't bring yourself to perform this thinning practice on all the plants, I suggest you try it on half. When you see the results, you will want to do all of your plants next year. This procedure will diminish the number of fruit per plant, but the quality and the size of the remaining fruits will more than make up for their lesser number. Imagine a slice of Big Boy tomato, big enough to cover a slice of bread; or eggplant Parmesan with slices of eggplant as big as saucers. And what about super-big bell peppers, so big that one stuffed pepper will feed two people? Oh, by the way, you can only encourage large fruit from plants that are genetically capable of producing them. Don't expect Tiny Tim or cherry-type tomatoes, or baby eggplants, or firecracker peppers, to grow into something gigantic; nature did not program them to do that. But, even with these miniature fruits, one can use hand-thinning to encourage a better quality product.

"Disbudding" is another form of pruning, one that produces those exhibition-size chrysanthemums and dahlias of large-flowering species. Disbudding is the removal of side (lateral) buds; only the terminal bud remains to mature. For example, as the chrysanthemum's terminal flower bud starts to expand, you will notice several side flower buds beginning to form at the same time. These buds develop lower down on the stem at the axils of many of the leaves. If all its buds were allowed to grow, the mum would produce average-size flowers. Removal of the side buds a few days after they have formed allows only the terminal flower bud to develop. It likely will mature into a very large, exhibition-type mum.

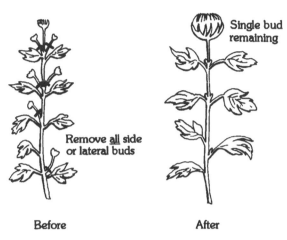

Before   After

Disbudding

This same practice of disbudding is used in commercial, long-stem rose and carnation production. Disbudding is a very labor-intensive cultural practice. If being grown under greenhouse conditions, allowing only one flower per stem to develop sends the cost per square foot of greenhouse space soaring. If some cut flowers seem rather expensive, the end product—the single, prime, grade-A specimen bloom—is worth it.

MODIFYING FORM

Espalier

Remember that pear tree, apple tree, peach tree, or whatever kind of tree, that looked as if it were flattened against a stone wall or wire fence? You can see a lot of them in the old formal gardens of estates or arboretums. They are the result of a pruning technique, espalier, practiced and guarded as a secret by European gardeners for centuries, and by today's gardeners, as well.

Well, let me expose the secret. A plant you wish to grow directioned to the left should be pruned above a bud pointing to the left; a plant you wish to grow to the right should be pruned above a bud pointing to the right. Espalier made simple. If you want to grow a peach tree flat against a wall, prune away any buds appearing to grow *away* from the wall, and any buds seeming to grow *into* the wall. On the "arms"—the branches pointing to the left and right— prune just to the outside of a bud pointing in the direction you want that branch to grow. This bud then becomes the terminal or apical bud that will grow in the direction in which it is pointing. Spend a little time during the spring and summer studying the bud locations, and then prune the branches to maintain and continue shaping your tree.

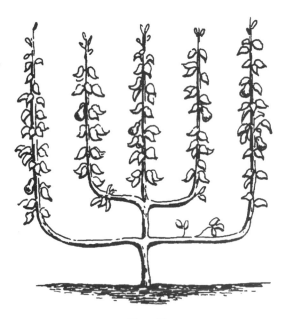

Espalier

Almost any plant that has terminal growth points can be trained as an espalier. Some popular plants include the many varieties of the shrub pyracantha with its bright-orange or red berries, and many dwarf fruit trees, such as crab apple and quince. Indoors, even a *Ficus elastica* (the common rubber plant) or a *Dracaena marginata* (the dragon tree), can become an espalier. Following the peach tree example, locate the buds pointing in the direction that you wish the plant to grow, and then prune just above or to the outside of those buds.

Hedge Clipping

Hedges are most often grown along property lines to provide privacy; you don't want to see your neighbor and you don't want your neighbor to see you. After several years have passed, however, it is not uncommon for a homeowner to notice his privacy screen

getting rather thin at the bottom. If he is relaxing in his backyard and can observe his neighbor doing the same, so much for privacy. Either the hedge has not been trimmed at all, or it has been pruned improperly.

Loss of lower foliage usually results when hedges are clipped so the sides are straight up and down or slightly "V" or vase-shaped. The upper part of the hedge then shades the lower portion. By pruning the hedge in a slightly A-framed fashion—slightly narrower at the top and slightly wider at the bottom —adequate light will reach the lower leaves. A home owner practicing this type of pruning, the A-shaped type, should not see, or be seen, by his neighbor. If the passing years have left your hedge with little or no foliage at the bottom, it still may not be too late to correct the problem. Start clipping back the sides near the top and allow the bottom to grow slightly wider. The lower branches may develop enough new foliage to provide the originally desired screening. Deciduous hedges of privet, viburnum, and hawthorn, and evergreen hedges of taxus, ilex and euonymus respond very well to this corrective pruning.

Other unnatural pruning practices that modify form include "poodle" or "powder-puff" pruning. These are methods used to create topiary (odd or ornamental) figures.

Incorrect "V" shaped

Correct "A" shaped

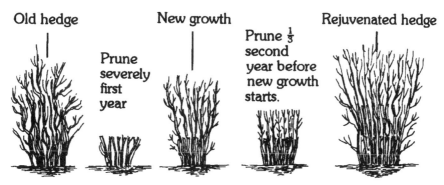

Old hedge

Prune severely first year

New growth

Prune ⅓ second year before new growth starts.

Rejuvenated hedge

Hedge Rejuvenation Pruning

REMOVING UNWANTED GROWTH

Earlier, I mentioned rhododendrons that were blocking a picture-window view, and the California privet that had grown to almost treelike proportions. With proper pruning techniques, we can return most overgrown plants to a manageable size. We speak, here, of "drastic" pruning. Caution: Not all plants can be pruned drastically.

Most textbooks referring to drastic pruning encourage it in late winter or early spring. I once recommended in the northeast that pruning of this nature be done in March and April, but some years back, the New York area recorded 98 degrees in April! Heavy or "drastic" pruning in that type of weather at that time of year may have killed some plants. So now, I say perform drastic pruning before there is any chance of hot, dry weather. The buds that are lying dormant in the older, woodier tissue then have a chance to expand and break through that tissue before it dries out. If pruning is done after hot weather sets in, many buds cannot develop properly, or at all.

Another factor that makes early spring an ideal time for drastic pruning is the location of the food within the plant. In late winter or early spring, the upper part of the plant is lowest in nutritional storage and the root system is highest. By doing drastic pruning just before spring growth begins, the food that is stored in the root system will be feeding far fewer buds on the upper parts of the plant, thus encouraging quicker recovery from drastic pruning.

Many species of evergreens, such as rhododendron, azalea, laurel, andromeda, leucothoe, boxwood, taxus, ilex and junipers, can be pruned drastically in late winter or early spring because they all have dormant buds that can grow from the older wood. If pruning is done in early spring, the growth buds will have a chance to develop before the arrival of hot, dry weather. As I said earlier, drastic pruning must be undertaken cautiously. Even some of the above-mentioned plants may not respond as you wish. In general, I recommend taking a chance with drastic pruning when a plant has grown to such a size that it will probably be replaced otherwise. In this case, I would "close my eyes" and do it.

As for deciduous plants—those plants that lose their leaves over wintertime (such as the privet hedge and viburnum)—drastic late-winter or early-spring pruning encourages multiple shoots to develop from the ground. These new shoots, characteristically wispy, will require pruning several times throughout the growing season to encourage branching. Repeated clipping or pruning will encourage a denser, thicker hedge with multiple stems.

Drastic pruning—pruning for renewal of growth—also may be done in the fall to effect one of two additional changes. In fall, a larger percentage of stored food is located in the aboveground parts; the lowest percentage of stored food is in the root system. If drastic pruning is done in the fall, you are removing recently manufactured food from the upper parts which normally would be returned to the root system for overwintering and for pushing spring growth. By drastically pruning the upper portion of the plant, a dwarf-growth characteristic is likely. Always keep in mind that such severe measures may kill a plant.

If you have a small tree or shrub in a very confined area, you might consider drastic pruning in the fall to instill in the plant a dwarfed-growth characteristic. Of course, drastic fall pruning or drastic spring pruning, whichever it might be, will definitely reduce the potential of flowers on spring-flowering plants in the coming season. For example, rhododendrons set their flowering mechanism this year for next year's bloom. Also, fruit trees, such as apples, peaches, and pears, set their flowers this year for next spring's bloom. So remember, if we do drastic pruning in the fall, or drastic pruning in the early spring before flowering, we cut off the flowering mechanisms that formed over the past season.

MAINTAINING ATTRACTIVENESS

The red-twig dogwood is a classic example of a plant that requires proper pruning in order to encourage a beautiful exhibition of bright-red twigs during wintertime. By cutting out the oldest branches (two-year-old growth) during early spring, you encourage multiple, juvenile shoots to sprout from near the base of the plant. It is in the juvenile shoots that the beautiful red pigments are developed. Similarly, the same pruning practice is used to keep the yellow-twig

Remove oldest stems immediately after bloom.

Before   After

Pruning Multiple Stemmed Shrubs: Forsythia

dogwood in bright-yellow color.

Forsythia, because of its beautiful yellow blossoms developed on last year's juvenile growth, is another plant that must be pruned properly to maintain its attractiveness. It is the young, wispy growth that creates the cascading fountain of bright-yellow blooms each spring. My rule of thumb is to remove the oldest canes or stems annually, right after bloom. Pruning forsythia at any other time of the year would mean cutting off the new growth that holds the potential of bloom for the following year. If your forsythia branches have become so long and gangly that you decide they must be pruned in fall, take care not to prune *all* new growth. Any pruning on the forsythia in the springtime, before bloom, also cuts off the potential of flower for that season. If you wish to cut a few branches in late winter or early spring to bring indoors for forcing, do it; your forsythia won't mind. Select branches randomly to prevent the appearance of "holes" in the upcoming seasonal display.

Overgrown shrub Remove ¼ oldest canes immediately after bloom (years 1, 2, and 3) Rejuvenated shrub (year 4)

Thinning Process Rejuvenating Multiple Stem Shrubs

Mock orange, lilac, and spirea plants also should have multiple canes or stems removed to encourage new juvenile growth. For older plants that are well established, my general rule of thumb is to remove one fourth of all of the oldest canes immediately after bloom, allowing a half dozen or so of the juvenile shoots to develop each year. This practice is particularly valuable for lilacs. By pruning only one fourth of the oldest canes, and leaving selected juvenile shoots, many unpruned branches remain for bloom every year. Once a lilac branch is cut, two years pass before that specific branch flowers again.

REPAIRING INJURY

Broken branches in a tree or a shrub should be pruned, no matter what time of year it is. Wind storms, snow storms, and ice storms all tend to cause varying degrees of damage. When damage is extensive, or high in a tree, I always suggest contacting a professional who has the skill, training and equipment necessary to make hazardous repairs. In large trees, a broken branch can become a "widow-maker," that is, it can fall and kill someone.

I recall making a house call to inspect a gigantic Norway maple tree damaged by a severe winter ice storm. This grand old maple tree, with a trunk diameter of more than four feet, had many lateral branches of twelve or more inches in diameter, which the owner thought were great for hanging kids' swings. Two of the lower branches, about fifteen feet above the ground, had cracked under the weight of a massive accumulation of ice and snow. The home owner, an orthopedic surgeon, had adapted his knowledge of repairing broken bones to repairing broken branches. The two broken limbs, splinted with wooden and metal splints and wrapped in what appeared to be miles and miles of Ace bandaging, were suspended in sling-type rigging from high in the tree. Even the breaks themselves were "stabilized" by eight-inch-long lag bolts screwed through the wood tissue. It was a valiant effort, but to no avail. The doctor of human bones was missing one important piece of knowledge: Wood tissue never heals. New layers of xylem cells can grow over broken tissue, but unlike an animal

bone that grows back together, a tree branch never will. Since the break would always be the weakest spot on the branch, and a definite hazard to anyone walking below, I recommended that he contract with his professional arborist to remove the branches immediately. He did just that.

Branches that cross within a plant can rub on each other, causing physical damage to the bark and creating a wound open to disease and insect problems. In a tree, the solution is to remove one of the two branches that will not leave a gap or empty space in the tree. For hybrid-tea roses, prune branches that are growing into the center of the plant by locating buds that point out from the center cane; prune just above them. This encourages stronger canes to develop and creates a much more open growth habit. The better air circulation around the foliage will greatly reduce the potential of black spot and mildew.

REMOVING DEAD, DISEASED, OR INSECT-INFESTED WOOD

Last, but not least, we prune to remove dead, diseased, or insect-infested material, no matter what time of the year it is. By being vigilant and pruning properly, many potential problems can be eliminated or greatly diminished.

I think of the old lilac bush I rejuvenated some years ago. My wife enjoys the smell of lilacs in our home, but with a height of almost twenty feet, the blossoms on this particular plant were so high that only the birds could enjoy them. There were other problems, too. Every year, the leaves were covered with a white powdery mildew and the oldest canes were infested with scale and borers. In fact, there were so many borers that it looked as if someone had discharged shotgun pellets through the stalks. The grayish-white, dusty, scale-type material was so thick that you couldn't see the bark.

It was springtime, right after bloom, when I finally got up enough courage to take on this plant and rejuvenate it. I pruned one fourth of all the oldest canes, which immediately reduced the twenty-foot height to about twelve feet. Remember, the oldest canes are the tallest. Each spring, for the next three years, I removed one fourth of the oldest canes until I finally had a brand-new lilac bush, six to seven feet tall, and in full bloom. As I mentioned earlier, if you cut back the top of a lilac, even after bloom, you will stop that branch from blooming for two more years.

The only other pruning I do on my lilac is to remove the flower seed head right after bloom. This stops seed production. By pruning my old, overgrown lilac in the fashion I have just described, I have eliminated the borers, reduced the scale problem to a minimum, and greatly diminished the possibility of powdery mildew, a major leaf problem of the lilac.

THE PRUNING ARSENAL

Every trade has its special tools and, as a gardener, you will require a few basic tools if you are to do your own pruning. It is not necesary, nor do I recommend, that you buy out the hardware store or your local garden center. A pair of hand pruning shears, a small curved pruning saw, and a pair of safety glasses may be all you need. Assess the potential pruning needs of the plants that are growing. If your garden consists only of house plants or a few flowers or vegetables on the deck or patio, you may need only a pair of hand-held pruning shears. If you add trees and shrubs to your garden landscape, the curved pruning saw will doubtless become a necessity. As for safety glasses, I cannot stress too strongly the need for them. Never attempt to prune branches, with either pruners or a saw, without wearing safety goggles to protect your eyes. A branch stub or falling sawdust can cause irreparable damage to your sight.

My first piece of advice is to purchase the best pruning equipment. You will find that there is a wide price range and variability in quality and craftsmanship. If you take care of quality tools, they will, most likely, last you a lifetime. Keep all cutting surfaces clean and sharp and keep all movable parts well lubricated. Wooden handles must be kept dry and covered with a protective coating of linseed oil or linspeed oil. This oil keeps the wood from cracking and splintering. Metal parts should be coated with a light layer of oil to prevent rust.

A second piece of advice: Don't lend your pruning tools. I once lent a pair of loppers to a neighbor only to get them back in such bad condition that they had to be replaced. The loppers had been used to cut a branch that was much too large, causing the jaws to spring open, and bending the steel blades out of shape. My hand pruning saw was returned with some missing and chipped teeth. I tried to question the fellow in an upbeat manner, hoping to drive home a subliminal message that he might want to replace the tools, but all I got was a mumbled "I must have hit a nail." I sure learned my lesson. And I don't lend my pruning tools anymore.

Basic Tools
Hand-held Pruning Shears If you grow house plants, annual flowers, vegetables, perennials, or trees and shrubs, you will need a sharp pair of hand-held pruning shears. There are two types of cutting actions from which to choose: the anvil and blade, and the scissor-type. Both are used to prune stems up to one-half inch in diameter. The anvil-and-blade-type works as the blade, which must be kept very sharp, hits squarely on the anvil surface in a crushing fashion. The scissor-type works as one blade passes by the other. I prefer the scissor-type for most of my pruning chores because it will make a more flush cut on small stems. And the scissor-type is usually easier to sharpen, needing only one side of the beveled blade to be sharpened with a whetstone or file.

One other point to consider when purchasing hand-held pruning shears is the safety lock. I prefer to have the safety lock where the thumb of the hand that is holding the shears can open and close it, as opposed to its being located at the base of the handle where the other hand must be used to lock it. Never put a pair of pruning shears in your pocket unless the blades are in a closed and locked position.

Lopping Shears Lopping shears are long-handled pruners used to cut branches up to one and a half inches in diameter. The long handles, made of either wood or metal, provide added leverage to the cutting action. Loppers are particularly valuable for pruning branches from fruit trees and removing multiple stems of deciduous shrubs, and are available in both scissor and anvil-action types.

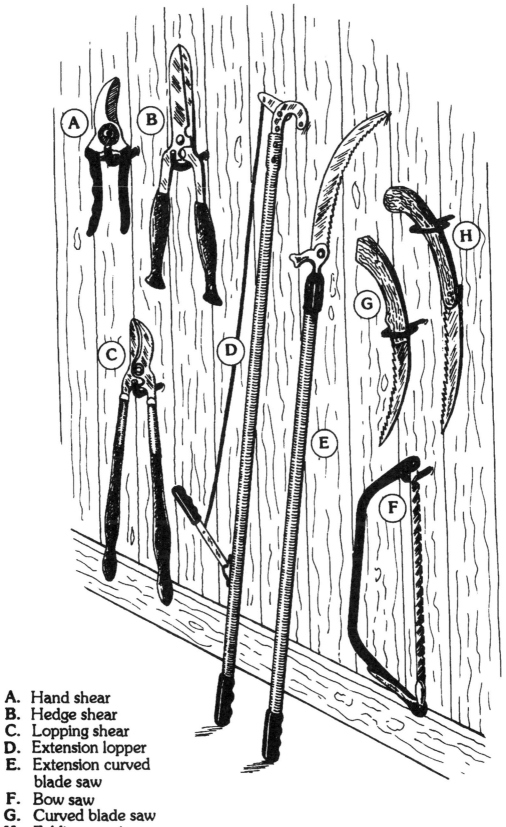

A. Hand shear
B. Hedge shear
C. Lopping shear
D. Extension lopper
E. Extension curved
   blade saw
F. Bow saw
G. Curved blade saw
H. Folding pruning saw

Pruning Tools

Curved-blade Pruning Saw The one other tool you are apt to need is a narrow, curved-blade pruning saw. If you have ever used a carpentry saw you know that it works with a pushing action, and, since most tree pruning is performed with the arms elevated, you will discover that only two or three pushes in an upward motion will wear you out. The hand pruning saw works on the pull, with the weight of your arms, hands and shoulders doing all the work. Just pull the saw as it cuts. The latest version of the hand pruning saw has a collapsible handle that protects the blade while in transport or storage. If you select the collapsible handle saw, always check to see that the blade is locked into position before starting the cut.

Other Accessories

Depending upon your intensity of gardening, you may find it necessary to invest in one or more additional pruning tools:

Hedge shears Scissor-action blades with long handles used to clip formal hedges, creating flat surfaces of foliage.

Electric or Gas-powered Hedge Shears Although either must be used with *caution*, both will make quick work of large hedge pruning jobs. Read the owner's operating manual before each use.

Bow Saw A lightweight saw with a replaceable blade that cuts with both the pull and the push strokes. It is a handy tool for removing larger branches.

Extension-pole Saw A curved-blade pruning saw, mounted on an extendable pole, that is used to reach small overhead or hard-to-reach branches. This small, curved-blade saw also works on the pull. CAUTION: NEVER USE EXTENSION POLE EQUIPMENT NEAR ELECTRICAL WIRES. If you have an area like this, call a professional!

Extension-pole Loppers Lopping shears with a scissor-action blade mounted on an extendable pole to reach small overhead branches.

The latest addition to the pruning arsenal is the multipurpose extension-pole unit, a one-unit consisting of lopper and curved saw.

RESPONSES TO PRUNING

Plants respond to pruning because, by removing or reducing the number of leaves, branches, and/or flowers, the remaining parts of the plant have more water and nutrients available for growth. I have often suggested to gardeners who are planting new trees during the heat of summer, to hand pull off at least one third of all the foliage. This reduces the quantity of water required to conduct transpiration, leaving more water available to the remaining foliage for manufacturing food for growth, and for the root system to repair itself. Removing a portion of the foliage greatly reduces transplant shock as well. The application of an antitranspirant to the remaining foliage will also help reduce the rate of transpiration.

The reduction of flower buds will generate another response, as discussed earlier in the section dealing with pruning practices to increase quality and abundance. By removing a percentage of the flower buds, we redirect the water supply and mineral nutrients to fewer buds, causing the formation of much larger and better fruit and flowers. The more water and mineral nutrients made available to a given flower or fruit, the larger the potential for that flower or fruit. However, there have been many times when I have recommended that *all* flower buds be removed on a newly set plant. Doing this allows the plant to become better established before returning to its flowering cycle. Once a plant has developed flowers, it will do its best to go completely through the seed-production cycle, a process that steals much of the energy required by the plant to establish itself in its new environment.

PLANT METABOLISM AND THE TIME OF YEAR

The time of year for pruning will influence the growth responses that will occur within the plant, which is why it is necessary to know the amount of food and its location within the plant at any given time. As you can imagine, the amount of stored food is greatest in the fall, just before leaf drop, after the plant has spent an entire growing season manufacturing food. It is also important to know about the amount of foliage retained after pruning, because enough foliage must remain to perform photosynthesis, especially during the growing season. During winter, or the dormant season of a deciduous plant, leaf consideration is not important, because it is a natural cycle of the plant to drop its foliage.

By being aware of the location of the food supply in the plant at any given time, you can determine how much pruning can be done and the effects it will have on the plant. A general rule of thumb is: Food stored in the plant is *lowest* in the top from December to March; food stored in the plant is *highest* in the top late in the growing season.

Heavy Fall Pruning Versus Heavy Spring Pruning

In the fall, manufactured food is translocated down through phloem tissue to the root system for overwintering and root growth. Heavy fall pruning of the top growth from a plant reduces the food reserves in the plant for overwintering purposes. If this food is missing or depleted, a dwarfed growth condition may occur or possibly even death, because the loss of food will inhibit normal root growth.

Heavy spring pruning will yield a greater quantity of food to be allocated to a fewer number of buds. If the root system has high nutrient content storage in late winter to early spring, the plant is encouraged to develop stronger, wispier growth, that is, the quick recovery of that hedge.

PLANT PHYSIOLOGY OF PRUNING

It is necessary at this time to look at a cross section of the plant in order to understand the pruning and healing process that takes place within the plant itself. The center or woody portion of a deciduous or evergreen plant is called xylem tissue. As discussed in Chapter I, xylem tissue transports water and dissolved minerals up through the plant to the leaves, where it is used in the process of photosynthesis. Outside the xylem tissue is a microscopic layer, called cambium, that contains meristematic tissue. This tissue develops the callus and healing layer. And on the outside of the cambium layer is the phloem tissue, which translocates manufactured food back down to the root system. The outermost layer of the plant is bark.

In order for the healing process to take place, there must be a continual cycle of water and dissolved minerals to the leaves, and the return of manufactured food to the callus tissue.

If you examine a wound on a tree trunk that occurred some years ago, one where a large section of bark was removed, you will notice the new layer of bark, called the callus, developing from side to side, not from top to bottom. On a completely closed wound, it seems that Mother Nature has closed the wound with a zipper.

A PRUNING CUT

The old philosophy in removing branches was to cut them off as close as possible to their point of origin, flush with the trunk of the tree. Recent research, however, has shown that pruning damage can be reduced by cutting just outside the lines of the branch bark ridge, which is the slightly swollen area that the tree forms for natural shedding. This area, called the branch collar, contains phenolic compounds that are nature's inhibitors against decay organisms; the swollen tissue is usually visible to the eye. The old procedure of flush cutting removed this important collar and allowed introduction of decay pathogens.

In years past, it was also a recommended procedure to treat cuts or wounds with a tree-wound dressing, such as commercial tree paints, orange shellac, asphalt paints, house paints, and/or grafting wax. Today, research has shown that the wound dressings are not only *not* effective, but they may prolong the period of susceptibility to wood-rotting organisms, because the dressings prevent proper drying of the wood tissue.

A PRUNING PRACTICE FOR LARGER BRANCHES

For branches too large to hold in one hand and cut off with the other hand using a pruning saw, undercutting of large branch first will eliminate the breaking of the branch and the peeling of the bark as the cut is finished. The first sawing cut should be made *upward* from the underside of the branch, penetrating the woody tissue by as much as one fourth the thickness of the limb. A second sawing cut can then be made *downward* from the upper side of the branch until both cuts meet. The branch will fall away from the main trunk without causing the damage referred to above.

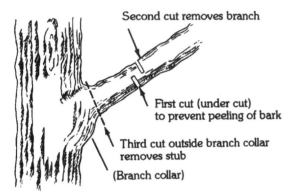

Pruning Large Branches

RULES FOR PRUNING FLOWERING TREES AND SHRUBS

It is not absolutely necessary to know the name of a plant before you prune it, though it *is* necessary to know when it blooms. In general, my philosophy is this: Plants that bloom in June or before are plants that bloom on last year's growth; prune these plants right after bloom. Some examples are: rhododendrons, azalea, laurel, andromeda, forsythia, spirea, as well as other plants that give beautiful springtime bloom. Pruning right *after* bloom allows adequate time for new growth to develop flower buds for the following year.

However, in my garden, there is one major exception to the blooming time theory:

Rhododendron maximum often blossoms in early July, but is a plant that produces its flowering mechanism on last year's growth. I still prune it right after bloom but it just doesn't fit the "June or before" part of my previous statement.

Plants that bloom after June can be pruned in the early spring while they are still dormant. Crape myrtle, hibiscus, rose of Sharon, abelia, butterfly bush, heather, and spirea all benefit from early spring pruning, because they all bloom on new growth.

The other main rule of pruning is to remove all dead, diseased, or insect-infested plant parts upon observing them. Do this immediately, regardless of the time of year.

ROOT PRUNING

Of all gardening techniques, root pruning is probably the least understood and practiced. Gardeners just can't bring themselves to do it, fearing, perhaps, that it will kill the plant. The opposite is the rule rather than the exception. Root pruning can, and often does, stimulate flowering. If done at the right time of year, root pruning can help create a desired dwarfing effect for a new plant, or it can ensure success when transplanting established trees and shrubs.

FORCING BLOOMS

The lilac and the wisteria can be two stubborn plants when it comes to forcing blooms. Proper pruning on the upper part of either of these plants is part of their care. Don't prune back on the lilac's last year's growth; this plant blooms on two-year-old growth. Leave the wisteria's short stems of last year's growth that are at least eight to ten inches long; they contain the blossoms for the coming season. Root pruning also helps these plants to bloom. Sever some of the roots, as instructed earlier in the root-pruning section. The plant may think it is dying. Mother Nature's instinct of preservation signals a priority emphasis on reproduction. The plant's natural reaction produces flowers and seed, and, ultimately, blooms.

Root pruning semidwarf apple trees helped

to reduce an extremely lush growth of foliage. It also induced the setting of flower buds. The nitrogen-rich soil in which the trees were planted had encouraged negative characteristics that root pruning could counteract. In previous years, the trees had produced hundreds of sucker shoots and extra-large leaves, but no flowers. The root-pruning process resulted in the trees setting flower buds during the next growing season, and apples one year later.

KEEPING PLANTS IN BOUNDS

House plants can also benefit from root pruning. New growth will be slowed by trimming and removing the outer layer of roots on the root ball. To root prune a house plant, moisten the soil slightly so it will stay together; if the soil is too dry it will fall away from the root system. However, don't make the soil so wet that it becomes a mushy mess. Slip the plant from the container and shave or pare back the sides of the ball to remove the solid mass of feeder roots. This may be a thin layer on small potted plants but as much as one inch on plants large enough for a 12-inch container. Sometimes a coil of roots will develop at the bottom of the soil ball. Pull on it like a bed spring and prune it back as well. After pruning, fill the spaces (once filled with root growth) with fresh potting soil and thoroughly water the new soil to settle it around the roots. It should match the soil already in the container. Keep the plant out of direct sun and wind for a few days while the roots heal and redevelop new hair roots necessary for the intake of moisture.

Repeated root pruning will enable you to grow plants such as schefflera, ficus, and dracaena for many years in the same size pot and to maintain their tops at a manageable height. If the root pruning process accidentally removes too many roots, the plant begins to drop a lot of its leaves. Don't panic and start overwatering. Just place the plant, pot and all, into a greenhouse environment. You can do this by making a tent of a large piece of clear plastic sheeting; a painter's thin drop cloth works well. Leave the plant inside the makeshift greenhouse until new shoots or leaves begin to sprout.

Every spring, before placing them outside for the summer, I root prune my spider plants and hanging baskets of asparagus fern. These plants develop root systems that grow so fast and become so dense that they literally jack the plant up and out of the pot. Root pruning enables me to grow these plants in the same size container year after year. After all, there is a practical limit to the size of hanging basket containers.

To create dwarfed plants or to slow top growth, root pruning is done at the time of year when the root system is richest in stored nutrients, usually late winter or early spring. Severe root pruning at this time of year destroys much of the stored food that would have promoted spring growth. This is essentially the same concept practiced in root pruning Bonsai plants.

TRANSPLANTING AND ROOT PRUNING

Trees and shrubs well established in one location may, for many reasons, need to be transplanted to another location. For instance, you may want to build a patio, install a walkway, change a view, or just move a plant because it grew too big for its present site. Whatever the reason for transplanting, you can do it if you root prune the plant a year in advance.

The procedure for root pruning a tree or shrub is quite simple. Draw a circle on the ground just inside the drip line that is beneath the tips of the outward-reaching branches. Using a sharp, long-bladed, flat nursery spade or shovel, thrust the blade into the ground as deeply as possible, following the circle surrounding the plant; the blade on my flat spade will cut a gash eighteen inches deep. Although the shovel will sever most roots, there are always a few large enough to require extra effort. The tree or shrub will not miss the portion of the roots from the outside of the drip-line that has been pruned away. New fibrous roots will develop from the inner root system.   Root pruning a plant in the fall prepares it to be moved the following spring; plants that are root-pruned in the spring may be moved in the fall.

Larger trees should be root pruned over a

two-year period by cutting only one half of the roots during one growing season and the other half the following year. Root pruning large trees is best done by a professional who understands the root system of the particular plant and who has the proper equipment. This process requires trenching instead of just shoving a spade into the ground.

Professional growers root prune their nursery field stock mechanically with a tractor-mounted blade. It cuts the roots that reach out to the sides as well as undercutting roots that grow straight down. Until the plant reaches a salable size, this process is usually carried out every other year to develop a strong, massive root system inside the ball. A properly root-pruned, balled and burlapped specimen plant at your garden center or nursery should have adequate roots inside the ball to ensure success at planting time.

BARE-ROOT PLANTING

Just before a plant is placed in the ground, it may be necessary to do a little root pruning to correct damage caused by the digging process. This is particularly true for bare-root transplants, some of which will have roots that are extra long, too long to actually fit in the hole. Instead of bending or curling the roots inside the hole, we prune the root back or dig a larger hole. Often one or two long stringy roots are attached to the main root system and generally can be pruned back without causing a problem. In fact, doing so can stimulate the development of new and stronger fibrous roots within the root system. Broken or ragged ends should be cut off cleanly so they will heal more quickly and soon begin to send out new hair roots. Strawberries and astilbe are examples of bare-root perennials that should have their long, stringy roots clipped back to make planting easier and to stimulate new root growth.

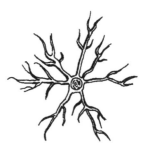

1. Unpruned root system

2. Phase One— cut ½ of roots.

3. Phase Two—cut balance of roots to complete circle

4. Cross section—root pruning.

Root Pruning for Transplanting

QUESTIONS AND ANSWERS

1. Q. **Is it necessary to prune shrub-type roses?**
    A. Shrub roses bloom on active new growth. If shrub roses are left unpruned, they become a mass of tangled, nonproductive brambles with many dead canes. It is necessary to remove these nonproductive plant parts to develop an attractive bush with fresh new canes and quality flowers.

2. Q. **When should old-fashioned roses and climbers that bloom only once a season be pruned?**
    A. Roses that flower only once a year bloom on the previous season's growth, so they should be pruned immediately after blossom.

3. Q. **Every spring when I remove the winter mulch from my roses, I find a few canes have suffered from winter damage. Is spring a good time to prune out winter damage and prune roses in general?**
    A. Winter damage should be pruned immediately upon observation. In general, hybrid-tea, floribunda, and grandiflora roses should be pruned in early spring just as the buds begin to swell.

4. Q. **I am growing hybrid tea, climber, and miniature roses in containers. Do I need special tools for pruning roses?**
    A. The pruning arsenal for roses includes a fine-toothed, curved-blade saw for cutting old, woodier canes; a pair of scissor-action, hand pruning shears for clipping spent blossoms; and a pair of loppers for removing thick canes on climbers and hybrid teas. For your protection, a pair of heavy-duty leather gloves are needed.

5. Q. **How severely should hybrid perpetual roses be pruned?**
    A. A safe rule to follow is to prune the strongest shoots the least and the weakest shoots the most severely. Heavy pruning encourages longer stems for flower production. Light pruning may result in a mass of roses in June, but the stems will be short and the quality of the blooms inferior.

6. Q. **What is heavy, light, and moderate pruning of hybrid tea roses?**
    A. Heavy pruning results when only three or four eyes are left upon each shoot. Light pruning consists of merely cutting out wood that has winterkill. Moderate pruning is cutting shoots back about one half of their length.

7. Q. **Are the terms *rambler* and *climber* synonymous when referring to pruning practices for roses?**
    A. Yes.

8. Q. **How should ramblers be pruned, and when?**
    A. Various climber or rambler roses should be pruned as soon as they finish flowering, to prevent seed production. Pruning at this time results in the growth of long, willowy canes, which bloom the next year.

9. Q. **When can I prune my large-flowered, everblooming climbing roses? It completely covers a chain link fence.**
    A. Well-established, everblooming climbing roses are pruned while they are still dormant in early spring by selectively removing the oldest, woodiest canes but retaining six to eight of the shiny green canes of the past season's growth. It is these canes that produce the flowering mechanisms for the coming season.

10. Q. **Why are some flowering shrubs pruned severely each spring?**

A. Summer flowering shrubs bloom on new growth. The more new growth, the more the potential for bloom during that season. Pruning stems of summer-flowering shrubs, abelia and rose of Sharon by about one half during spring encourages multiple shoots with better blooming potential.

11.   Q. When is the best time to prune a dogwood tree in order not to affect flowering?
A. Pruning flowering dogwood, *Cornus florida*, should be done right after bloom. Pruning at this time allows the maximum time for production of flower buds for the following season.

12.   Q. Should I remove away suckers that grow from the base of a purple-leaf plum tree?
A. Yes. When they are about two to three inches long, try pulling them off instead of pruning them. If you remove suckers by pruning, additional sucker growth develops from the bases of the ones that were pruned away.

13.   Q. When do I prune pussy willow to produce more branches?
A. To encourage multiple stems, prune last year's growth back to two or three buds per stem immediately after the opening of the "pussies" in early spring. The more you prune, the more pussy willows you have.

14.   Q. When can I prune a barberry hedge?
A. Prune the tips of new growth just as they begin to mature in late spring. Tip pruning will ensure a denser inner growth.

15.   Q. Can I rejuvenate an overgrown deutzia shrub?
A. Yes. Cut out the oldest, woody canes immediately after the flowers fade to allow light to reach the new developing shoots. This thinning practice can be carried out over a two- to three-year period.

16.   Q. Mountain laurel tends to grow into a tall, leggy shrub with little or no foliage near the base. Can I cut the old stems back severely to bring the plant down to a smaller size?
A. Drastic pruning of mountain laurel is always chancy and should only be tried in early spring, long before the blossoms open. It must be realized that some times new breaks *do not* develop from older wood and the plant dies. To keep a mountain laurel from becoming leggy, prune out the spent flowers immediately following bloom.

17.   Q. I have low-growing junipers planted along a walkway. Will it hurt their growth habit to remove shoots that grow onto the walk?
A. Prune the junipers as needed to keep the walkway clear and from becoming a safety hazard. This corrective pruning for safety should be done at any time when needed.

18.   Q. Can I prune back, by one half, a white pine tree that is planted at the corner of my house? It is growing into the gutters and causing damage.
A. White pine *cannot* be pruned in the fashion you want, as it will not develop a new growth leader. In general, the branches of white pine are pruned as the candles begin to elongate in the spring. If the plant is damaging your home, have it removed.

19.   Q. When can I prune an arborvitae to thicken its growth?
A. Shear the tips of branches as new growth begins in early spring. The clipping breaks apical dominance in the stems and initiates new growth from buds on older wood.

20.   Q. Why do clipped hemlock hedges become thin near the bottom?
A. The foliage on the lower branches is not receiving enough light. You are either pruning the hedges straight up and down on the sides or your pruning is creating a

vase-shape. To ensure retention of lower foliage, prune hemlock hedges so they are slightly narrower at the top and slightly wider at the bottom.

21. Q. **Can I cut a few long branches from *Juniperus horizontalis* (spreading juniper) for use in making a holiday decorations, without hurting the plant? What branches should I remove?**
    A. If spreading junipers are of sufficient size, they can supply greens for making holiday decorations without any harm. A branch growing from below another can be removed without leaving a hole in the growth habit.

22. Q. **My French hydrangea, *Hydrangea macrophylla*, annually produces tall canes with lush green leaves, but no blue flowers. I feed it with aluminum sulfate and prune all of the canes each spring because they look dead. What could be wrong?**
    A. French hydrangea set their blooms during fall on canes produced last year. If you are pruning away all of the canes in the spring, you are removing the flowering buds. Clip off any winter damage to the canes, but cut back by no more than one half to retain the flower buds.

23. Q. **When is the best time to prune snowhill and peegee hydrangea?**
    A. Both species bloom on new growth, so both are pruned in early spring.

24. Q. **Why is it recommended to remove spent blossoms of tulip, daffodil, and hyacinth bulbs?**
    A. Removing spent blossoms before seed-pod formation directs energy, that would be used for making seeds, into next year's flower production. Do not prune the foliage until it yellows, as it is manufacturing food to complete the bulb-growing cycle.

25. Q. **When can I remove foliage from a bed of naturalized daffodils? The dead leaves are rather unappealing.**
    A. Foliage can be cut from naturalized daffodils as soon as it begins to yellow. The yellowing is a sign the bulb has completed its growth for the season and is going into its summer dormancy.

26. Q. **Can I clip a taxus hedge in mid summer to make it look more even? It seems to produce many "rabbit-ear" shoots that make it look uneven.**
    A. A light clipping to remove "rabbit-ear" shoots can be done before the end of July or after mid September. Avoid pruning during August and early September, as it can initiate growth that may not harden off before the first killing frost.

27. Q. **When should azaleas be pruned to keep them from growing into other plants that are part of my foundation planting?**
    A. Clip or shear growing tips of azaleas immediately after flowering. This pruning stops seed formation and encourages new shoots from older stems.

28. Q. **I have a *Rhododendron maximum* that appears as though it is growing from a stump. Could this be?**
    A. Yes. Most *Rhododendron maximum* are collected from the wild. Before they are harvested, old plants are cut back drastically, leaving a stump, in order to cause multiple new stems to break from the base. If this had not been done, the plant would likely be all stems with a little foliage at the top.

29. Q. **Why should I prune out wilted flowers on *Rhododendron roseum elegans*?**
    A. Removal of spent blossoms, immediately after bloom, breaks apical dominance in the stem, allowing several growth buds to develop simultaneously. Branches that do not have spent flowers removed before seed formation develop only one stem that gives the rhododendron a "leggy" look.

30. **Q. I have both male and female American holly trees. When should I prune them to encourage dense growth?**
    A. Clip the tips of American holly branches during early spring just before new growth begins. A light clipping will have little effect on the flowering and fruiting capabilities.

31. **Q. Any suggestions for creating a straight line when pruning hedges?**
    A. Simple. Place a stake at each end of the hedge and stretch a cord between the two stakes at the height you want to prune. Use the straight line as your guide.

32. **Q. When planting a privet hedge from bare-root transplants in the spring, should they be pruned at that time or allowed to grow without pruning?**
    A. Cut back privet transplants at planting time to six to twelve inches above the ground to encourage growth of multiple shoots the first year. Clip the tips of these new shoots when they reach twelve to fifteen inches tall.

33. **Q. Can an arborvitae be clipped to keep it from getting too large?**
    A. Yes. Clip or shear the growing tips of all branches during the beginning of every growing season.

34. **Q. Does it harm lilac shrubs to cut branches for enjoyment indoors?**
    A. No. This pruning will only reduce the blossoms for next year. Branches where blooming stems were removed will not flower again for two years, so take them randomly.

35. **Q. My overgrown lilac is at least twenty feet tall and has many shoots. What pruning should I do to reduce its size?**
    A. If the lilac has multiple tall stems prune away one-fourth of the oldest canes just above ground level right after bloom. Each year allow no more than five or six *new* stems to grow, removing the rest. Repeat this pruning practice annually for the next four years and the lilac will be back to the five- to seven-foot height without affecting its bloom.

36. **Q. How often should a privet hedge be sheared?**
    A. Shear a privet hedge just as new growth begins during spring to encourage shoots from inner stems. Clip the new growth from spring as it begins to harden in early summer. Complete the growing season with a final pruning in early fall to even the hedge for winter.

37. **Q. When should I prune clematis?**
    A. Timing for pruning of clematis depends on the blooming period. Those which bloom on old wood, last years growth, need little or no pruning other than removal of dead or diseased twigs. Clematis that bloom on current season's growth are pruned in early spring before growth begins.

38. **Q. Can an overgrown privet hedge be restored by pruning?**
    A. It is worth the effort, but not always a success, to prune an overgrown privet hedge during early spring to a six-inch height above the ground and let it start all over. If pruned drastically during early spring when the root system is fullest in stored nutrients, many new shoots should sprout from the base and ground.

39. **Q. Can wisteria be pruned to keep it in bounds and still have it bloom?**
    A. During mid summer, prune back the longest runners or vines by about one half their length to encourage spurlike shoots. In late winter, prune these shoots again to leave no more than three to four inches at their base. The flower buds will be apparent at this time.

40. **Q. Is it necessary to pinch out spent blossoms of minor bulbs such as chionodoxa, colchicum, crocus, and lily of the valley?**
    A. I have never heard of anyone spending time to remove spent blossoms from minor bulbs. If the bulb bed is of any size, the time involved would be prohibitive. Time spent fertilizing in late winter or early spring would probably benefit their production more.

41. **Q. When should lily stalks be removed?**
    A. To reduce possible disease, prune off lily stalks at ground level once the foliage and stems have browned.

42. **Q. Should stalks and leaf stems be cut off tender gladiolus corms before they are stored for winter?**
    A. Yes. Clip the stalks and leaf stems just above the corm to help harden off the corm for storage.

43. **Q. Shrub roses have become popular as landscape plants. Are there special pruning techniques to keep them healthy and in bloom?**
    A. Prune a few of the oldest canes to the ground each spring, remove dead or diseased wood whenever it is seen, and prune to keep the plants in bounds.

44. **Q. Can asters be pruned to keep plants from getting too tall?**
    A. Pinch or prune asters by early summer to create a bushier plant.

45. **Q. Should hardy chrysanthemums be cut to the ground in the fall after they bloom?**
    A. Yes. Prune stems to an inch or so above the ground after they are killed by a freeze. If the prunings are not disease-infected they can be used as a mulch to provide wind protection for the remaining stems.

46. **Q. My hardy chrysanthemums grow too tall and end up bending over to the ground when they bloom in the fall. Can I help them?**
    A. As soon as their new growth reaches six to eight inches tall during spring, cut it back by one half. Six weeks later, cut or pinch them again by one half. Depending upon the variety and when you want them to bloom, another pinch may be done no later than mid July.

47. **Q. Can spruce be clipped to form it as a hedge?**
    A. Except to preserve the uniformity of a hedge, spruce is pruned very little. As spring growth begins, pinching out the strong buds at the base will help make the hedge bushier at the base.

48. **Q. Can the growing tip—leader—of an evergreen be cut back?**
    A. Removal of leader growth from many species of evergreens will tend to make more compact tops. But for white pine, spruce, and fir, it ruins their shape; they tend to develop a crooked neck as a new leader.

49. **Q. Is it true the faded blooms of andromeda should be removed?**
    A. Removal of faded blossoms is highly desirable, because seeds are formed at the same time as next year's clusters of flower buds are being set. If flower clusters are promptly removed, energy intended for seed production will go into bud formation instead.

50. **Q. During winter we invariably have one or two ice storms that leave broken branches dangling from the trees. Can we wait for spring to repair the damage?**
    A. For safety's sake, have dangling branches removed as soon as possible. The repair of the damaged tissue should wait until the temperature is above freezing to avoid damage to the bark and cambium tissue.

51. **Q. Can evergreens, that have been allowed to grow too tall be topped or pruned back severely?**
A. Only those evergreens that "bud" readily from old wood, such as holly, taxus, and boxwood can be pruned severely. Severe trimming, however, may leave large evergreens in an unsightly condition. Pine, fir, spruce, and Douglas fir are not to be pruned by topping.

52. **Q. Does it harm a spruce or pine to cut branches from it for indoor decorations?**
A. Cutting branches from spruce and pine will not hurt the tree if care is taken in the selection of the branches. Their removal can only spoil the looks. Make sure there is a branch that will cover the gap created by the one that is removed.

53. **Q. Can branches loaded with berries be cut from American holly during winter?**
A. Small branches may be cut randomly from the fruit-bearing holly without harming the tree.

54. **Q. Will pinching back growing tips of an azalea encourage fuller growth?**
A. Yes. Pinching off the end of growing tips will force several side buds to develop and result in a bushier shrub.

55. **Q. Should lilacs be pruned?**
A. Yes, prune out all but five or six young suckers and all of the dead or diseased wood each year. Some of the older branches could be cut out to allow more light to reach the branches in the center of the plant. Prune just *after* blooming.

56. **Q. How should spirea "Anthony Waterer" be pruned?**
A. Spirea "Anthony Waterer" is a late bloomer, producing its flowers on the current season's growth. Prune by cutting back one half of each cane just as growth begins.

57. **Q. Will pruning encourage snowberry bush, *Symphoricarpos rivularis* to produce more white berries?**
A. Yes. Prune the snowberry to the ground in late winter.

58. **Q. How many branches should be left when a shrub is espaliered against a trellis or wall?**
A. Spacing is determined by the character of the shrub. Evergreens and small-leaved deciduous plants average about one feet apart. Enough branches should be left so that the wall or trellis is well covered when the branches are in full leaf during the growing season.

59. **Q. What are the reasons for root pruning?**
A. Plants are root pruned to promote formation of fibrous roots for transplanting purposes, to induce blossoming, and to check excessive shoot and leaf growth.

60. **Q. My neighbor is growing apples, peaches, pears, and plums along a stone wall and fence. He claims this way of growing plants, called espalier, saves room and has been used for centuries. What is an espalier?**
A. An espalier is a plant that has been subjected to a special technique of training growth in one plane, against a wall, trellis, or fence. The secret to this Old-World practice is identifying growth buds and determining the direction they will grow.

61. **Q. What is meant by disbudding?**
A. Disbudding is a pruning technique used to increase the size of specific flowers. It is the removal of certain buds while they are small, in order to force the remaining buds into flowers of larger size. Plants commonly disbudded include carnation, chrysanthemum, dahlia, peony, and rose.

62. **Q. When should spring-flowering shrubs be pruned?**
    A. Shrubs that bloom during spring bloom on last season's growth. They are pruned right after bloom to remove spent blossoms, seed pods, and to encourage new growth.

63. **Q. When is the best time to prune fruit trees?**
    A. Fruit trees—apple, peach and pear— are pruned in late winter before the sap starts to move.

64. **Q. When is the best time to prune ornamental trees?**
    A. Maple, oak, sweetgum, ash, and so on, can be pruned in early summer after the leaves are out, so you can see just what you are doing.

65. **Q. I planted pachysandra ground cover but it does not seem to be filling in as fast as it should. Will it help to prune the tips of each stem?**
    A. Pinching or pruning the central leader of each stem will encourage pachysandra to develop multiple side shoots.

66. **Q. How often should I mow a bluegrass lawn?**
    A. The general rule for mowing turfgrass is to remove no more than one third of the grass blade at any one time. As to the frequency, that is determined by how fast the grass is growing.

67. **Q. Should lawn clippings be removed after mowing?**
    A. With the new technology in mowing equipment it is seldom that grass clippings need to be removed from the lawn after mowing. The size of the clippings and their density is what determines the need for removal. If clippings accumulate, and can be seen after twenty-four hours, it is probably an indication that the grass blades were too long when they were mowed. In this case, the clippings should be removed, either by raking or by use of a lawn sweeper.

68. **Q. What is the difference between shearing and pruning?**
    A. Shearing is a form of pruning in which all growth extending beyond a definite line is cut off. Pruning is the removal of individual shoots or branches with a view toward improving the tree or shrub.

69. **Q. How should one prune a forsythia hedge the first year?**
    A. To develop a dense growth, cut back all shoots to within six to twelve inches of the ground at planting time. To encourage the natural growth habit of the forsythia, do no more pruning until after bloom the following spring.

70. **Q. Do all hedge plants need to be trimmed several times during the growing season?**
    A. No. Most evergreens can be kept neat with one shearing. The same is true of such deciduous shrubs as althea, barberry, buckthorn, and spirea.

71. **Q. As a new homeowner, what pruning tools should I purchase?**
    A. The pruning equipment depends on the landscape material you will be pruning. You will most likely need a pair of hand pruning shears, a pair of long-handled loppers, and a small curved-blade pruning saw. Purchase the best quality and keep them sharp. Good equipment will last for many years if you care for it.

72. **Q. When I pruned a maple and dogwood last spring, they dripped sap for many days. How can I keep tree wounds from bleeding?**
    A. Maples, birches, and dogwoods are among the "bleeders" when it comes to springtime pruning. This is a temporary situation and although it is unsightly, it does not harm the tree. To avoid bleeding, prune at another time of the year.

73. **Q. We planted a ten-foot tall oak tree and the central leader broke out of it. Will it grow into a tree, or should we replace it?**

A. If there is a strong side shoot just below the break, tie a support cane securely to the trunk and let it project two or three feet above. As the side shoot grows, bend and tie it to the cane.

74. **Q. Can pruning aid in controlling plant disease?**

A. Yes. Pruning is recommended for canker on roses, gall on forsythia, and fire blight on trees and shrubs. Affected limbs must be cut off well below the diseased tissue, using tools disinfected after every cut.

75. **Q. Will pruning reduce infestations of scale insects?**

A. Yes. If branches are *dying* from heavy scale attack, the branches should be removed. If the branches are an important part of the plant and are still alive, apply a recommended insecticide according to the label directions.

76. **Q. How can I prune my Swedish ivy hanging basket to keep it from looking out of control? The top looks dead.**

A. Pinch, pinch, and pinch your Swedish ivy plant. Clipping the tips of every stem every few weeks will cause new growth to develop from buds further in on the branch structure.

77. **Q. Is there any special pruning practice that will make a plant grow in a particular direction?**

A. Yes. Prune just above a growth bud, located at a node, that is pointing in the direction you wish to have the plant develop.

78. **Q. How can I avoid tearing bark on the trunk when cutting off large limbs?**

A. Make the first cut from the underneath side of the branch, cutting upward until the saw bind slightly. This cut will eliminate peeling of bark as you make a cut from above to remove the limb. If a stub remains, you may now cut it off with safety by holding it with one hand while the few last cuts with the saw are being made.

79. **Q. An arborist wants to prune my large shade trees in late winter. Is it all right to trim trees at that time?**

A. Yes, provided the temperature is not too low. Large cuts made just before bud break will "bleed" due to the hydrostatic pressure of sap in the plant. The bleeding is beneficial in reducing decay organisms that might infect the wound.

80. **Q. When is the best time to prune a tree?**

A. The answer depends on the desired effect. If it is to dwarf or check growth, prune trees when they are actively growing. Ordinarily, trees are pruned when they are dormant, in the fall or late winter. Dormant pruning stimulates strong shoot growth.

81. **Q. Can pruning be used to dwarf plants?**

A. Pruning at specific times of the year will reduce stored food in plant tissue. Heavy pruning of above-ground plant parts during fall eliminates much food that was manufactured over summer. These nutrients would normally be translocated to the root system for overwintering and for pushing spring growth. Without the nutrient supply, dwarfness occurs. Root pruning during early spring, before growth starts, also eliminates much stored food.

82. **Q. If I root -prune a shrub ahead of time, is it possible to move it with greater safety?**

A. Yes. Start the root-pruning process during spring by plunging a sharp spade deeply into the ground a few inches inside the drip line. This severs many roots and induces the formation of fibrous roots. The shrub may be moved the following fall or spring.

83. **Q. What is a terminal bud?**
    A. The topmost bud on a stem is the terminal bud.

84. **Q. What are the reasons for root pruning?**
    A. Root pruning promotes formation of fibrous roots, induces blossoming, and checks excessive shoot and leaf growth.

85. **Q. When are plants disbudded?**
    A. Disbudding is practiced when the buds to be removed are large enough to handle, usually about the size of a small pea.

86. **Q. What is more important in pruning espaliers, the time of pruning or the shape?**
    A. The most important aspect of creating an espalier is having a mental picture of the final shape desired. Taking off a single wrong bud may retard the final shaping for a year or more.

87. **Q. When is the best time to prune forsythia to promote flowering growth?**
    A. Prune forsythia immediately after blossoms drop in spring. Remove the oldest stems to allow juvenile growth to emerge from the center of the plant. Forsythia bloom on last year's growth.

88. **Q. Should lilac flowers be removed after they fade?**
    A. Yes. Removing spent flowers stops seed production. To promote bloom for the following year, clip the flower head *just* below the lowest blossom.

89. **Q. What is the best way to prune an overgrown mock orange shrub?**
    A. Cut out the oldest and weakest shoots as close to the soil line as possible, immediately following flowering.

90. **Q. Can I prune my Christmas cactus to encourage better bloom next year?**
    A. Pruning will stimulate more stem development, which has the potential of bloom, if flowering conditions are right. Pruning is not the initiator of bloom.

91. **Q. I tried growing Brussels sprouts last year and got nothing but tiny sprouts, about the size of marbles, at the axil of each leaf. Do I need to feed more?**
    A. It is doubtful that feeding would correct the problem. To grow Brussels sprouts to their normal size or larger, during late summer remove the lower third of the foliage and pinch out the growing tip of each plant. The removal of the growing tip breaks the apical dominance, distributing growth energy to side shoots that are the Brussels sprouts.

VI

WATERING

IT CAN SAFELY BE SAID that water, in quantities either too great or too little, is the number-one killer of both indoor and outdoor plants. Insects and diseases kill plants, but it is my professional opinion, after many years of observation, that these two culprits take second place to water as the number-one killer. If only we understood the inter-relationship of water and the plant's growth cycle, water, indeed, would be the glorious "staff of life," not the dreaded destroyer.

Furthermore, water conservation methods should be the number-one priority of gardeners. Over the many years I have been gardening, water has been so plentiful that I fear we have become quite complacent in its use, and un-believably wasteful in our watering practices. Many homeowners have installed automatic water systems for their lawns and landscapes. While making watering a breeze, these systems can be very wasteful. Recently, several summers have seen restrictions placed on water usage: that is, forbidding sprinklers or irrigation systems, but allowing use of hand-held garden hoses or sprinkler-can watering. Household use of water was likewise limited: as little as fifty gallons of water per person per day and alternate-day watering of garden and landscape plants. In some cases, water for use in the garden was prohibited altogether.

What has brought this water crisis to our doorstep? It's a rhetorical question actually. To confirm that we willfully waste one of our most precious resources, drive through a neighbor-hood in suburbia during a summer rainstorm. You won't have to go very far before you come upon a lawn or garden with its automatic sprinkler pulsating away, delivering gallons of unneeded water. Most irrigation systems cannot tell if it is raining or even how much it has rained. What a waste.

If we learn the best techniques for watering, the best times for watering, and learn the real water requirements of our plants, we can con-serve water and make its use much more efficient.

Role of Water

The many uses of water within the plant itself should not be confused with the misuse of water in our watering practices. A plant starting to wilt is not necessarily thirsty. Water is used by the plant in photosynthesis, transpiration, cell elongation, cell growth, conduction, and turgidity. Water is absolute-ly essential in propagation, both vegetative and seed. Water is also a byproduct of respiration. A good understanding of how a plant uses water will provide the proper reference for our watering practices, par-ticularly relating to volume and frequency.

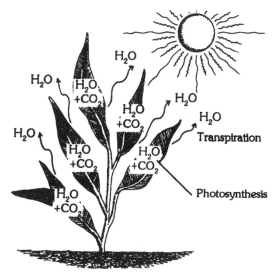

**Role of Water:
Photosynthesis and Transpiration**

PHOTOSYNTHESIS— FOOD MANUFACTURING

As discussed in Chapter 1, photosynthesis is the process by which building blocks, in the form of sugars, are manufactured for growth. Although the formula is quite complex, the essential ingredients include: light, proper temperature, chlorophyll, carbon dioxide, and water. Through the miracle of nature, food is produced that provides the energy for plant growth. By increasing or reducing the amount of water available to the plant, we can influence food manufacturing within a plant. A look at growth rings from a cross section of a tree trunk illustrates the availability of water to the plant during any growth season. The rings provide an accurate record of precipitation for that specific area. A year of drought will exhibit a much narrower growth ring compared to a ring laid down or produced during normal and above-normal rainfall.

The ability to control the amount of water, and the knowledge of the normal growth rate of a particular plant, allow us to speed up or slow down the food-manufacturing process within the plant. We can cause seedlings to grow faster or slower by adjusting the amount of water they receive. For tomato, eggplant, and pepper, I begin reducing the available water immediately after the seedlings emerge from the starting mix. However, to stop water completely would stop the photosynthesis necessary to maintain growth, and the seedlings would collapse and die. If seedlings are kept too moist, they tend to become "leggy", almost spaghettilike in growth.

TRANSPIRATION— PLANT PERSPIRATION

Transpiration is defined as the giving off of water (in most cases as a gas) through the aerial parts of the plant. You might call it plant perspiration. A typical sunflower plant grown over a 140-day period will transpire as much as 145 pounds of water. If you recall the saying "a pint of water is equal to one pound the world around," then this would be the equivalent of more than eighteen gallons of water for one sunflower plant during one growing season.

Ninety percent or more of the water that is not used in the plant for its growth functions evaporates as a gas through the stomata on the leaf surface. The balance of water, which could be as much as ten percent, is given off through the cuticle, a waxy layer secreted by the cells of the leaf. The function of this waxy substance is to inhibit loss of water and reduce desiccation. *Ficus elastica*, the large-leaf rubber plant, is a "shining" example of cutin on the leaf surface. In fact, it is the cutin that gives those leaves their natural shine. If you wash your plant leaves regularly, you notice that, after a few washings, the leaf surface takes on a rather dull look. That is because the cutin has been removed, and cannot be regenerated by the epidermal cells. The loss of cutin will cause the rate of transpiration to increase. To restore the leaf shine, several commercial products are available from your local flower and garden shop. The only down side I can find in the use of these products is that they become dust catchers which, in turn, requires additional washing of the leaf surface to keep the plant clean.

FACTORS AFFECTING THE RATE OF TRANSPIRATION

Dry Air Versus Humid Air

Relative humidity (RH), a measurement of the amount of water vapor in the air at a given temperature, is stated in a percentage. If you have a three-dial, indoor wall weather station, you most likely have a thermometer and barometer unit. Take a look at the third dial. It may be a humidity gauge which gives you the relative humidity.

Warm air holds more moisture than cool air, so it takes more moisture to give a higher measure of relative humidity indoors, especially during the heating season. I find that by maintaining an RH of 50 to 55 percent during the winter months, my house plants, particularly ivies, pothos, philodendrons, and schefflera, do quite well if all other factors, such as light, water, and temperature are maintained. When the relative humidity drops below 50 to 55 percent for an extended time, emerging growth is much smaller in size. During the heating season, it is not uncommon for the relative humidity in our homes to drop as low as 5 percent, or even less. It would be similar to the low humidity found in the Sahara Desert, and if you are growing bromeliad, aloe, and sansevieria, there is no problem. These are plants that thrive in an environment of low humidity. However, I find it beneficial for most of my tropical plants to add moisture to the air during winter. Though it is slight, there is an increase in the rate of transpiration from the stomata and the leaf cuticle in low humidity. This may be why new leaves on plants such as Swedish ivy, English ivy, pothos, and philodendron are somewhat diminished in size compared to those produced at a higher relative humidity.

Humidity Tray

If water vapor is not given off through the leaf, then it may be used in the photosynthesis process, building more food for growth. During the summer, when many of my tropical-foliage hanging baskets are enjoying their summer vacation outdoors, the new growth develops to its maximum size: pothos leaves are extra-large and colorful; Swedish ivy, grape ivy, and English ivy also end the summer with foliage fully expanded. As soon as I bring the plants indoors for the winter months, new growth, continual throughout the year on all four plants, develops but is reduced in size. In fact, each new leaf is progressively smaller than the one produced just before, by as much as 50 percent. I attribute this dramatic difference in leaf size to the change in the environment and, in particular, to the reduction of humidity around the plant. In general, the higher the humidity, the larger the foliage.

A winter visit to a northern greenhouse where tropical plants are being grown often results in wet shoes. Take a look at the walkways; they have been watered, too. It is the grower's way of introducing more moisture into the growing environment without continually wetting the foliage. In some greenhouses, you may also find a mist system in use. This is an automated method of introducing fine droplets of water into the air. Of course, we can't do either one of these procedures in the home.

Increasing Relative Humidity Indoors
When I was a child, one of my daily household tasks during winter was to fill pans with water. These pans were hung on the back side of the radiators. Some radiators even had covers with water trays on top that required daily filling. Our home was heated by a coal-fired, steam-heat boiler, which fed the radiators in each room. Every time they warmed up, the heated water caused moisture to evaporate into the air from the open pans. In addition to the water trays, my mother always kept a pot of water simmering on the stove. There were times, with so much moisture in the air in the dead of winter, that ice formed on the inside of the window glass.

During the heating season, if you don't have a humidity indicator indoors, but have an antique table that has not been refinished with the new poly finishes, take a look at the surface of the old finish. Because of a lack of moisture in the air, the surface of the tabletop will dry and shrink, giving it the appearance of a road map, side roads and interstates included. However, as soon as humidity is reinstated, the fine cracks will virtually disappear.

One method of increasing the relative humidity in your home is to grow a lot of house plants. Each plant releases water vapor into the air through the leaf structure, as well as through evaporation from the soil and pot. Collectively, these two sources of moisture are called evapotranspiration. So, the more plants you grow, the higher the humidity.

Humidity trays can produce much-needed moisture for your plants. Simply use a large, watertight baking pan or tray with one- to two-inch sides. After filling the pan with washed gravel or coarse builders' sand, place your plants on top of this medium. Fill the tray with just enough water so the pots are not sitting directly in the water. Roots that are continually immersed can develop a problem known as root rot. Continue to add water to the tray as needed. The moist surface area of the sand or gravel will increase evaporation action, making the air immediately above the tray higher in humidity. If the plants are growing in a warm environment, above 70 degrees Fahrenheit, the humidity tray will probably require water on a daily basis.

I find that windowsill orchid collections love the humidity tray. And when I grow a prayer plant on a humidity tray, it has few or no brown tips on the leaves. Without the humidity tray, tip dieback begins.

Hot-air furnaces often have a humidifier built into them. This system introduces moisture each time the furnace runs. However, if the automatic system is not maintained properly, it is a potential health hazard. Read the owner's manual carefully to know appropriate maintenance requirements.

Last, but not least, you might consider purchasing an individual room humidifier. These usually need to be refilled once a day, and sometimes twice a day; we have one that uses about twelve gallons of water per day. The disadvantage of the mist-type humidifier is its tendency to leave a white film on everything in the room, including plants. This white deposit is most likely comprised of minerals from your water—harmless, but a mess to clean up. Again, check your owner's manual for maintenance requirements. Like the automatic humidity system in the hot-air furnace, the individual room humidifier must be kept clean.

Soil Factors

Competition among plants for available soil moisture also affects their rate of transpiration. Less moisture available for a given plant means less moisture available for the cooling process. The cooling process prevents buildup of heat energy inside the leaf, a buildup that causes cell desiccation. A solution to the problem caused by competition is to increase the amount of available moisture during dry periods by giving your plants a drink. Or, if the competition for moisture is caused by the competitive presence of weeds, pull them out and use a mulch (see Chapter VII) to prevent their re-growth. When beds of living ground covers, such as ivy, pachysandra, or vinca, are grown under trees as part of the landscape, it is often necessary to water both trees and ground cover during extremely dry periods.

Air Temperature

Temperature of the air surrounding a leaf can have a direct effect on the amount of water vapor released. When you cool the air temperature, less water vapor is released through the stomata and leaf cuticle, simply because the air can hold less moisture. On a hot, sunny summer afternoon, go into the vegetable patch and observe the leaves of the cucurbits: squash, melons, and cucumbers. The large leaves will likely appear to be somewhat wilted. Water vapor from the leaves is being released at a rate too fast for the root system to replenish. Revisit the garden in the early evening, after the warm sun has disappeared, and you will likely find the leaves restored to their full turgidity. The cooler temperature limits the amount of moisture escaping into the surrounding air. If the leaves do not show a turgid response to the cooler temperature, there may be other problems. Check the soil to make sure there is sufficient moisture available, and check the stem of the plant for possible borer infestations (see Chapter VIII for pest management).

Reducing the air temperature around the plant foliage reduces the rate of transpiration, allowing the plant to "live" on less water. I have often recommended to plant lovers who are about to go on a vacation that they simply turn down the heat a few degrees, or set the plants out of direct sun, if the plants can't be tended. I have been able to add as much as a week to a vacation without worrying about my plant's water supply.

Air Movement

Air circulation is good for a plant, but a windy condition can spell disaster. The plant may be unable to take up enough water to compensate for the increased transpiration rate created by the pulling action of the air as it flows across the leaf surface. The relative humidity of the microclimate immediately adjacent to the leaf surface is greatly increased in "still" air. This increase in humidity reduces the rate of transpiration because of air, already saturated with moisture, stagnating due to lack of circulation. As soon as air begins to circulate the stagnant microclimate of higher humidity next to the leaf is replaced with air lower in moisture. This exchange of air allows greater evaporation of water vapor by the leaf, both through the stomata and the cuticle. If the plant cannot take up enough water to replace that which is given off, it loses its turgidity; that is, it wilts.

One winter I had a colorful coleus collection of five different varieties growing on a sunny windowsill. They were fantastic; the leaves were extra colorful and large. One day, it was a little warm in their part of the room and I decided to open the window to cool things down. Within just a few moments, my "fantastic" coleus plants began to look very sad. They were wilting right before my eyes. The fresh air, though much appreciated by me, was not being enjoyed by my coleus collection. The loss of high humidity around the leaf surface of my plants was allowing them to transpire at a rate much greater than their ability to take up replacement water. Without adequate moisture to provide turgidity, my plants wilted. As soon as I realized the problem, I closed the window. Doing so reduced the air movement around the foliage, allowing the microclimate of high humidity to be reestablished, and the plants to recover.

Light

When light strikes the surface of a leaf, heat energy is generated inside the leaf, because the chlorophyll and other pigments become solar collectors. Absorption of light by the darker colors creates warmth. This heat energy not only increases the rate of photosynthesis, but also increases the rate of transpiration. The cells of the plant require enough water to accomplish both functions. Without a sufficient amount of moisture in the cells during a warm condition, the plant will exhibit signs of wilting. By reducing the light intensity, temperature inside the leaf drops, and it requires less water. One simple practice to reduce water needs is to shade a plant.

Rhododendrons and azaleas are classic examples to demonstrate the reaction of light on foliage. When the ambient temperature is below 32 degrees Fahrenheit, the foliage on these plants will be pointing in a downward direction. If the temperature is well *below* 32 degrees, the leaves will be pointing downward and will be rolled up in the shape of a cigar. You might think the plant is showing typical signs of severe stress and wilting, but it isn't. This posture is nature's way of reducing the rate of transpiration from the leaf. As soon as the sun's rays reach the leaf surface, the cells inside the leaf absorb the light and generate heat energy, which increases the rate of transpiration, as well as other growth functions.

Outside my kitchen window, I have two, twelve-foot-tall, *Rhododendron maximum* specimens that have become my wintertime thermometer. They grow in an area shaded by the house from morning sun and when I get up on a cold morning, I look out the window to check the position of the foliage. If the leaves are drooped, I know it is below freezing and I had better bundle up for the day. If they are curled up in addition to pointing downward, I know it is *very* cold and probably time for the long underwear. As soon as the sun reaches the leaf surface, the leaves begin to unroll and return to their natural shape.

To demonstrate how light is absorbed by dark colors and how it generates heat energy, on a cold day put your hand on the body of a dark-colored auto which is parked outside in a sunny location. The surface will feel warm. Then put your hand on a white auto that has been parked in the sun. Since white reflects light, this car should feel cooler by comparison. Remember when you sat on the seat covers of that car parked in the sun? That's a perfect example of light generating heat!

CELL ELONGATION

Cell elongation is the irreversible stretching of the cell wall and it occurs during the primary growth cycle, a cycle true of all plants. This process contributes to the increase in the length of the plant. To facilitate the process, water must be present in sufficient quantities, within the cells, to provide the necessary pressure that will permanently stretch the primary cell wall. Plants without sufficient water pressure inside the cells to provide elongation will, at most, develop dwarfed growth. High transpiration rates will also reduce cell elongation.

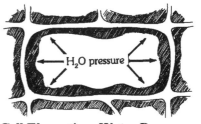

Cell Elongation: Water Pressure

CELL EXPANSION

Cell expansion is known as the secondary growth in a plant; it is the increase in girth or width of the cells. All plants have primary growth, but only woody plants have secondary growth and, again, moisture must be present in adequate quantities to fully expand the growing cells. A look at the growth rings of a woody plant will tell you whether there was an abundance or shortage of moisture for a given year.

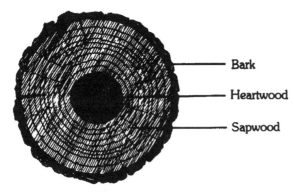

Annual Rings: Cross Section

CONDUCTION OF NUTRIENTS

Water is essential to the movement of minerals within the plant. Water, along with dissolved minerals in the form of ions, enters the hair roots through the processes of imbibition, diffusion, and osmosis. The dissolved minerals are translocated through the xylem tissue in the roots, stems, and into the leaves to the location where the manufacture of food occurs. Upon completion of the manufacturing process, food in the form of sugars is translocated down through the phloem tissue to the growth points in the leaves, stems, and roots, completing the food-movement cycle within the plant. If at any time water is not available to the plant, the food manufacturing process is jeopardized and the growth of the plant diminished. Withholding water, to a limited extent, is a technique used in the hardening-off process of new seedlings.

TURGIDITY

Water provides turgor pressure in the plant cell that ensures normal rigidity in the plant structure. When a plant is not turgid, it is said to be wilting. For example: Blow up a balloon. The air inside provides pressure on the inner balloon wall, thus making it "turgid". As soon the air is released, the balloon collapses or loses its turgidity.

Loss of Turgidity: Wilting

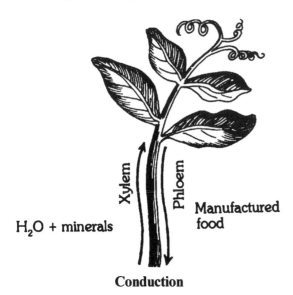

H_2O + minerals   Manufactured food

Conduction

PROPAGATION

Water is essential in all phases of propagation, whether it be sexual (seed) or asexual (vegetative).

Seed Propagation

The function of water in seed propagation starts with the softening of the seed coat, an event that facilitates the emergence of roots and shoots. Water carries in free oxygen that triggers respiration, a food utilization process that activates digestion of the stored food found in the cotyledons. Water then becomes the medium for movement of digested food to the seed embryo. The embryo is the living portion of the seed containing the epicotyl (shoot), the hypocotyl (stem), and the radicle (root). It is in the embryo that the cell elongation process and growth as we know it takes place. Without water, some species of seeds can lie dormant for centuries; they are actually in a state of reduced respiration.

Vegetative Propagation

For vegetative propagation, produced either by cuttings or grafting, water provides the necessary moisture to keep the cells from drying. When a cutting is taken from a plant, it no longer has the root system to supply its normal water needs. Cuttings taken early in the morning contain more moisture in their cells than those taken later in the day when water-using transpiration and photosynthesis have been at work. Moisture in the propagation medium keeps the cell walls soft, allowing additional moisture to be absorbed into the cutting. These soft cell walls allow roots to emerge with less resistance. It is also important to increase humidity around the cuttings in order to reduce transpiration. Remember, plants that have no root system are unable to take up moisture and must rely upon the water in the cutting itself for photosynthesis and the eventual development of roots.

In grafting, moisture must be present to allow new cells to grow on the cut surface of both the stock and scion. These new cells become either xylem tissue for the translocation of water and dissolved minerals upward, or the phloem tissue that carries manufactured food downward to be used by the lower parts of the plant.

RESPIRATION

Water is a byproduct of respiration. When free oxygen attacks the sugars, carbon dioxide and water are released. This metabolic process occurs mostly at night. Some of the water is given off as a gas and the balance of water is held within the cells where it may be used in the photosynthesis process the next day.

TIME FOR WATERING

As stated in the beginning of this chapter, it is my opinion and that of many other horticulturists that water is the number-one killer of plants. Every time I talk about watering practices during a gardening lecture, I begin by asking the audience a few simple questions: When is the best time of the day to water your plants? How often do you water your plants? How do you know if a plant needs a drink? How much water do you give your plants at any one time? The answers are many and varied.

When asked for the best time of day to water a plant, the audience responds with answers from "early morning" to "late at night." Occasionally, someone answers with "midday," another person will disagree using the qualifying statement, "No, if the sun is out, you'll burn the foliage."

Very seldom do I get the right answer, which is: You water a plant *when it needs it.* With regard to the efficiency of watering, one time of day may be better than another, but we will discuss that later. The time of day to water a plant is irrelevant if a plant is losing its turgidity or showing any other stress due to lack of water. If a plant needs water, water it! For example, if you notice a bed of coleus plants in the garden that are beginning to wilt in the afternoon, you had better water them that afternoon. It doesn't matter that someone told you morning watering is best or that you think another time is better. If you don't water when you see wilting signs, you may end up with dead coleus.

There are a great many plants that will begin to exhibit signs of water stress long before they are even close to reaching a terminal condition. You will have a much longer grace period before you must supply more water. My *Ficus elastica*, large-leaf rubber plant, is growing in a bright corner of the living room and it will display a need for water by losing turgidity in the petioles. They will begin to arch downward, causing the leaves to droop. In fact, this is the principal indicator I use in determining when this particular plant needs to be watered. Usually within an hour or so after watering, the petioles are rigid once again, and the leaves erect. After seeing the drooping leaves, I have waited to water this ficus for as long as three or four days without damaging the plant.

When I ask an audience how often they water their plants, I get answers that range from daily to weekly and everything in between. "Every Friday afternoon at two o'clock," was one answer. These answers many be right, or wrong. Frequency of watering depends upon many factors which all must be taken into consideration.

What species of plant is it? And where is it growing? Is it an annual, such as a marigold, growing in the flower garden? Is it a shrub, such as an azalea, growing in the foundation planting? Is it a ground cover, such as a bluegrass lawn? What about an ivy geranium growing in a window box on the terrace; a peace lily in a planter in the office; a spiny cactus in a sunny window at home; or an African violet growing under lights on a table?

If you know which plant you are growing, you will have some clues about how often to water it. At the very least, you will have enough information to seek the answers from others who are more informed. Accept the information as a guide, not as gospel, because growing conditions do vary. I knew of an ardent cactus connoisseur who lived on the East coast but subscribed to a newspaper local to a community in the desert region of the West. When the news reported rain in the desert, he would water his collection. I don't recommend this method, but the man received enjoyment from it and his plants were surviving.

Where is the plant growing, inside or outside? If the plant is indoors, is it located in the direct sun or is it in filtered light? As we have discussed, light conditions have a direct bearing on the rate of transpiration. The more sun, the more moisture required to keep the plant cooled.

If indoors, is the plant in an air-conditioned environment or one heated by dry air? Air-conditioning and dry heat increase the rate of transpiration from the leaves as well as evaporation of moisture from the soil. Under these conditions, it may be necessary to water more frequently. Another point to consider indoors is the growing position of the plant. If it is growing among other plants or in a grouping, you may find that a particular plant requires less water; its rate of transpiration is being affected by the moisture given off by adjacent plants. The air around and within a plant grouping will probably be higher in relative humidity than that found around a single plant.

If the plant in question is outside, is it in the sun, shade, or partial sun and shade? As with the indoor plant, if the plant is in full sun, the rate of transpiration will be greater than the plant grown in shade. In general, then, the plant grown in sun will need more water. Is the plant in an area where the wind exposure is extreme, such as a balcony on the twenty-second floor of an apartment building in New York City, or at the windy corner of a house? Air currents will pull moisture from the foliage, increasing both transpiration and evaporation and creating a greater need for moisture.

The type of soil a plant is growing in is as variable and different as the many types of potting mixes available for container culture. A quick trip to the garden center will convince you that available soil mixes are numerous. Outdoors in the garden are hundreds of soil types, depending on your locale.

You must know the basic characteristics of the soils you are dealing with. Soils high in organic matter tend to hold moisture. Sandy soils retain little moisture while clay soils absorb a lot. Use the tests we discussed in Chapter II to determine the composition of your soil. Rub a handful of soil between your hands. If it feels gritty, it probably contains sand or even perlite; if the soil feels very silky and smooth, it probably contains clay particles. And, if the soil leaves a black substance on your hands after rubbing them together, humic acid or decomposing organic matter are probably present.

Another test of the soil's ability to hold moisture is to determine its field capacity, which is the amount of water remaining in the soil after a twenty-four-hour period. Pour a given volume of water through a given volume of soil and see how much drains out. By pouring water through the soil sample and knowing the amount remaining in the sample after twenty-four hours, you then know the field capacity for moisture of the soil in question.

If it is a potted plant, either indoor or outdoor, we must know the type of container. Is it plastic, clay, wood, fiber, ceramic, metal, or fiberglass? Plants grown in clay, fiber, or wooden containers dry differently from those grown in plastic, fiberglass, ceramic, or metal. I find plants dry out the fastest when grown in clay, peat or paper fiber, or wooden containers because these pots "breathe." In other words, moisture evaporates from the sides of the container. On the other hand, ceramic, plastic, metal, and fiberglass containers do not allow moisture to escape through the sides and this, in turn, allows an increased amount of moisture to be served to the root system of the plant. Either of these characteristics can be an advantage or a disadvantage, depending upon the gardener.

Another consideration is, does the container have a hole in the bottom? A pot without a drainage hole is trouble, because it is almost impossible to gauge the quantity of water in the bottom layer of soil. If you wish to use a container without drainage holes—and many people do because they are very decorative—I highly recommend the double potting technique. Place the growing container which has drainage holes into the pot without the drainage hole. This arrangement allows a better chance of success.

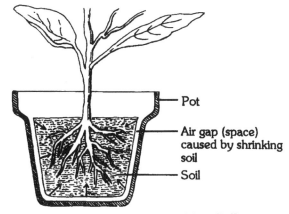

Cross Section: Shrinking Soil

Soil in containers will shrink as it dries, whether it be a soilless, artificial mix or one

that you have blended yourself of milled peat moss, garden soil, and sand or perlite. This phenomenon is quite evident if you compare the drying process of soil in a clay pot to that of soil in a plastic pot. As organic matter dries, it shrinks to the center of the mass, or the center of the force holding the mass, such as the root system. See for yourself by filling both a clay pot and a plastic pot to the proper planting level; water the soil thoroughly and then allow it to dry. The soil in the clay container will dry most evenly and without pulling away from the sides of the pot, because air passes through the sides of the pot and the soil mass simultaneously. In the plastic pot, however, you will note that the soil pulls away from the sides as it dries; it dries to the center of its mass. This is similar in concept to baking a cake or a loaf of bread; as the mix bakes and dries, it pulls away from the sides of the pan. You might have a problem watering a plant grown in a plastic container. If the soil has shrunk, the water will run off between the sides of the soil and the inside of the pot. You might be misled into believing the soil has plenty of water. To the contrary, the soil mass inside the pot is probably getting drier and drier, a condition that can only be remedied by a good soaking. The solution to this problem is discussed under "Watering Techniques."

How do you know if a plant needs water? Whether it is indoors or outdoors, here again it sure pays to know the name or type of plant, because most plants exhibit certain changes in growth characteristics that tell you when they need a drink. My pothos and heart-leaf philodendrons, growing as hanging baskets in a filtered, bright-light window, first show a slight change in their vivid green foliage color when they begin to exhibit water stress; the leaves take on a dull gray-green look. After this, there is a slight cupping of the leaves. When I see either of these symptoms, I know these plants are in need of a thorough watering. As discussed earlier, the drooping leaves of my *Ficus elastica* signal that it's in need of water.

In addition to the color change of foliage, I use the feel of the soil as an indicator; I probe the soil to a depth of an inch or so to feel for dampness. The surface of the soil may feel dry due to evaporation, but an inch or so into the soil mix there may be plenty of moisture. If you have smaller container plants, just pick them up; feel the weight. If you pick up a plant that you know has been watered thoroughly, your muscles will help you remember; the next time you can compare by feel. Your arm will assist your brain in deciding when the soil is drying. Certainly, the arm test is excellent for hanging baskets.

Another way to judge moisture is to squeeze a mass of soil in the palm of your hand. If the soil crumbles easily when you open your hand, it is presumably dry; but if the soil particles stick together in a ball, the soil is probably moist enough.

To test for soil moisture in my outdoor gardens, I slip the blade of a hand trowel into the soil about six inches deep. When I pull it out, if moisture and soil appear near the tip of the trowel, there is adequate moisture for the roots of my garden plants. However, if the trowel is dry, I consider the need for water. There are also electronic water meters for determining the moisture content of soil. Some meters even talk to you saying, "I'm dry" or "I'm wet"; some ring a bell. These are good teaching tools, and I prefer to use them only in that way.

How much water is enough at any one time? In general, I prefer to give my indoor plants a thorough soaking and then allow them to dry a bit. There are exceptions, though. My African violet, begonia, coleus, fittonia, prayer plant, and fern are a few of the plants to keep slightly moist at all times. I never let them dry as much as my *Ficus benjamina* or *elastica*, yucca, or virtually all species and varieties of corn plants; all of those are allowed to dry considerably between waterings. My cactus collection receives even less water. We return again to the need to know specific water requirements for a given species or plant group.

For plants growing on the deck or patio, don't forget to consider exposure to wind, sun, and rain when determining how much water to give them. Assuming you keep good garden records, particularly when it comes to rainfall, you should have a pretty good idea when your plants need to be watered.

It is recommended that bluegrass turf, for example, receive an average of one inch of water per week during the active growing season, again depending on other weather conditions (such as sunshine or clouds, wind or calm, and soil and drainage conditions). When I water my lawn, which is a mixture of Kentucky bluegrass, rye grass, and creeping fescue, I water long and deep, not short and shallow. A good, thorough watering of the lawn encourages your plants to develop a deeper root system which, in turn, will enable the turf to put up with drier conditions during the hot part of summer. Applying water for short periods of time moistens only the soil near the surface and causes the development of shallow root systems. Shallow roots can spell disaster for a lawn that is put under stress during hot, dry weather, because the roots are not deep enough to search out needed moisture. Such a lawn turns brown much more quickly than one with a well-established root system. One sign that grass is losing its turgidity due to lack of moisture is to walk across your lawn and see your footprints remain. Grass that is showing water stress will also tend to have a grayish-green look, not the lush green of well-watered turf.

Newly planted trees and shrubs, whether they were balled and burlapped, container grown, or bare root, will need more frequent watering than those already well established. The root system of a well-established plant reaches wide and deep for its water sources. In fact, you may find that well-established plants don't need extra watering at all, or only during extremely prolonged dry periods. Seedlings, such as tomatoes, eggplants, peppers, petunias, marigolds, and zinnias must be watered immediately after planting. I call this "watering-in." Even though your local weather forecast may be predicting torrential downpours, the "cats and dogs" rain may fall only on the other side of town without one drop falling on your garden. A new seedling needs water to settle the soil around the roots and to keep it moist while regenerating hair roots that have been damaged. Allowing seedlings to go into water stress can cause transplant shock that could result in immediate death or, at least, retarded and delayed growth. A thorough watering-in will also help anchor the plant into its new location. The need for water is most critical when transplanting if you wish to establish a healthy plant. Subsequent waterings are determined by weather and soil conditions.

Time of year is another factor in determining how much water a plant will need. During the dormant season, deciduous plants require very little moisture to sustain life, but a constant supply must be available during active growth. Evergreens transpire year-round and must have access to moisture at all times. During winter months, when the soil is frozen, they will suffer winter burn or desiccation of the leaves if they are deprived of an adequate supply of moisture. To avoid this problem, the northern gardener can apply an antidesiccant spray material to seal off the stomata. The antidesiccant spray is cheap insurance if your plants have experienced winter burn in the past.

WATER SOURCES

There is no better source of water for your plants than that of a gentle rainfall, that is, if it is not an acid rain. I will not address what makes acid rain, but if you know the source of your weather patterns, you will have a general idea of its quality. If your municipality uses water from lakes or deep wells, call your local water company and inquire about the quality. What is its calcium content? What is the pH? Does it contain iron? By knowing the answers to some of these questions, you can adjust your feeding practices to compensate for surplus or missing elements. Hard water and alkaline soils make it very difficult to grow acid-loving plants, such as gardenias, rhododendrons, azaleas, and camellias. An alkaline condition will reduce the ability of the plant to absorb trace elements for growth. The use of acid fertilizers and rich humus will help alter alkaline conditions caused by hard water. An application of iron chelate, available at most garden centers, will help alleviate iron chlorosis. However, in alkaline conditions, the iron must be supplied on a regular basis.

The old-fashioned rain barrel has once again become the "in" thing in many water-starved communities. The only caution in their use is not to let them become a mosquito breeder. Keep a tight lid on the barrel and do use the water. Don't just let it stand.

Water treated with a softener contains sodium that may accumulate in the soil and harm your plants. Thus, softened water is not recommended. In my home, I have installed a tap on the incoming side of my water supply that bypasses the softened water. If this is not possible in your home, draw water from your system just before the softener cycle begins, when the sodium content is at its lowest. You can check the time clock on the softener to determine the frequency of cycles. My softener runs every three days.

SELECTING PLANTS

Conservationists are now encouraging you to plant species that are native to your area. Select plants that are indigenous to your region; they tolerate the available water supply once they become established. Follow this general rule: In the desert region, don't try to grow plants that require constant moisture, and in the tropics, stay away from plants that appreciate dry conditions.

EQUIPMENT AND METHODS OF WATERING

Water conservationists, which we all are today, know to water a plant only when it needs it. In many gardens this may be only a couple of times a year. We know to water-in our newly planted trees, shrubs, perennials, annuals, and seeds and to water when a plant begins to wilt.

Sprinklers

An overhead sprinkler is probably the easiest system to use, but in many cases, it is the most inefficient. If you set up a sprinkler in the vegetable patch or flower garden, it not only waters the plants, but also irrigates the walkways. And, what grows in the walkways? Weeds! Who wants to grow weeds? However, for the lawn, the sprinkler is the most efficient, because you can water large areas with the least amount of effort.

A secret to overhead irrigation is in knowing the delivery capacity of the sprinkler. The nozzle size of the sprinkler may be a half inch per hour or even less. To test the sprinkler, place a rain gauge within the water pattern and take a reading after each hour. I think you will be surprised to find that it may require as many as three hours to deliver one inch of water from most sprinklers. If you don't have a rain gauge, place a measuring cup or straight-sided can in the water pattern and measure the contents with a ruler each hour.

Oscillator sprinkler

Rotary arm sprinkler

Overhead Sprinklers

Drip or Emitter

The most efficient water-delivery method to use in the flower garden, vegetable patch, and for landscape planting is the drip or emitter system of plastic tubing. Water is released at the base of each plant, not in the walkways. The drip or emitter system can be controlled to allow only a precise amount of water to be delivered to a given plant at a given time. The slow speed at which the water droplets are released ensures a more thorough soaking of the soil without potential erosion, runoff, or leaching of nutrients. The drip system eliminates compaction, which is often a problem with clay soils when overhead sprinklers are used. To measure the amount of water released from a given emitter, catch the drops in a measuring cup over a ten- or fifteen-minute period. You can then calculate the gallons per hour. I believe you will be amazed at how gradually and gently your plants are being watered.

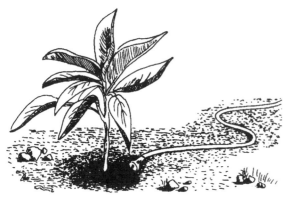

Drip System

I install a drip system in my vegetable patch each spring, after preparing the soil and before starting to plant. By using my prepared garden plan, I know where every

transplant will be located, and I can install the precise size emitter at a designated site. It is best to lay out the plastic tubing before planting because of potential damage to your many transplants if done afterward. I speak from experience. There are many manufacturers of quality drip and emitter watering systems for installation in the landscape and garden, and many of these systems are available in kit form through your local garden supply dealer.

If you presently have a sprinkler system for watering your landscape trees and shrubs, you should consider converting to a drip or emitter system. Conversion kits are available. These emitter drip systems use about 30 percent of the amount of water used in an overhead sprinkler system, and, of that, 90 to 95 percent goes directly where you want it—to the plant's roots.

Soaker Hose or Ooze Tube

Another system that delivers water to a limited area is the soaker hose or ooze tube. It looks like a porous garden hose. Both the tube and hose allow water to leak out along the complete run of the hose. I use the soaker hose when growing borders of annuals, when I do not want to water adjacent plants. In the vegetable patch, after planting bush beans, I stretch out one run of soaker hose along each row. I give the newly planted seeds a thorough watering with the soaker hose to start germination and after this soaking, depending on the weather, I may not need to water again until the beans begin to flower and form pods. Once the bean pods start to develop, I turn the soaker on, as needed, to keep the soil slightly moist at all times. By supplying adequate moisture to the beans as they begin to expand in the pod, I can easily grow beans to twice their normal size. I have also noticed a definite difference in the tenderness between those beans that were watered and those that were not. Another advantage to the soaker-type watering system for my beans is that the foliage remains dry. Wet foliage can and will encourage diseases that could greatly reduce the harvest.

Soaker Hose

Subirrigation

If you bury an ooze tube in the ground, you have subirrigation. This is a new watering procedure being developed for turf. Leaky tubes or pipes are installed underground to supply the roots with water. This works well where the soil type is consistent. If you use a subirrigation system, care must be taken not to cut the pipes during planting. After years of using the ooze tube on top of the soil near my bush beans, I buried a soaker hose ten inches deep and planted bush beans in the soil above it. After planting, I turned the water on for one hour to thoroughly soak the soil and to start the germination process. Once my bean seedling emerged, I watered for no more than five minutes per week, right up to harvest. Releasing the water deep in the soil encouraged deeper rooting of the plants and resulted in less evaporation of water from the surface of the soil. The only problem I had with this system was in the fall when I tried to dig up the hose; I accidentally cut it with the garden spade.

Self-water Pots

When we speak of self-watering pots, don't be misled into thinking that the pot does all the work; you must occasionally fill the water reservoir inside the container. Self-watering pots are a great convenience, because they reduce the frequency of watering. If you grow plants that enjoy having a constant moisture supply, such as coleus, African violets, or ferns, or if you are away from home a lot, self-watering containers are for you. I have said many times never to trust a friend to water your plants. But if you have self-watering systems, you might trust them to fill the reservoirs.

Many commercial establishments with plant displays use self-watering pots to reduce the maintenance schedule. Plant rental companies use the self-watering systems because they can water, feed, and clean the plants in one trip and be assured that the plants will be sustained until the next visit.

There are two basic types of self-watering pots to consider: the wick-watering unit and the reservoir unit. There are many versions of the wick-watering pots. Water is "pulled" by capillary action from the water reservoir, which is usually below the plant, into the pot of soil above. The system was named "wick-watering," because a wick connects the soil to the reservoir of water. A very simple wick system can be made when you pot the plant. Insert a cotton or fiberglass thread through the hole in the bottom of the pot, making sure the thread inside the pot is spread out into and making good contact with the soil. This thread must be long enough to allow the other end to be suspended into the water supply below. To ensure a continual supply of moisture, you must prevent the wick from

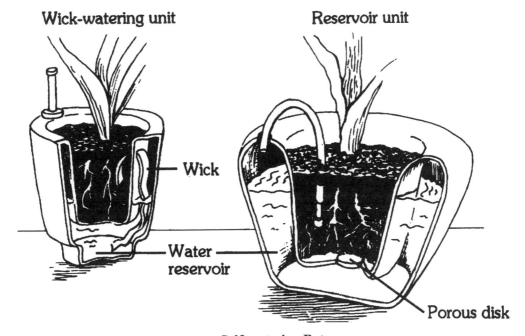

Wick-watering unit   Reservoir unit

Wick

Water reservoir

Porous disk

Self-watering Pots

Wick Watering: Clay Brick

Hand Watering

I refer to hand watering as the "teacup" method. It is the mechanical delivery of water to a plant by a cup, watering can, or even the garden hose. There is nothing wrong with hand watering. You just need to know how much water is enough, and you will learn that from experience. Many people have told me they give their rubber plant a large glass of water each week, and the plant looks great. They don't even know the volume of the glass, let alone the size of the container or the type of soil. I guess if their system works for a particular plant, that's fine, but my best advice for learning how much to hand water a plant is to know the plant, know its water requirements, and know the growing conditions.

In the garden, hand watering can be even more difficult and frustrating to figure out. How much water does it take to reach ten inches down into the soil? If you pour water on the surface of the soil, most of it will run off, particularly if there is not a water well around the plant. If you know you will be hand watering, use soil to create a dish around the base of each plant. This dish-type construction will create a reservoir to hold the water. Test the penetration of moisture by inserting a stick, as deeply a possible, after water has soaked into the soil. If you fail to water enough to reach the roots of the plant, the root system will tend to grow near the surface and your plant will need watering more often, particularly during hot, sunny weather.

drying out; it cannot be exposed to outside air. Set the growing container directly on top of the reservoir, but not in the water supply itself. With clay pots, set a block of floral oasis or an unglazed clay building brick in a tray of water and place the clay pot on top. The brick will act as "the wick" between the clay pot and the reservoir of water.

The reservoir self-watering unit has an airtight water chamber built into the walls and bottom of the pot. Water flows into the soil through a tiny hole in the bottom, as long as there is no vacuum in the airtight reservoir. When the soil dries, the vacuum is broken, and water again flows into the soil. The only way to tell when the unit needs more water added is to pick up the pot and check its weight or shake the water inside the reservoir. Since this is impossible to do with large pots, you will need to open the reservoir fill cap and insert a stick to measure the water. However, this will break the vacuum and allow water to flow.

Thread: Wick-Watering System

Watering Methods

OVERWATERING

A heavy watering hand can be detrimental to plants and to soil. Too much water can compact the soil and drive out air held between the soil particles. This results in an anaerobic condition, moisture without oxygen, which leads to root rot. The hair roots, which take in water to the plant, are destroyed. When the hair roots cannot develop, the plant begins to wilt. Most of the time a wilting plant is one that is signaling that it needs more water, but not in this case. To add water under these circumstances would only add to the already overwatered condition.

Overwatering also leaches nutrients from the soil, which can be either beneficial or detrimental. If there is too high a concentration of mineral salts, flushing great quantities of water through the soil will help remove the excess. This practice is often used in greenhouse bench-growing, where adjustments must be made in mineral salt concentrations when one crop is removed and another is planted. The high concentration of minerals that remain in the soil after a crop has matured would very likely destroy new seedlings or rooted cuttings.

A detrimental result of overwatering is the removal of beneficial nutrients. Even though you may have been feeding your plants, your fertilizer could be disappearing through the hole in the bottom of the pot. Overwatering can also change the soil pH range. If you suspect you have been overwatering, do a pH test to determine if there has been any change.

SHADING PLANTS

Providing shade for plants is one method of protecting them from sunburn or other adverse weather conditions. Shading reduces transpiration by cooling the plant tissue. For my newly planted tomato transplants, especially if I have had to plant on a sunny day, I erect a cardboard shield over them to block out the hot afternoon sun, and I leave the shield in place for three to four days. This little protection reduces transpiration, allowing the water already in the plant to be available for photosynthesis and the establishment of a new root system.

As winter protection, shading reduces water loss due to transpiration. An evergreen exposed to hot sun during the winter months can dehydrate unless moisture can be available to the plant. If you know the soil is frozen and your plant is in the direct sun, consider shading it, particularly during the sunniest part of the day.

SHADING TO CAUSE CHANGE

Although it does not have anything to do with the direct use of water in the plant, shading can cause change within the internal clock of certain plants, inducing them to start their flowering cycle. A classic example is the commercially grown

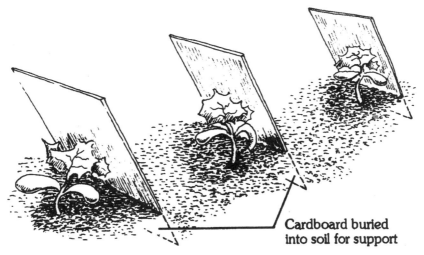

Cardboard buried into soil for support

Shading Transplants

poinsettia plant. The poinsettia, originally from Mexico, blooms during late winter after it has been exposed to long nights, fourteen hours of darkness for approximately forty nights. In order to make the poinsettia bloom in time for the Christmas holiday, a grower must provide artificially long nights. For older varieties of the poinsettia, place the plant in total darkness starting on October 1 at six o'clock in the evening and return it to full light after eight o'clock the next morning. This procedure must be followed for at least forty consecutive nights. Each day the plant must be returned to light. If for any reason you fail to put the poinsettia in total darkness for fourteen hours each night, add at least three more nights to the original forty nights for each forgotten night. A large coat closet is a great place to put the plant at night. Check the door to be sure that it closes tightly and that no light can creep in. You might even put a sign on the door to prevent accidental entry: DON'T OPEN THIS DOOR.

Several newer varieties of poinsettias have been bred to produce colorful bracts and flowers within fall's natural length of day. This has made poinsettia culture much easier. The grower of the newer varieties, those that will set the flowering cycle with shorter nights, is able to have a poinsettia crop in bloom for the holidays without spending the time and materials to provide artificial nights. Prior to these new varieties, commercial growers used a black shade cloth pulled over each bench of poinsettias in order to provide darkness.

Chrysanthemums also require controlled periods of darkness and light in order to initiate the flowering cycle at a specific time.

The number of consecutive hours of total darkness varies with the variety. Some varieties require seven hours of uninterrupted darkness, and other varieties require much more. A greenhouse grower of pot mums can make a crop bloom at a specific time by adjusting the length of time that the plants are exposed to total darkness. The grower will install a lighting system above the potting bench that automatically turns on at a given time during the night to interrupt the consecutive hours of natural darkness. This interruption reduces the consecutive hours of darkness below the number that would usually initiate flower-bud induction for that variety. Control of the night keeps the mums in a vegetative state.

To start the flowering cycle, the grower discontinues the programmed period of artificial light interruption. By knowing the exact number of hours of continual darkness needed by a particular variety for flower-bud induction, a chrysanthemum can be made to bloom at any time. This is why we have flowering pot mums available year-round.

If you wish to grow hardy chrysanthemums in your garden, plant them where they will not be exposed to night light. They will then come into bloom during their natural cycle. I have seen many chrysanthemum displays planted around yard lights and next to porch lights. They were the best-looking foliage plants, but never blossomed. In those cases, the lights were turned on after dark; the mums lived in a vegetative state and the flowering cycle could not begin. In my garden, some hardy chrysanthemums begin blooming in July, and others bloom as late as November.

QUESTIONS AND ANSWERS

1. **Q. When is the best time to water a plant?**
   A. There is only one answer to this question: When it needs it. There are times of day preferred for watering, but if a plant needs water, water it. Don't wait until "the right time of day" to do it; the plant may be dead by that time.

2. **Q. If I have a choice, is it better to water during evening or morning hours?**
   A. For the most efficient use of water, early morning is preferred. There is less evaporation, allowing the moisture to soak into the soil.

3. **Q. Our source of irrigation is a well that produces very hard water. I am planning to plant Christmas tree seedlings. Will this water harm my plants?**
A. Water that is alkaline would be harmful to broad-leafed evergreens, such as holly and rhododendron, and would be unhealthy for narrow-leafed evergreens like spruce, pine, or fir. The damage to the plant occurs when the alkali gets into the soil.

4. **Q. We are in the middle of a drought and I am concerned about the trees and shrubs on my property. Should they be watered?**
A. If local or city ordinances do not prohibit watering during a drought, you will know to water a particular plant when it shows sign of wilt; leaves droop and are limp. If you water at the first sign of wilt, your plants should recover quickly. It is normal for the sycamore tree to drop a portion of its leaves when there is an inadequate supply of moisture.

5. **Q. My rhododendrons wilt when we have several days with very high temperatures and no rain. How much water should I give them?**
A. Wet the soil thoroughly—the equivalent of two inches of rainfall. Do this every two or three weeks.

6. **Q. When I use a sprinkler to water landscape trees and shrubs during dry weather, it seems to do very little good. Any suggestions?**
A. Water wets the soil from the top down and a daily, light, surface-sprinkling is of no use to shrubs or trees. Most trees and shrubs have deep roots, so—water "long and deep" when you water.

7. **Q. Do self-watering pots really work?**
A. Yes, they are a great convenience if you remember to add water to the reservoir. Whether it be the airtight reservoir or the wick system, it is always advisable to try out the system before you go away or depend on it for the first time.

8. **Q. What type of self-watering pot can I use on the patio?**
A. The only criterion I look for in a self-watering pot for outdoor use is its ability to provide overflow of water. Without an overflow, if a heavy rain should occur, your plants would be overwatered.

9. **Q. Can I grow African violets in self-watering pots?**
A. Yes. Many growers of African violets use the wick system for maintaining even moisture in the potting mix. The wick must be installed at the time the plant is potted to ensure that moisture will be evenly distributed to the root system. There are several commercially available wick watering kits.

10. **Q. How can I provide moisture for my house plants when I am away from home? They are potted in clay containers.**
A. Place a block of floral oasis in a deep baking dish or similar container and add water to just below the top edge of the block. Oasis is a dried foam material that absorbs many times its weight in water, and is used as a water supply for cut flower arrangements. Place a clay pot on top of the oasis and apply enough pressure to make a slight indentation in the oasis. This ensures good contact between the pot and floral oasis. Water absorbed by the oasis is transferred to the clay pot and into the soil.

11. **Q. Would wrapping a piece of plastic around a clay pot reduce watering?**
A. Yes. Plastic sheeting would retard evaporation of moisture from both the sides of the pot and from the top of the soil. Fold the plastic so it covers the soil surface up to the stem of the plant.

12. **Q. Do plants that are growing in clay pots require more water than those growing in**

plastic pots, if they are grown under the same conditions?

A. If clay pots are made of a porus, unglazed clay, yes. The clay absorbs moisture from the soil and allows air to pass through the pot wall.

13. Q. **What is a root-watering needle? Is it the same as a root feeder?**

A. Yes. A root-watering needle and a root feeder are one and the same. A root-watering needle is a mechanical device used for injecting water deep into the soil. The "needle" is a hollow metal tube with holes near the tip end. Water supplied by the garden hose is released through the holes after the needle is inserted into the soil. When it is used as a root feeder, water and nutrients are both injected into the soil.

14. Q. **Does a root-watering needle really work?**

A. Yes, it's one of the most efficient ways to water to small trees and shrubs—injecting water to the direct area of the roots. However, the watering needle must be moved frequently, because it only waters the immediate area of each site. Make several probes around the base of the plant.

15. Q. **Is it necessary to create a bowl-shaped impression in the soil at the base of a newly planted tree or shrub?**

A. The bowl is created to facilitate watering. The dished-out area catches water and reduces run-off.

16. Q. **I heard the term *ooze* tube the other day. Is it anything like a soaker hose?**

A. As the term would indicate, water oozes from the "ooze tube." It waters the area immediately adjacent to the tube, whereas the soaker hose produces a fine mist of water that may cover a foot or more of ground on either side of the hose. They are both great tools for use in limited areas such as border plantings or hedgerows. The "ooze tube" is particularly great for watering rows of plants in the vegetable garden.

17. Q. **How long should a soaker hose be allowed to run?**

A. A soaker hose delivers water slowly so it can seep into the soil. The length of time depends on the soil condition and crop being irrigated. As with all watering, provide a thorough soaking.

18. Q. **To create an atmosphere more conducive to shopping, our mall has placed container-grown trees along the sidewalks. Other than keeping them well watered, is there any other particular care that we should be concerned about?**

A. Feed them on a regular basis with an appropriate formula for the tree and the soil. Mulching the soil at the top of the container will certainly help to conserve moisture. If you live in an area of the country that knows hard freezing, you will want to place these containerized plants in a cool building over winter. Water them well before the soil freezes.

19. Q. **Is it better to water a Kentucky bluegrass lawn with a sprinkler, or, since my lawn is not large, can I water it with a hose?**

A. Use a sprinkler if you want it done right. It is recommended to provide the equivalent of an inch of rain per week. This encourages turf to produce a deep root system, one which will better withstand the hot, dry periods of summer. Watering with a hose would have to be done day after day and would only wet the top of the soil, encouraging a shallow-rooted turf. If you water "long and deep," you will have to water less often, and your lawn will be less susceptible to the occasional days of summer drought.

20. Q. **Why is thorough watering recommended, as opposed to running the sprinkler on a daily basis?**

A. A thorough watering will wet the soil to a depth of a foot or more. The roots grow *down* to the moisture and the cooler soil. A short run of the sprinkler each day only encourages roots to stay near the surface. The plant with deeper roots will also be more stable, less likely to fall over.

21. **Q. My neighbor waters his flower garden with a sprinkler after he gets home from work in the evening. Will it harm the plants?**

A. Foliage that does not have time to dry before darkness is more susceptible to fungi, such as black spot and mildew disease on roses, rust on zinnias, and mildew on phlox and lilacs.

22. **Q. I have a small greenhouse that is used for growing transplants of annuals such as petunias, impatiens, tomatoes, peppers, and eggplants. Often I am not able to water until late afternoon or early evening. Will this harm the plants?**

A. In a greenhouse, it would be advisable to water in earlier in the day so foliage can dry before nightfall. If this is impossible, care should be taken not to wet the foliage. Moisture remaining on leaves during darkness encourages diseases such as mildew, botrytis, and damping-off.

23. **Q. What is the best approach to follow when you water established trees and shrubs?**

A. You must soak the soil thoroughly, to a depth of two feet. If you find it necessary to loosen the soil in order for the water to penetrate, do so. Or, use a root feeder—a pointed rod designed to inject water below the soil's surface.

24. **Q. Is it necessary to water an herb garden?**

A. Transplants or new plants from seed need water to become established. Mint, and a few other herbs, require a generous source of water. Most herbs, however, do best when they are left to rather dry conditions; they have better taste and enhanced scent.

25. **Q. How can I control humidity in my greenhouse?**

A. A wet-bulb thermometer will indicate the relative humidity. To control this element, one must balance three important factors: heat, ventilation, and moisture.

26. **Q. Will it hurt plants if I water when the sun is shining on their leaves?**

A. Generally, no. It would be better to water in the early morning or the late evening, so water has a chance to soak into soil before it evaporates.

27. **Q. My episcia has stopped growing and the leaves are turning brown at the tips. It gets sun early in the morning; I water it whenever the soil is dry; and I mist it on a regular basis. Can you tell me what's wrong?**

A. Lack of humidity. This plant will never produce lush growth in a dry environment. You might consider growing it in a terrarium where you will have better control over the humidity levels. You might also consider purchasing a small humidifier to place in the growing area.

28. **Q. The leaves on my jade plant are falling off, after they turn limp and dry at the tips. What causes this?**

A. When the leaves are limp, it means the plant does not have enough water. The soil is either too dry or you have watered so heavily that the roots have rotted. The jade plant requires well-drained porous soil. Good watering practice dictates enough to thoroughly moisten all of the soil, and then let the plant dry out between waterings.

29. **Q. Our home has a water softener. Will this water help, or harm, my plants?**

A. Ion-exchange water softeners can cause sodium to build up in the soil, which will be injurious to your potted plants. It would be better to install a line where water can be taken from the pipe before it enters the softener. Collected rainwater would be an alternative if you don't want to call a plumber.

30. **Q. My old house was heated with a baseboard, hot-water system. Our new house has forced hot-air heat and now my plants do not do well when the heating season comes along. Is there anything I can do?**
   A. As you suspect, the air in your home is too dry. Check your heating system; make sure the humidifying device is working properly. You might consider purchasing a room humidifier, or placing pans or trays of water on the hot-air registers. It will help your plants and your family.

31. **Q. My prayer plants show brown tips on the leaves as soon as the heating season begins. How can this be avoided?**
   A. Humidity trays may work for individual plants. Place each pot in a tray filled with pebbles; add water to the tray until it is just below the bottom of the pot. The water will evaporate from the pebbles to effect a higher rate of humidity in the immediate area of the particular plant. If you bunch plants together, each plant will benefit from a more moist and humid environment created by the group.

32. **Q. What are some house plants that will do well if they must be maintained on the dry side?**
   A. Most succulents, including most cacti, will do well with very little watering; aloe, sansevieria, beaucarnea, crassula, or echeveria, to name a few.

33. **Q. We live in a mountainous region. What would be a good ground cover for a steep slope? A type that will do well with whatever water Mother Nature provides?**
   A. *Sedum stoloniferum*, a hardy member of the subgenus *Sedum*.

34. **Q. Should I water roses during dry weather?**
   A. Yes. Roses like lots of water; they grow better and produce more flowers if thoroughly watered at least once a week.

35. **Q. Will using a water-retaining polymer with my potting mix reduce the number of times needed for watering a hanging basket of impatiens?**
   A. Water-retaining polymers, mixed in with a potting soil at planting time, absorb as much as one hundred thirty times their weight in water. The polymer granules become reservoirs of water that can release as much as 95 percent of the water retained. From personal experience, I have been able to reduce the frequency of watering ten-inch hanging baskets of impatiens from every other day to once every ten to fourteen days.

36. **Q. Can a water-retaining polymer be used in the soil when I plant my vegetable garden?**
   A. Yes, but it must be mixed into the soil to at least the normal depth of the root system for each particular crop. Polymers applied to the soil surface will do absolutely no good.

37. **Q. I have a windy spot on my terrace where plants grown in containers dry rather quickly. What can I do to increase the moisture-holding capacity of the soil?**
   A. Vermiculite or a water-retaining polymer can be mixed into the soil to increase the moisture-holding capacity. If the container is made of a porous clay, wrap the outside of the container with plastic to reduce evaporation of water through the pot walls.

38. **Q. Does vermiculite increase moisture retention in the soil?**
   A. Vermiculite holds hundreds of times its weight in water. It is the gold-colored component in soilless potting mixes, seed-starting mixes, and standard potting soils.

39. **Q. What happens to a plant that gets "wet feet?"**
   A. "Wet feet" is a condition of too much water around the roots of a plant. When water

stands for more than twenty-four hours, it loses its free oxygen. The lack of free oxygen inhibits root-hair development and promotes root rot.

40. Q. **Should I let water come to room temperature before using it to water plants?**
    A. No. It is not necessary to go to the trouble to draw water and let it stand overnight. Just don't use cold or hot water.

41. Q. **We have chlorine in our city water supply. Will it hurt my plants?**
    A. The chlorine in your drinking water is in such dilute quantities that it is not a problem. In addition, chlorine is a gas. As soon as water containing chlorine is poured over soil, it dissipates into the air.

42. Q. **At the end of summer, we drain our swimming pool. Can we use water from the pool for our trees and shrubs?**
    A. It is recommended to run the circulator pump for a few days, without adding additional chlorine, before using swimming pool water. The chlorine in the water will be given off as a gas.

43. Q. **Why is it recommended to "water-in" a transplant?**
    A. "Watering-in" ensures moisture availability to the damaged roots of a transplant. It helps settle soil around the root system.

44. Q. **Why is it necessary to soak the roots of a bare-root transplant before planting?**
    A. Soaking roots of a bare-root plant restores lost moisture to epidermal cells. This moisturizing initiates growth and repair of hair roots, important to root growth and water uptake by the plant.

45. Q. **Should I use large or small pots for growing plants on the patio?**
    A. The size of pot definitely has a bearing on watering practices. The larger the pot the greater the volume of soil for holding moisture. The smaller the pot, the more frequent the watering, because there is less volume of soil.

46. Q. **Although an automatic sprinkler system provides water two or three times each week to my lawn, it still dries out. Should I water daily?**
    A. Check the length of time the system is running in one location and measure the amount of water delivered. Frequent light watering is encouraging the grass roots to develop near the surface, not deep into the soil where they should be. Either turn off the automatic part of the system and run it manually, or set the clock to run longer in any one position to provide deep watering.

47. Q. **My neighbor has a beautiful lawn that never browns out during the heat of summer. My lawn, even though I water regularly, turns brown at the first sign of hot weather and does not green up until fall. Should I apply more water?**
    A. The answer does not lay in watering. The species and even the variety of grass determine how a lawn puts up with summer heat. Your grass is going dormant to protect itself from adverse conditions.

48. Q. **When I apply water with a sprinkler in the vegetable garden, water tends to puddle after a short time. Does this mean the soil is wet enough?**
    A. Not necessarily. Turn off the sprinkler and let the moisture seep into the soil, then water again. If soil is compacted, moisture will open soil pores and allow penetration of additional water.

49. Q. **How often should a newly seeded lawn be watered during the germination process?**
    A. The frequency of watering depends on weather conditions. If it is sunny and windy,

the soil will need to be moistened more regularly than it would if it were cloudy and calm. The rule to follow is: Once your have moistened seed to start germination, never allow them to dry out. Continue watering until the seeds are established.

50. **Q. What procedure should I use for watering newly potted tropical plants?**
A. First, be sure the soil ball is thoroughly moistened before transplanting. Handling moist soil places less stress on the root system. After potting, water once again.

51. **Q. After I transplant a tropical hibiscus that I am growing as a house plant, it wilts. Am I not giving it enough water?**
A. The damage to hair roots during transplanting reduces the plant's ability to take up adequate moisture for transpiration. Reduce the rate of transpiration by increasing humidity by removing the plant from bright light, and/or by pinching off some of the foliage.

52. **Q. How can I tell when the soil in a pot is dry?**
A. Test the soil for moisture by feel, sight, or hearing. Tap the side of the pot and listen for a hollow "ring." If present, water the soil.

53. **Q. Is it really necessary to water a vegetable garden?**
A. Watering has a direct effect on the quality and quantity of produce, particularly during dry weather. Plants that have been watered regularly will have a root system nearer the surface of the soil when compared to those that are not watered. It is important to continue watering those plants that have been receiving supplemental water, to avoid damage to roots due to water stress. Vegetable plants that are not watered other than by rainfall are better fitted to withstand long, dry periods, because their roots penetrate the soil deeper in search of water.

54. **Q. Which vegetable plants need extra water during dry weather?**
A. Extra water given to plants that produce seeds in pods will enlarge the crop. These include lima beans, bush beans, and peas. Those most susceptible to drought injury are celery and leafy crops of lettuce and spinach.

55. **Q. We returned from a vacation, during the heat of summer, only to find wilted tomato plants. After a thorough watering, the plants perked up once again, but all of the ripening fruit split open. What caused the splitting?**
A. During the ripening process of tomatoes, the outer tissue of the fruit stops growing and hardens-off. The additional water was taken up by the plant and translocated through the xylem tissue into the inner cells of the fruit. The pressure from the expanding inner cells caused the splitting.

56. **Q. How can I water lettuce and spinach without getting the leaves wet? I don't have money to purchase a soaker hose.**
A. Dig a shallow irrigation trench alongside the row of plants and gradually fill it with water. If there is any slope to the soil, place the trench on the high side of the row.

57. **Q. We live in a ranch-style home with wide overhangs from the roof that shade the foundation plants. Several of the foundation plants have to be replaced each spring. Are the overhangs blocking out too much light?**
A. The death of the landscape plants is most likely due to lack of water reaching them, rather than lack of light. Planted under the protection of the overhang, plants receive little or no rain. They will need supplemental water year-round.

58. **Q. The flower buds on tuberous begonias drop off before they open. What is the cause?**
A. Bud drop is due to either underwatering or overwatering. Keep the soil slightly moist at all times. Tuberous begonias are very sensitive to erratic watering practices.

59. **Q.** **How can I water a flat of seeds without disturbing the seeds?**
A. Watering a seed flat with a fine overhead spray, using a watering can with a sprinkling device attached to the spout.

60. **Q.** **How long should I let a seed flat stand in a tray of water when bottom watering?**
A. The length of time needed to bottom water a seed flat depends on the consistency of the seed starting mix. Some mixes contain wetting agents that absorb water more quickly. Do not leave it in water any longer than it takes for moisture to show on the surface of the mix.

61. **Q.** **Every winter my *Ficus elastica*, rubber plant, drops its bottom leaves one by one. The leaf drop starts at the bottom of the stem and works its way up. It stops when I put the plant outside for summer. What causes the leaf drop?**
A. Leaf drop on ficus during the heating season is primarily caused by lack of humidity. Provide more moisture in the air by grouping other plants around the base of the ficus, or by running a humidifier in the growing area.

62. **Q.** **How do you water a cyclamen when it is in bloom? Mine always collapse soon after I purchase it.**
A. Cyclamen must be kept very moist and in a sunny location in order to continue the blooming cycle. Set the pot in a two-inch-deep saucer and add water each morning. If water remains in the saucer at night fall, pour it out. The cyclamen must not stand in water overnight. Repeat the watering practice daily, particularly on sunny days.

63. **Q.** **Can I grow an herb garden in an arid location?**
A. The majority of herbs do best in rather dry conditions. If additional water is needed, water the plants thoroughly. Mint, being an exception, requires continual moisture.

64. **Q.** **Can I use a water meter to tell when to water plants?**
A. Yes, but I would use a water meter only in conjunction with other telltale signs. If the meter indicates a need for water, check the soil by touch, lift the pot for weight, and examine the soil visually.

65. **Q.** **Why do flower buds drop from my Christmas cactus before they open?**
A. Bud drop on Christmas cactus is caused by overwatering, poor drainage, and warm night temperatures. During active growth, keep the soil slightly moist at all times. As soon as flower buds appear, reduce the water in both amount and frequency.

66. **Q.** **What are the advantages of using a drip watering system in a vegetable patch?**
A. The greatest advantage of a drip system is water conservation. Water delivery to a specific plant can be precisely controlled in both volume and duration. Slow release of water reduces or eliminates runoff. And, the emitter releases water only to the targeted plant and not to the weeds growing in walkways.

67. **Q.** **Would you spend money to install a drip or emitter watering system in a garden? I'm going to be gardening in an area where there is little rainfall.**
A. If you plan to continue gardening, the answer is yes, absolutely. To save money, use a kit available at your local garden center or hardware store. You don't need a plumber, as you can install it yourself. A drip system will return your investment through water saved. Drip irrigation systems use less than 30 percent of the water used by overhead sprinklers.

68. **Q.** **Are there house plants that need little water to survive? I travel frequently and have no one I can rely on to water them.**
A. Classic house plants for the traveler include the snake plant, *Sansevieria trifasciata*; yucca, *Yucca pendula glauca*; century plant, *Agave victoriae-reginae*; and the elephant-

foot tree (ponytail palm), *Beaucarnea recurvata*. They can all be allowed to dry substantially between waterings.

69. **Q. What is "gray" water?**
A. Gray water is recycled, household-waste water, other than from the toilet. It includes bath water, rinse water from dishes, and the second rinse from laundry. For recycled laundry-rinse water, do not use bleach or boron-based detergents. Before using "gray" water for gardening, check with your local health department for possible use restrictions.

70. **Q. Do you have any tips on sources of water that can be used to water plants during chronic water shortages?**
A. An often overlooked source for usable water is the shower. When taking a shower, set a bucket or large dishpan in front of you in the stall. It will amaze you just how much water misses you and falls into the container. Another source is drinking water. We often turn on the tap before filling the glass. Place a pan in the sink to catch every drop of water. Even leftover drinking water will do.

71. **Q. Last year, many of my gardening friends said they were using rain barrels to collect water for their plants. What is a rain barrel?**
A. Rain barrels are used for collecting and storing water. The old-fashioned, fifty-five gallon wooden rain barrel has been replaced by the sixty-gallon plastic garbage can. They are used to catch rainwater from the roof by directing the downspout from gutters into the barrel. Plastic wading pools are also usable as rain barrels.

72. **Q. What is xeriscaping?**
A. Xeriscaping is landscaping with water conservation in mind. It is gardening with water-efficient plantings by selecting drought-tolerant species, and by using proper horticultural techniques.

73. **Q. What points should I consider when planning a xeriscape?**
A. There are basically seven steps in planning a xeriscape: proper design; soil improvements; planning practical turf areas; efficient use of mulches; use of low water demand plants; efficient irrigation; and good maintenance.

VII

MULCHING
AND
WEED
CONTROL

WHAT DOES ONE Sunday issue of the *New York Times*, strips of used carpeting, a bale of bedding straw, and a roll of black plastic sheeting have in common? Answer: They all make excellent mulches for use in the garden.

Let us define a mulch. A mulch is nothing more than a covering over the surface of the soil. In addition to the above, it could be wood chips, shredded pine bark, sawdust, pebbles, salt hay, buckwheat hulls, cocoa hulls, marble chips, volcanic rock, or the new landscape fabrics. It could even be a living mulch, like English ivy or pachysandra. The list goes on and on, and they all help to block out garden weeds and to conserve moisture in the soil. Mulching offers many and various benefits.

FUNCTIONS OF A MULCH

To Control Weeds

In my gardens I use mulches for many purposes, but the number-one reason is to suppress weed growth. Consider four basic criteria in selecting mulch: its ability to block sunlight; thickness and required quantity for coverage; whether the mulch itself might become a favorable site for weed germination; and purity of the chosen material.

No Light A mulch must block out light. In Chapter I we discussed the food manufacturing process in the plant, and its dependency on temperature, chlorophyll, and light for photosynthesis. As soil temperatures rise in the spring and as moisture becomes available to seeds, germination begins. It is completed thanks to essential food stored in a part of the seed called the cotyledon. To continue growing and maturing, the seeds must manufacture additional food through photosynthesis. Without sunlight there is no food production and, without food, the seedling dies. So, if you are using a mulch to control weeds, it must be sufficiently dense to prevent light from reaching the weed seedlings. Black plastic sheeting, the new landscape fabric, or at least five layers of newspaper will block out enough light to provide weed control.

Before putting down a mulch for weed control, take care to eliminate any existing weeds. I cultivate the soil with a scuffle hoe to a depth of one-quarter inch to be sure that the roots of any actively growing weed seedlings are useless. This ensures that growing weeds cannot raise up the mulch, which they will do otherwise in search of light required for growth. Other seeds will germinate underneath the mulch, but they will die without light.

In the part of my vegetable patch where I grow squash, melons, cucumbers, and other plants that enjoy warm root systems, I use a large sheet (twenty-five by fifty feet) of six-millimeter (or heavier) black plastic to cover the prepared planting bed. Besides inhibiting weed growth, it acts as a large solar collector and encourages faster rooting and growth of the vegetables that will sprout through holes that I cut in the plastic. Use six-millimeter or thicker black plastic to ensure that you can walk on it to plant and harvest without tearing or poking holes through it. Wherever a hole is made, guess what will grow right through it? That's right, weeds!

The outer edge of the plastic sheet is trenched into the ground and anchored with soil to keep it from flying into the air. Provide additional anchorage by placing stones, culled from the garden, in several places atop the plastic sheet. When I am ready to plant either transplants or seeds, I cut an X-shaped opening, about twelve inches square, and fold the flaps underneath. It is important to fold the flaps under, because their flapping in the breeze can beat your plants to death. The seeds and transplants can be watered through the openings by hand or with an automated drip system. If plastic sheeting is used in a flat garden area with no slope for runoff, after a rain, poke tiny holes where puddles of water have collected. Water will seep through the tiny holes to the soil below and reduce the possibility of stagnate pools of water, breeding habitats for insects.

The new landscape fabrics, as well as black plastic, can be used for row plantings. Simply prepare the soil for planting, roll out the fabric or plastic mulch material, anchor the edges, and make the X-shaped opening for each plant. I use this method for weed control when I plant tomatoes, eggplants, and peppers. The new landscape fabrics block out the sunlight but allow air and moisture to penetrate to the soil and roots.

Five layers of newsprint make an excellent mulch, particularly for those plants that enjoy cool soil around their roots, such as broccoli, Brussels sprouts, and cabbage. The paper's light color reflects sunlight, keeping the soil cooler, as opposed to black plastic, which helps to warm the soil. Since there is no lead in printers' ink anymore, it is safe to use the black-and-white sections of the newspaper. Newspaper is now being recycled in large composting operations, so why not "recycle" by using it as a mulch in your own garden? Note the several *musts* to installing newspaper:

- Always use *at least* a five-sheet thickness. If you use less, enough light penetrates to let weed seedlings grow.
- Overlap the edges of the layers by two or more inches. This prevents light from falling through the cracks to the weed seedlings.
- Never put the paper down on a windy day. You will be chasing it all over the neighborhood.
- Wet the paper immediately after putting it down. Wet paper tends to adhere to the soil for better anchorage.
- Cover the newspaper with a thin layer (one to two inches) of grass clippings,

straw, or wood chips. This layer will help hold down the paper and give your garden a neater appearance during the growing season. Also, by covering the paper, you don't have to read the same stories all summer. At the end of the gardening season, all of the organic ingredients—grass clippings, straw or wood chips, plus the newspaper layers—can be tilled into the soil to provide beneficial organic matter.

Proper Depth A second criterion when considering mulch for weed control is to be sure it is *deep enough* or thick enough to block out light. If a mulch does not naturally act as a barrier between light and seeds, if it does not normally inhibit light from reaching weed seeds, then that mulch must be applied in greater quantities to create a barrier thick enough to block any light from reaching the weed seeds.

Wood chips and bark nuggets are materials that must be applied in more substantial quantities to create an effective barrier against sunlight. Because the large chips *do not* pack down and *do* allow light to penetrate between the chips, it is necessary to create a barrier depth of at least six inches. The smaller mini-nuggets tend to pack and settle tightly together, allowing less chance for light to reach the seedlings. If you are interested in using chips, large or small, and want to save some money, cover landscape fabric or black plastic sheeting on the soil surface with a thin layer of chips. But don't be "penny-wise and pound-foolish." Use enough mulch to adequately cover the fabric or plastic —about a two-inch thickness should do.

Not A Growth Medium A mulch must not favor weed growth. For this reason alone, I do not recommend compost or peat moss as a mulch. The only legitimate use for compost or peat moss is as a soil additive during soil preparation or at planting time. Many gardeners love to put a fresh layer of rich compost or peat moss around their landscape plants every spring, but later in the season they usually end up with a bumper crop of weeds. Both compost and peat moss are ideal growing media for all types of seeds—including weed seeds.

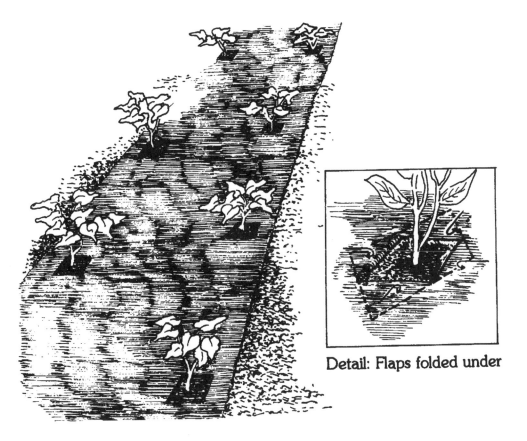

Detail: Flaps folded under

Garden Mulch: Plastic or Landscape Fabric

Newspaper Mulch: 5 Sheets Thick

No Weed Seeds A mulch should not be full of weeds to start with. A very popular mulch used in the vegetable patch is bedding straw, used more appropriately in barns to soak up animal waste. This straw is not sterile. Every weed that grew in the farmer's field will very likely show up in your garden if you choose straw mulch. Bedding straw is *loaded* with weed seeds. On the other hand, a gardener can use salt hay, even though it too is loaded with weed seeds. Salt hay is different since it is harvested from coastal areas whose weed seeds will not grow in your garden, unless you garden in a salt marsh. Weeds from a salt marsh need a salt marsh type of environment in order to germinate.

The following story of weed-contaminated mulch hopefully makes my point:

When I was director of a botanical garden in New York, we were fortunate enough to receive all the horse manure and stable sweepings from the city's mounted police academies. Each week we would receive as much as fifty barrels of waste to add to our compost piles.

One day in late fall, after a quarter-million tulips had been planted, we received an extra-large delivery for our compost pile. A staff horticulturist, who shall remain nameless, decided to use this extra manure and straw as top dressing and mulch for the tulip beds. He believed that by spring the manure would be broken down enough to provide beneficial nutrients to the soil, as well as to the bulbs.

He was right in one respect because, and much to our surprise, along with the emergence of the tulip foliage came billions of tiny seedlings of "oats"—probably enough to produce a hundred bushels per acre! He had not considered that the straw sweepings and manure contained the remnants of the horse feed: oat seed! The seeds lay dormant over winter only to germinate in the spring. Since we could not use a weed killer in the tulip bed after the bulb foliage started to grow, it was necessary to spend many hours on hands and knees, carefully pulling the tiny oat seedlings from between each plant. In beds where the tulip foliage had not yet emerged, we were able to use a scuffle hoe to cut the oat seedling's roots without damaging the tulip foliage. They never again used manure and stable sweepings as mulch. Now, they compost it first to eliminate weeds.

To Conserve Moisture

During dry seasons, I am concerned with conservation of precious soil moisture. Any gardener who uses a mulch also conserves soil moisture. A mulch is a barricade to evaporation, and it also reduces runoff during heavy rains. In my garden, there have been many summers when I used a mulch around my tomatoes, eggplants, and peppers to conserve moisture. Never have I had to apply additional water to what Mother Nature provided.

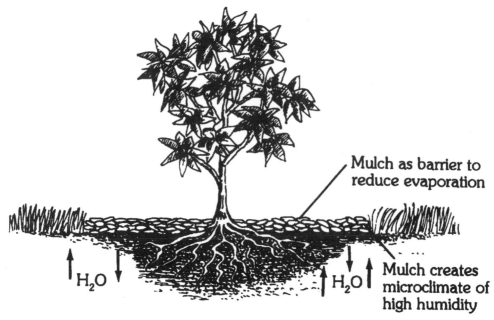

Mulch as barrier to reduce evaporation

H_2O

H_2O

Mulch creates microclimate of high humidity

Mulch Barrier: Moisture-Loss Reduction

A mulch creates a microclimate at the soil surface that is extremely high in humidity. This microclimate, supersaturated with moisture, reduces evaporation of moisture from the soil particles. Use caution mulching wet areas; this mulch must be a material that allows moisture to evaporate from the soil. Black plastic sheeting is not recommended for wet or damp areas. Without a proper balance of free oxygen and moisture in the soil, anaerobic conditions will develop and so will root rot.

For container culture, a mulch can be placed on the surface of the soil in each pot to reduce evaporation. The resulting reduction of moisture loss can add several days between waterings. I use a one-inch-thick layer of pine bark mini-nuggets on the soil of window boxes and large planters, once they have been potted and begin to grow. During hot, windy days water stress on the plants is reduced; aesthetics also are improved.

To Prevent Erosion

We all know that good soil is a very precious resource. Wind and rain can and do cause billions of dollars of erosion damage to our farmlands annually. During the dust-bowl days, had the agricultural industry known the benefits of using a mulch to stabilize the soil, much of the soil from Kansas would not have blown all the way to the peach orchards of Georgia or washed down the Mississippi River to the deltas of Louisiana. Even on a small scale in our own gardens, soil can and does end up at the bottom of the hill after a heavy rain or wind.

In the sloping part of my garden, I use a mulch to prevent soil erosion. A mulch cushions the force of water droplets, whether they fall as rain, or from overhead irrigation, or even from a watering can. The impact of water on bare earth breaks the soil particles apart, resulting in both erosion and compaction.

The soil of containers, whether on the patio or indoors, can erode as well. Every time you give a plant a drink from a watering can, an uncushioned stream of water forces soil from the surface roots of the plant; a stream of water can dig a hole. Even a thin layer of mulch on the surface of the soil eliminates soil erosion in container culture.

To Prevent Cultivation Damage

In the vegetable patch, mulch not only keeps down the weeds and conserves moisture, but also prevents cultivation damage to the roots and reduces compaction of freshly tilled soil. Every time you cultivate

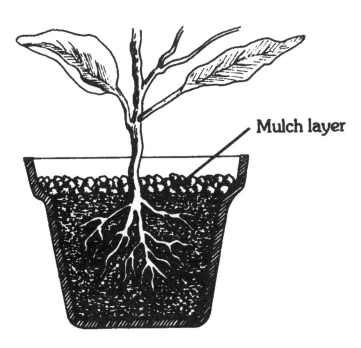

**Container Culture: Mulch Layer on Soil Surface
to Reduce Evaporation**

around a plant to loosen the soil or to remove the weeds, whether it be in the vegetable patch, flower garden, or landscape, you end up cutting and destroying some surface roots of the desirable plants. These surface roots are important for healthy growth. In the vegetable garden, cultivation damage can be one cause of the dreaded blossom-end rot on tomatoes, the rotten black spot on the bottom side of the fruit.

I once set up an experiment in my tomato garden to test the theory of cultivation damage on tomatoes. I planted three plants through a black plastic mulch, and three plants with no mulch. On almost a weekly basis, I had to cultivate around the plants with no mulch to keep the weeds from crowding out the plants. The weeds included crabgrass, purslane, and chickweed, to name a few. After just a few weeks of growth, I could see a definite increase in growth and overall vigor of the plants not being cultivated, as opposed to those that were. On the cultivated plants, as soon as they started flowering and setting fruit, the tomatoes showed signs of the blossom-end rot, a problem without cure until the first killing frost in the fall. I know this was not a scientific analysis, even though I fed and watered the plants in similar fashion, but it was enough to convince me that cultivating around tomatoes was a practice to be avoided.

Evergreen landscape plants, such as taxus, rhododendron, and azaleas, do not appreciate having their root soil cultivated either; anytime their roots are damaged, leaves begin to yellow and fall. If you cultivate around azaleas or rhododendrons while they are in bloom, you might cause the flowers to wilt. Damage to taxus may manifest itself as yellowed inner leaves that drop immediately. All these plants possess a shallow network of very fine, fibrous roots for intake of moisture. If these roots are damaged or destroyed, an immediate strain cripples the plants' physical and chemical processes. They cannot take up needed moisture required for turgidity and transpiration, or for photosynthesis. Remember, evergreens need a continual supply of moisture because they hold their foliage year-round.

The solution to cultivation damage: Use a mulch instead!

To Prevent Temperature Fluctuation

A mulch can blanket the surface of the soil, insulate it for either soil coolness or warmth. I use a mulch to help keep the soil frozen longer in the springtime so that bulbs will not emerge too soon. In our area of the country, premature spring, with its several thaws and freezes, often arrives before the season's permanent warmth is expected.

Gardeners in the north know a winter mulch can be very beneficial to plants put into the landscape in the previous fall. A three- to four-inch layer of pine bark nuggets, wood chips, or even shredded bark, will act as an insulating mulch. The mulch will reduce heat radiation from the soil. The soil stays warmer longer and the roots of the plants continue growing. For newly planted evergreens, particularly those classified as broad-leafed (azaleas, rhododendrons, hollies, boxwood, and taxus), the warmer soil allows root growth right up to the time the soil freezes. The plant is thereby better established for overwintering.

For bulbs planted in early fall, mulch application generally is not necessary; there is plenty of time for the bulbs to develop roots before the ground freezes. If you cannot avoid planting the bulbs until late fall or early winter, but before the ground freezes, a mulch of straw or salt hay over the bulb bed will insulate the soil against freezing temperatures for a period of time. The time for rooting is extended.

There is one problem with mulching bulbs in late fall, and that is rodent damage. Late one fall, but before the ground froze, I placed a five- to six-inch layer of straw over a tulip bed, but not one bulb emerged in the spring. Raking off the mulch revealed field mice had made their home under it, and they had eaten well—all my bulbs.

If you mulch a bulb bed after the ground freezes and leave it in place until spring, that mulch will reduce the potential of early emergence during a January thaw. The mulch, acting as an insulator, helps to keep the soil frozen longer into spring. This mulching technique can delay the initial flowering time of tulips, daffodils, and hyacinths. To inspire spring growth, remove the mulch and let the sun warm and thaw the soil.

Permanent Mulch A permanent mulch is one put on the surface of the soil and allowed to remain in place "forever." In the forest, Mother Nature spreads a permanent, organic mulch every fall when the leaves drop. These leaves not only act as an insulator, but also decompose, adding humus and nutrients to the soil below.

The same process occurs when you permanently place an organic mulch (such as wood chips or pine bark) around your landscape plants. Each succeeding year may require a few additional bags of mulch to freshen up the landscape and to replenish mulch decaying underneath. If you scrape away a small area of mulch and examine the soil below, you will see the benefits of decaying organic matter. The soil will be crumbly to the touch, dark in color because of the extra humic acid, and very likely loaded with healthy, tiny, fibrous roots. The soil will contain billions of beneficial micro-organisms and probably a great many earthworms. When I want bait for fishing, I just go to my deepest mulch pile, scrape away the surface, and dig it out. Decaying organic matter is heaven for night crawlers, and I find them eight to ten inches long.

In early fall where freezing is probable, pull away permanent mulch from around woody plants to allow proper hardening-off of the stem tissue. Mulch piled around the woody stem during its growing season holds moisture against the bark. Pulling the mulch away, by as much as two to three inches over a few weeks' time, allows the stem tissue to dry and harden for winter. Mulch can be reapplied in late fall or early winter, but a good practice doesn't allow mulch to accumulate against the bark. Failure to remove the mulch can result in frost damage to the cambium layer and to splitting of the bark. In either instance, the plant will probably die.

Summer Mulch When we refer to a summer mulch, we are generally talking about mulch in the vegetable and flower garden to conserve moisture and to prevent weeds. The mulch should be applied after the soil is sufficiently warm for planting.

Winter Mulch A mulch can either keep the soil frozen or prevent freezing. In the north, it can protect plants from severe cold, reduce wind and sunburn, and keep plants from heaving during the fluctuating cycle of freezing and thawing. After the ground starts to freeze in early winter, I mulch my strawberry patch with a three- to four-inch layer of salt hay. This insulator protects them from the winter wind and sun, and keeps them from waking too early in the spring. One winter when I failed to mulch my strawberry plants, I lost them all to winter dehydration and heaving in the early spring. The ground was so dry during that winter that you could kick up dust from the frozen ground. When the rain did fall, the freezing and thawing action literally jacked the plants from the ground, exposing their roots to the winter's drying wind and sun.

The Results of Using a Mulch
Increased Yield Add up all the reasons for using a mulch—weed control, moisture retention, erosion prevention, elimination of cultivation damage, and reduced temperature fluctuation—and the result will be increased yields from vegetable patches, flower gardens, and landscapes. Vegetables, such as tomatoes, eggplants, peppers, and cabbage, will be bigger and better. Whether they be annuals (such as petunias, marigolds, zinnias) or perennials (roses, daisies, rose mallow), the flowers will be larger and more brilliant. Landscape plants (rhododendrons, azaleas, laurels) display their much-improved blossoms and a greener, lusher foliage.

SELECTING A MULCH

Expend as much time and effort selecting the mulch as you would to actually apply it.

Effects on Soil pH
Over time, a mulch can have an effect on soil acidity or alkalinity. In general, organic mulches such as wood chips and pine bark acidify the soil as they decay. The end product of decaying organic matter is humic acid, naturally acidic. On the other hand, lime chips make it more alkaline as calcium is leached into the soil.

Aesthetics or Beautification
Numerous and varied mulch materials can be used to accent the landscape. Decide what you want to accomplish before selecting a decorative mulch. A light-colored

mulch, such as marble chips or washed beige gravel, provides a backdrop against which a plant with green foliage stands out as an individual. Just imagine the dark-green needles of a juniper or mugho pine surrounded by a mulch of white stones at its base. A dark-colored mulch, such as pine bark mini-nuggets or redwood bark chips, blends a plant with green foliage into the landscape, giving a more natural appearance.

MULCHES FOR THE HOME GARDEN

As noted earlier, "A mulch is nothing more than a covering over the surface of the soil." There are almost as many materials for use as mulch as there are plants to put mulch around. Many come in three-cubic-foot bags and are available at your local garden center, nursery, or plant shop.

The quantity of mulch to cover a given area is calculated by this rule of thumb: 1 cubic foot = 12 square feet, 1 inch thick; 1 cubic foot = 6 square feet, 2 inches thick; 1 cubic foot = 3 square feet, 3 inches thick.

Large building-supply centers and landscape contractors handle some mulches in bulk, sold by weight or by the cubic yard. The popularity and price of a particular mulch material is largely determined by its availability in a given locale. Redwood bark chips are popular on the Pacific Coast, shredded pine bark and pine bark nuggets in the Northeast, and washed gravel along the sea shore.

The following materials are only suggestions you may wish to consider when selecting a mulch for your own landscape and garden.

Landscape fabrics and fiber weed barriers are long-lasting, and the newest of mulch materials. These weed barriers are made by weaving synthetic cloth fibers together (woven) or by bonding short or continuously spun fibers together through heat bonding, spin bonding, or other processes (all non-woven), in such a manner as to allow water, air, and nutrients to penetrate, while at the same time providing an efficient barrier against light. The new fabric mulches are available in a black or dark brown color. I use landscape fabric in row plantings in my vegetable patch, and also as a weed barrier under a decorative mulch in my landscape plantings. In the vegetable patch, at the close of the season, I pick up the landscape fabric and store it for reuse. I am in my fifth year for one roll of fabric. Used as a weed barrier under mulch, landscape fabrics will last for years. But I just recently learned of a potential problem with landscape fabrics made of cloth fiber. A caller to my *Garden Hotline* radio program related a story about his *disappearing* landscape fabric. The caller said he noticed that someone had been disturbing the decorative bits of bark chips which he had placed around his foundation plantings. It was a puzzle why anyone would want to do such a thing. Upon closer examination, he discovered strips of landscape fabric were also disappearing from underneath the bark mulch. Surveillance soon exposed the culprit: A friendly squirrel was spending his early morning gnawing away sections of landscape fabric with scissorlike precision. Apparently, the squirrel desired this fabric for a more perfect nest.

Black plastic is long lasting, but does deteriorate over time due to weather conditions. Black plastic sheeting, in blanket form or roll, has been around for over forty years and is still the most popular barrier to weed growth in the garden.

Arborist wood chips are probably the cheapest mulch you can find. I call them arborist wood chips because today the tree services in my area have to grind or chip all the prunings and brush they remove from the landscape, instead of hauling it in bulk to the dump. Now that most sanitary landfills or garbage dumps do not allow dumping of garden waste, such as wood chips, the arborist usually is quite willing to leave them with you at no charge. I use wood chips to cover the newspaper mulch in my vegetable garden, and for making pathways. Fresh wood chips, usually light in color, soon darken from the effects of weather, making them a natural-looking mulch for landscape beds. The chips break down over time and become an important organic addition to the soil.

Pine bark nuggets, large and small, are among the most popular landscape mulches in my area. The different sizes available make them useful for the largest of planting areas or the smallest. Mini-nuggets, chips about the size of your thumb-nail, are a very attractive mulch in containers. In the garden, these chips do decompose over a period of time, so replenish them periodically. Each spring I purchase a few bags of new mulch and spread them over the existing mulch to give my landscape a fresh, new look.

Shredded bark—hardwood or pine bark —is ideal for mulching around plants grown on a slope. The consistency of the shredded material is quite stringy. Spread on the ground, shredded bark tends to mat down and stay in place, making it valuable in erosion control. Hardwood shredded bark will last for several years, since it is slow to decompose.

Redwood bark chips come in several grades, from large-chunk bark to mini-chips. They are one of the most popular and least expensive mulches on the West Coast, where redwood forests abound. The farther away from the West Coast you get, the more expensive they become. Redwood bark does become flammable after drying for several seasons, so it should be used with caution in areas prone to fire. The chips are one of the most attractive and decorative materials for use in extensive landscape plantings. I have used the large redwood bark chips to accent evergreen landscape plants, such as junipers and mugho pines planted next to an outcrop of stone. Large redwood bark chips add a visual strength to the landscape.

Sawdust—used alone—packs, crusts, dries, and is difficult to remoisten. Fresh sawdust will steal nitrogen-fixing bacteria from the soil, culminating in nutrient deficiency known as nitrogen chlorosis. The addition of nitrogen to the sawdust mulch usually clears up chlorosis in the plants. Sawdust can be mixed with shredded bark or bark chips with success. I prefer to use sawdust as an organic component in my compost pile, as opposed to using it as a mulch, because it breaks down into a fine organic additive.

Newspaper—one Sunday edition of the *New York Times* or *Los Angeles Times*— makes a great mulch for the vegetable patch. It is not uncommon for a Sunday issue to be three inches thick, enough mulch for a ten-square-foot garden, if the paper is at least five sheets thick for each layer. Overlap the layers by at least two inches so light does not get to the weed seedlings, and cover the

paper with an additional mulch, like grass clippings, straw, or wood chips. At the end of the season, all the ingredients, such as grass clippings, straw or wood chips, including the newspaper layer, can be tilled into the soil as additional organic matter. One caution when using newspaper: Be aware that paper is flammable.

Carpeting, that is, used carpet strips, can be a decorative as well as functional mulch in the vegetable patch. Cotton and other natural fibers will decompose over time. Nylon carpeting can be used for several seasons if rolled up in the fall and placed in dry storage. I find carpeting cut in three-foot-wide strips to be ideal for mulching the walkways between crop rows. I put down the carpet in the spring after planting, and take it up in the fall after the first killing frost. To prevent mold and decay, be sure carpeting is dry before storing it for winter. You can dry carpeting by laying it in the sun for a few days before it is rolled up.

Oat straw, also referred to as bedding straw, is relatively inexpensive and is a good mulch to spread over newspapers. Oat straw is also used as a thin mulch cover over newly planted grass seed. It keeps the soil slightly damp during seed germination. Straw will also reduce compaction and erosion caused by overhead sprinklers. Disadvantages of bedding straw are the probability that weeds will be introduced into the garden, and it tends to blow away.

Salt hay is a marsh grass generally available locally only in coastal areas. It is sold by the bale and often hard to find at times other than fall; fall is when salt hay is harvested. When I purchase bales, I usually buy several so that I'll have enough for the following gardening season. I stack them in an out-of-the-way location and keep them dry with a plastic sheet. A bale of salt hay used in the perennial garden will last for several years, because it does not break down or decompose nearly as readily as bedding straw. I use salt hay as a mulch around and over many perennials that need winter protection, then rake it off in the spring, pile it in an out-of-the-way spot in the garden and cover it with a piece of plastic to keep it dry until I need it for mulching the following fall or winter.

Washed gravel is relatively inexpensive, depending on locale, and is available in tan, gray, white, and blended colors. It is often used in commercial installations as a decorative, permanent mulch with weed barriers of black plastic, landscape fabric, or fiberglass. Keeping gravel or other nonorganic mulches clean can be frustrating. Do not try to rake leaves that have accumulated during the season. Raking will crumble the leaves and make the stone mulch look dirty. Use a leaf blower to remove the leaves and other debris. A positive feature of gravel is that it is fireproof.

Coarse sand comes in colors that vary from white to brown to red, depending upon location. Coarse sand is often used in rock and water gardens, and oriental landscapes. The sand can be raked lightly, but will show accumulated debris. A thin layer of new coarse sand is often needed to provide a clean, fresh look. As with gravel, sand is fireproof.

Marble chips, available in white and various colors, are used as a decorative mulch to make plants stand out as individuals. Take care when removing leaves accumulated on white marble chips. Use a leaf blower to clean washed gravel, or pick up the leaves by hand. Do not rake them or you will have bits and pieces of leaves mixed in with the marble chips, giving your landscape a really dirty look. Marble chips are fireproof.

Volcanic landscape stone is also fireproof. Due to this single characteristic, volcanic landscape stone has become one of the most popular landscape mulches in areas prone to fire. Landscapers recommend its use around wooden structures, where you would not want to use a flammable organic mulch. It is considered by many landscape gardeners to be the most decorative mulch. Volcanic stone is available in three basic colors: deep red or earth-tone; slate black (a gray-black); and a blend of brown and deep red, and comes in sizes from one-quarter inch to one and three-quarter inches in diameter. Volcanic landscape stone does not degrade or fade with age as do organic mulches.

Ground corn cobs are not generally used in landscaping, but they are very satisfactory when used to mulch the vegetable patch and flower garden; they are weed-free, clean, and easy to handle. A layer, two to four inches deep, will sufficiently control most weeds and conserve moisture. As ground cobs decompose, it may be necessary to correct nitrogen deficiencies in the crop being mulched by adding extra nitrogen. At the finish of the gardening season, the cob material can be incorporated into the soil as an added source of organic matter.

Fiberglass bats, squares of flexible fiberglass sheets sold as wall insulation at building supply houses, have a fireproof characteristic that makes them an effective permanent mulch for use underneath a decorative mulch, particularly adjacent to wood structures. After installing the landscape plants, lay out the fiberglass bats as if you were putting together a puzzle, trimming the fiberglass layers to fit the landscape bed. A one-inch-thick layer of fiberglass bats *without* the foil backing will allow moisture, nutrients, and air to penetrate to the roots of desirable plants, and at the same time stop the growth of any potential weed seedlings. Decorative mulches, such as redwood bark, volcanic landscape stone, or washed gravel, are often used over fiberglass. The expense of fiberglass bats has kept them from becoming a popular mulch.

Cocoa bean hulls are very dark brown in color and will last for about one season. Some years ago, I went to my local garden center to purchase cocoa bean hulls for my herb garden, only to find they were no longer available. Much to my surprise, the chocolate manufacturers in my area had switched to using artificial chocolate, thus, no cocoa bean hulls. Now that manufacturers have returned to using real chocolate, the hulls are back.

The job of spreading a bag of cocoa hulls is probably one of the most pleasant you will ever have. You will think you are in Willie Wonka's Chocolate Factory; you can inhale the aroma of chocolate, but not gain one pound. There are a few disadvantages, however. If used repetitively in the same area, enough potash may be released to cause root burn on shallow-rooted plants, and the hulls often contain enough sugary material to support a mold growth of white mycelium. The growth of the mold is easily checked by letting it develop for two or three days and then stirring the mulch with a rake to allow air to penetrate.

Buckwheat hulls are another of my favorites for use in the herb garden, and their dark color makes them attractive in the perennial garden. Their use is limited by availability. Because they are extremely light in weight, they cannot be used in a windy location or they blow away. A terrace gardener on the twenty-fourth floor of an apartment building in New York City told me he had used a mulch of buckwheat hulls on the soil in his vegetable containers only to find that by the end of the first windy day, not one buckwheat hull remained.

Leaves, of all the natural mulches, are best known as Mother Nature's mulch. Whole leaves can be used as a winter mulch around perennials, as long as they do not pack down when wet. I prefer oak leaves. I do not use maple leaves since they do pack and smother the plants underneath. A caution: Do not use leaves as a mulch around evergreens and fruit trees if rodents, like field mice, are a problem during winter. The mice will make a homey nest in the leaves and then eat the bark of the trees or shrubs. Remember, too, that dry leaves are flammable and should not be used in areas at risk from fires.

Dried grass clippings can be used to cover landscape fabrics and newspaper in the vegetable patch. Dry the grass clippings by exposing them to the sun in an out-of-the-way spot in the garden. Do not use fresh or green grass clippings, because heat energy is released when they begin to break down. If you've ever left fresh grass clippings in a pile for just a few days and then tried to gather them up with your hands, you probably were surprised by the heat you felt. Respiration occurring in the green tissue of clippings creates very high temperatures. Don't ever pile fresh grass clippings at the base of a shrub or tree; the heat will cook the cambium layer of the bark, which will probably kill the plant.

Living mulch—ground covers like pachysandra, English ivy, or vinca—can shade the soil during summer and provide an organic insulation over the soil during winter. Living mulches also provide excellent weed control, if they are encouraged to grow into a dense mat. I grow vinca or pachysandra under shallow-rooted trees, such as the Norway maple and the flowering dogwood, so I don't have to mow grass that would otherwise try to grow there. Without a living mulch I would be forced to mow an area sparse in grass and with exposed roots. Result: dull mower blades and injured root systems. During a prolonged dry season it may be necessary to water your living mulch because there will be competition for moisture from both the tree and the ground cover.

QUESTIONS AND ANSWERS

1. **Q. What does mulching mean?**
   A. Mulching is the placing of a cover over the surface of the soil. Gardeners use various materials to cover the soil surface in order to prevent weeds from growing, to conserve moisture in the soil, to prevent soil compaction, to eliminate cultivation, to keep the soil warm, to keep the soil cool, and to prevent erosion.

2. **Q. If roses need winter protection, what is the best method?**
   A. In northern gardens, hybrid tea and most hybrid perpetual roses need winter protection to prevent water from standing around the crown of the plants. Water damage can be prevented by hilling up soil (eight to ten inches) around the base of the plant, where the crown is located. After the soil freezes, several inches of mulch, such as salt hay, evergreen boughs, or straw, will keep the soil frozen, protect against the cold, and conserve moisture in the plant.

3. **Q. How do I protect perennials for winter?**
   A. Established hardy perennials enjoy a light mulch protection against winter wind dehydration. After the ground freezes and the plants are completely dormant, cover them with a thin layer of straw, salt hay, or evergreen boughs. You should be able to see as much as 50 percent of the plant when looking through the mulch. A light

mulch reduces alternate freezing and thawing during spring and also reduces heat buildup that causes premature sprouting.

4. **Q. How do I protect peonies over winter?**
   A. Peonies are hardy perennials. They generally do not require winter protection after they have been established for a year. However, if you feel it necessary, you might use a light covering of salt hay or oak leaves. It is important to use a mulch that does not pack down.

5. **Q. Can the pine bark mulch around my evergreens remain year-round?**
   A. Yes, and do not disturb the mulch. Leave the mulch around your evergreens in all seasons, especially if they were new transplants.

6. **Q. Do pine bark, sawdust, or wood chips have any nutrient value when used as a mulch?**
   A. As an organic mulch decays and becomes humic acid, it releases nutrients to the soil. Fresh pine bark, sawdust, and wood chips can cause a deficiency of nitrogen on a temporary basis. To prevent this deficiency, add a nitrogen fertilizer to the bark, sawdust, or wood chips.

7. **Q. What is the best mulch to put around rhododendron plants?**
   A. Pine needles, pine bark chips, and shredded pine bark are all good. Oak leaves are also good, but they have a tendency to blow away more easily. Whatever you use, you should add to it each year.

8. **Q. What is a good mulch for mountain laurel, andromeda and glossy abelia?**
   A. All three plants prefer an organic mulch. Pine needles and oak leaves are good. The decomposition of these materials is very beneficial to the growth of these plants.

9. **Q. Should I cultivate the soil around my evergreens?**
   A. Cultivation disturbs the surface roots, which harms the plant. You can prevent the soil from hardening by applying a permanent mulch, either wood chips or leaf mold.

10. **Q. What is a permanent mulch?**
    A. A permanent mulch is a covering over the surface of the soil that is left in place year-round.

11. **Q. We have evergreen seedlings that have not been transplanted as yet. How can I help them over winter?**
    A. Water the plants thoroughly just before the first hard freeze, and then mulch them with a covering of dry oak leaves or straw.

12. **Q. I have tons of maple leaves. Can I use them as a mulch in my perennial garden?**
    A. No, not as is. Maple leaves tend to pack down and become soggy over winter. They smother the plants below. Mix maple leaves with oak leaves or straw before using them as a mulch; otherwise, add them to your compost pile.

13. **Q. How can I prevent winter wind burn on my evergreens?**
    A. Evergreens that are susceptible to winterburn or scorch should be planted where they will have some protection from the brightest winter sun. The timely application of an antidesiccant, according to the label directions, also reduces winter burn.

14. **Q. What can I do for evergreens in the winter when I can't water them?**
    A. The plants can be sprayed with an antidesiccant to cut down on transpiration of moisture from the leaves. If the plant is very small, you can protect it from sun and wind with various barriers, including a burlap screen.

15. **Q. What kind of care is required during the winter for junipers and pines?**
   A. If the plants are established, they shouldn't require any special protection. If they were recently planted, water the soil thoroughly and apply a mulch around the base of the plants just before the ground freezes.

16. **Q. I recently planted a couple of Fraser fir trees, and since I have access to a large quantity of oak leaves, I was going to use them for mulch. Is that OK?**
   A. Yes. An oak-leaf mulch will not harm fir trees. However, these leaves do have a tendency to blow around and may not be the best mulch to use. A more stable mulch would be shredded pine bark, pine needles, or wood chips.

17. **Q. When should I mulch my azaleas?**
   A. I recommend a permanent mulch as soon as you have planted, whether it be spring, summer, or fall. At the least, put down a mulch before the first freeze of winter. The mulch keeps the soil warmer longer into winter allowing continued root development.

18. **Q. Last year, an arborist was working on my trees and left me a free load of wood chips that I used as a mulch in my vegetable garden. I noticed the plants didn't produce as well and they looked pale and washed out. Was this caused by the wood chips? If so, what can I do?**
   A. The yellowing of the plants is most likely due to nitrogen chlorosis, a condition caused by using fresh wood chips. Any fresh organic matter can cause nitrogen deficiencies in the soil. Add a water-soluble nitrogen fertilizer to correct the problem.

19. **Q. Does black plastic make a good mulch?**
   A. Black plastic acts as a solar collector by absorbing light energy, and it blocks out light that would reach weed seedlings. Crops that prefer warm roots, such as tomatoes, eggplants, melons, cucumbers, and squash, benefit from the use of black plastic mulch. Use a film of at least six-millimeter thickness. Thinner layers tear and puncture. Make sure it is securely anchored and punch an adequate number of holes to allow water to seep through.

20. **Q. Can I use pine needles as mulch around my cedar and spruce trees?**
   A. A mulch of pine needles can be used for all plants, but it is especially good around evergreens, which prefer an acid condition.

21. **Q. Why cultivate the surface of the soil?**
   A. Cultivation reduces compaction, helps aerate the soil where a crust forms, and helps to kill weeds. Cultivated soil creates a loose surface that allows rain to soak in more quickly, instead of running off.

22. **Q. What is salt hay?**
   A. It is hay that is cut from salt marshes, which are located near a coast. It is often used as winter protection for plants.

23. **Q. How does a pine-needle mulch affect the soil? Every fall I let the needles that drop from the pine trees accumulate on the soil.**
   A. Water leaching through pine needles acidifies soil. As the needles decompose, they become humus.

24. **Q. What is a good way to keep grass seed from washing off a steep slope?**
   A. Anchor cheesecloth or a commercially prepared fiber cloth mulch, which is biodegradable, over the newly sown seed to keep it from washing away. Do not try to remove the cloth mulch after the seeds have germinated; you will pull the seedlings out of the soil. Allow the mulch to decay in place. If the slope is very steep, you might want to install sod.

25. **Q. In the fall, when should I mulch my flower beds (astilbe, coralbells, phlox)?**
A. If you are gardening in an area where frost penetrates the ground, wait until it freezes. When mulch is applied in these circumstances, it is meant to keep the soil frozen, preventing periods of freezing and thawing. Also, because of this late-application technique, mice will be discouraged from making the flower bed their home. Rodents can do a lot of damage to perennials when they eat the growth buds during winter.

26. **Q. Is there any circumstance when perennial flower beds should be mulched *before* the ground freezes in the fall?**
A. Yes. Late-planted perennials are mulched before the ground freezes to give the roots more time to become established. The mulch, in this case, keeps the soil warmer, longer into winter.

27. **Q. Is it absolutely necessary to dig up the gladiolus bulbs each fall?**
A. To ensure next year's crop, if the gladiolus are nonhardy varieties, dig them up before the ground freezes. If you garden in an area where the soil does not freeze deeply, a heavy mulch of straw and leaves can occasionally be used. However, the gladiolus corms will become overcrowded if you do this very often. It is best to rotate your crop to replenish nutrients and to discourage a build-up of disease problems. Dig your bulbs just before the ground freezes.

28. **Q. I have a rooftop flower and vegetable garden with plants grown in boxes. Would it help the plants if I were to apply mulch to the soil?**
A. Absolutely. A mulch will help hold moisture in the soil. Plants in a rooftop garden must always battle the drying effects of wind and sun. Mini-nuggets, wood chips, shredded pine bark, crushed cane, or leafmold could be used, but always keep in mind a mulch that will not blow away.

29. **Q. Should I wrap the branches and buds of my rhododendron in winter?**
A. No. Air has to circulate around the plant. You can provide protection with a screen of burlap, leaving it slightly open at the base for air circulation.

30. **Q. What is the best way to protect my rhododendrons in winter from strong, prevailing winds?**
A. Properly constructed burlap screens will give protection from wind, and provide some shade during the winter months. Apply an antidesiccant spray to the foliage before setting up the screen. The antidesiccant reduces water loss from the foliage and flower buds.

31. **Q. I have a taxus growing near the house, and this plant takes much abuse from heavy loads of snow and, sometimes, ice. Is there anything I can do to prevent the branches from breaking so easily?**
A. Before winter, loosely entwine the shrub with cord. This will give added support to the branches and may help prevent breakage. When possible, try to dislodge the snow and ice before it becomes a real problem.

32. **Q. Is it necessary to cover boxwood after it has been transplanted?**
A. Yes. If the weather is hot, a shade will help reduce water loss. In addition to shading, the application of an antitranspirant is recommended. It is a good idea to repeat the same protection the first winter after boxwood has been transplanted.

33. **Q. What is the best way to protect my boxwood during winter? It's a prized specimen and I don't want to see the plant damaged.**
A. Boxwood should never enter winter with dry roots, so water them thoroughly if the ground is dry. Prune out any dead or diseased wood. Avoid pruning the current

season's growth during late summer, as this pruning will initiate new growth that does not harden-off before winter. For additional protection, I suggest you construct a frame that will support a burlap cover for the plant over wintertime. This cover reduces sun- and windburn potential.

34. **Q. What is the best type of winter cover for a bulb bed?**
A. If you are lucky enough to have them, I suggest pine boughs, branches from a pine tree with the needles attached. They are easy to work with and should be applied after the surface soil has frozen solid. Remove them when the danger of very hard frosts is past.

35. **Q. I collect "used" Christmas trees and turn the trunks into tomato stakes and bean poles. What use can I make of Christmas tree branches?**
A. Branches cut from Christmas trees, such as pine, spruce, or balsam, are ideal for use as a winter mulch. They hold their needles well after being cut. Use them after the ground freezes to prevent dehydrating wind from reaching the crowns of perennial flowers, bulb beds, or fruiting plants such as strawberries. The branches are easy to apply and remove.

36. **Q. What is erosion?**
A. Erosion is what happens when runoff of surface water washes away the soil because the soil is bare and, perhaps, lacks the necessary humus to absorb moisture. Erosion can occur on level soil as well as slopes.

37. **Q. What nutrients do I have to apply to sawdust when I use it as a component in a mulch?**
A. Fresh sawdust takes nitrogen from the soil. Provide additional nitrogen. This can be done by using any regular lawn and garden fertilizer such as 10-6-4, sulphate of ammonia, nitrate of soda, or urea.

38. **Q. I have heard some gardeners say one thing about when to put down mulch for winter protection of plants, and other gardeners say the opposite. Should I do it before the ground freezes or after?**
A. Mulching for winter protection depends on the plant. If it is not a hardy type, such as the edible fig and camellia, then it must be protected before freezing temperatures set in, or the plant may die. If the plant is a hardy type, such as the perennial chrysanthemum and daisy, the plant should be protected after the onset of cold weather and after the top layer of soil is frozen. Hardy plants are usually mulched to protect them from alternate freezing and thawing of the soil.

39. **Q. Is their any advantage to using mulch paper, as opposed to other mulches?**
A. It depends on the other mulches. Mulch paper is difficult to use, in that it tears easily and is hard to keep in one place. However, as with other mulches, it will keep down weeds, conserve moisture in the soil, and should eliminate the need for cultivating.

40. **Q. Is it OK to use debris such as dried brush, grass, or leaves as mulch around pine trees or other evergreens?**
A. Care should be taken when using garden debris as a mulch, as it may harbor insect and disease problems. In addition, undecayed plant material will sometimes cause a temporary nitrogen deficiency. It would be better to compost this material first, and then use it as a soil additive. If composting is not an option, then supply additional nitrogen by using a complete fertilizer, or any other source of nitrogen.

41. **Q. Is it necessary to mulch strawberries for overwintering?**
A. In cold climates where freezing occurs, a light mulch of straw, salt hay, evergreen boughs, or oak leaves over strawberry plants will greatly enhance their ability to

overwinter in an exposed area. Mulch will help prevent winter dehydration of the crown of the plant; heaving caused by freezing and thawing; and it will help conserve soil moisture. The berries will also be cleaner the following spring because the mulch will prevent mud from splashing on them. Apply the mulch after a couple of hard freezes, but before the temperatures become extremely low—20 degrees Fahrenheit.

42. **Q. How do I mulch my strawberry bed?**
A. Scatter straw, salt hay, evergreen boughs, or oak leaves over the bed to a depth of two to three inches. You should *just* be able to see the plants through the mulch layer.

43. **Q. What is the best summer mulch to control weeds in a strawberry patch?**
A. Hay (marsh or salt), straw (wheat, oat, rye), and pine needles are all good for mulching around strawberry plants. Care should be taken not to smother the crown of the plant. The runners will grow out over the mulch. Sawdust and wood chips are OK too, but you may have to supplement the nitrogen loss in the soil that these mulches create.

44. **Q. When is a winter mulch removed from a strawberry bed?**
A. Remove the winter mulch just as the new leaves are beginning to grow from the crown. Allow mulch to remain between the plants and the rows and leave only a light covering on the plants. Leaves will push up through the remaining mulch and when the berries form, they will rest on the straw, which keeps them clean.

45. **Q. Is it OK to use grass clippings as a mulch?**
A. Yes, if they are allowed to dry first. Never pile green grass clipping over the roots or around the stems of a desirable plant. The heat generated by the decaying process will cook the living tissue.

46. **Q. In the fall, we have a lot of leaves to rake. Can they be used to mulch around shrubs?**
A. Mother Nature has been using leaves as a natural mulch since the beginning of time. If you use them, do it with caution. Leaf piles make a wonderful environment for field mice and other rodents. If the mice make a home in the leaf pile, they may eat the bark from stems of trees and shrubs.

47. **Q. Is it necessary to apply mulch around peach trees for winter?**
A. No. A surface mulch will provide little protection to the roots of a peach tree. A protective wire cage around the trunk may be of benefit, if you have experienced rabbit damage to the bark.

48. **Q. Can I use the animal manure to mulch strawberries for winter?**
A. Animal manure may provide too much nitrogen for fruiting plants. Manure works better as a soil additive after composting than as a mulch.

49. **Q. What is the advantage of using salt hay to mulch strawberries?**
A. Salt hay is much freer of weed seeds than other hay or straw. You do not want to introduce additional weeds into the strawberry patch.

50. **Q. Is it OK to use leaves that I rake in the fall as mulch on perennial plants? I have several different kinds of leaves all mixed together after raking.**
A. Leaves are OK, if that is all you have, but they tend to mat down on plants. If you pull most of the leaf mulch off the perennial plants as they emerge in the spring, then I would say go ahead and use leaves as a mulch.

51. Q. **Is it necessary to mulch everbearing strawberries?**

A. Yes. Treat them just like any other strawberry plants when it comes to winter mulching.

52. Q. **Almost every winter, I see news reports on television of southern growers who spray water on their plants to protect them from freezing weather. How does this process work to protect plants?**

A. The main idea is to use the heat from the water to keep the plants warmer; the temperature of water from a sprinkler is well above freezing, giving off one calorie of heat per degree temperature drop for every cubic centimeter of water. If the act of spraying water on plants causes ice to form, the very act of water turning to ice produces heat.

53. Q. **I have heard that oak leaves are good as a mulch, but I only have maple leaves. Will they work just as well?**

A. The reason oak leaves are recommended is that they tend to be rigid and stiff and do not "pack" as do maple leaves. When maple leaves pack very tightly, they can become soggy and a barrier to air. When they decompose, the alkaline they produce is not good for most plants.

54. Q. **My home is near the ocean and I have access to plenty of seaweed. Can I use it as a mulch, or will the salt cause harm to my plants?**

A. Seaweed works very well as a mulch. Your plants should not suffer any damage, unless you use the seaweed mulch to extreme. An added benefit to seaweed use is that decaying seaweed supplies trace elements to the soil.

55. Q. **Will coffee grounds work as a mulch?**

A. Coffee grounds make an excellent mulch, if not used in excess. Try not to layer more than a half-inch thick, or else the mulch will create a barrier to air.

56. Q. **Is it necessary to do more, once a permanent, organic mulch has been applied?**

A. Make sure the mulch doesn't pack or blow away, and replenish it as it decomposes.

57. Q. **Can mulch be applied in the early spring?**

A. In applying most mulches, it is best to wait until the soil has warmed. Two of the main reasons for mulching are to conserve moisture during hot, dry weather and to keep weeds down. Black plastic or landscape fiber can be applied in early spring to act as a solar collector to warm the soil.

58. Q. **After almost every rain, the soil in my garden forms a crust. Is there anything I can do to prevent this?**

A. Use an organic mulch, something that will continually add humic acid to the soil as it decays. Also, each year, add organic matter to the soil when it is prepared for planting.

59. Q. **How do I anchor newspaper when I use it as a mulch?**

A. First, as soon as paper is placed on the soil surface, wet it; wet paper tends to stick to soil. A small amount of garden soil scattered on the paper will provide anchorage also. To make the newspaper mulch more aesthetically pleasing, spread a thin layer of grass clippings over the surface of the paper.

60. Q. **What type of mulch would be good in a perennial border?**

A. Shredded redwood bark, bark nuggets, bark mini-nuggets, crushed cane, buckwheat hulls, or cocoa hulls are my favorites for perennials, because they are dark in color and give a natural look. You might also consider pine needles, but remember, they tend to make the soil acid and this might not be a good idea for some plants.

61. **Q. Why would I ever want to use a light-colored mulch, such as beige gravel or white rock?**

A. The color of the mulch either allows a to plant stand out as an individual, or lets it blend into the environment.

62. **Q. Do wildflowers (the kind one usually finds in the woods) require a mulch?**

A. It would be good to mulch them with leaves. In their native state it is natural for them to have leaves around them.

63. **Q. Are grass clippings useful as a mulch in a perennial garden?**

A. I prefer to compost grass clippings and use the end product as an organic additive when planting perennials. Grass clippings can be the carrier of weed seeds, which you don't want in a perennial garden.

64. **Q. When you talk about a scuffle hoe, what do you mean?**

A. A scuffle hoe is a cultivator with a sharp blade that works with a forward and backward motion just under the surface of the soil. The blade severs the roots of weed seedlings, in addition to breaking up the soil's surface. If used properly, a scuffle hoe will not damage the root system of vigorously growing plants.

65. **Q. Should I mulch asparagus over winter?**

A. A permanent mulch can be placed over an asparagus bed to control weeds and conserve moisture. It is not necessary to use an additional winter mulch.

66. **Q. What are hot caps?**

A. Hot caps are miniature paper covers, usually in the shape of a tent, which are set over young plants to protect them from frost and wind. The hot cap is opened or removed on sunny days. As soon as the transplants become established, the hot caps are permanently removed.

67. **Q. Is it economically advisable to use hot caps?**

A. If you are one who "cheats" on the growing season, taking a chance in setting out tender transplants before the last frost date in your area, hot caps can be a very positive advantage. Anytime you can protect tender plants from wind, rain, and possible cold weather, it will ensure a better success rate for your transplants.

68. **Q. How soon after a rainfall can one hoe in the garden?**

A. Garden soil should have dried enough so that big quantities no longer stick to the hoe as you work.

69. **Q. What program should be followed to keep weeds out of my vegetable garden?**

A. The best program is to prevent weeds from growing in the first place, but no system is perfect. Mulch between rows and around individual plants, wherever possible. Those weeds that do appear near individual plants can be pulled out, carefully, so as not to disturb the root systems of the vegetable plants. If you cannot mulch, cultivate between rows with a scuffle hoe or Rototiller, but hand pull weeds that are near your plants.

70. **Q. Is a summer mulch necessary in the vegetable garden?**

A. A summer mulch will help control weeds, virtually eliminate cultivation damage, and help conserve moisture in the soil. A proper mulch will keep the soil loose and crumbly, a condition that receives rain well and prevents runoff.

71. **Q. What is "dust" mulch?**

A. This is a layer of dust-dry soil, one to two inches deep. Frequent shallow cultivation with a cultivator or hoe will produce this effect.

72. Q. **What can I use for mulch in the vegetable garden, besides peat moss?**

     A. I don't recommend peat moss as a mulch in the vegetable garden. It tends to be a nursery for weeds. There are so many other materials that one can use, such as salt hay, sawdust, wood chips, layers of newspaper, old carpeting, seaweed, dried grass clippings, black plastic sheeting, landscape fabric, ground corncobs, and buckwheat hulls.

73. Q. **Can peat moss be used as a mulch around a taxus hedge? It looks very dressy when it is raked level and clean.**

     A. Peat moss should never be used as a mulch around shallow-rooted plants. In fact, I recommend peat moss only as a soil amendment. During spring rains, peat moss, as a mulch, remains wet, encouraging shallow roots to develop. As soon as the spring rains stop, peat moss, containing the shallow roots, dries, causing damage or death to the roots. Peat moss also tends to crust as it dries, making it difficult to wet once again without using great quantities of water.

74. Q. **What type of plants can you suggest for erosion control on a steep slope where the soil is mostly clay?**

     A. If the slope is in the sun, try crown vetch, Hall's honeysuckle, bittersweet, barberries, or creeping phlox. Until the individual plants grow together, mulch the slope with shredded pine bark or shredded hardwood bark to help stop the erosion. Shredded bark, with its stringy characteristic, tends to hold together even when under the pressure of heavy rainfall.

75. Q. **How can I remove leaves that accumulate in white stone mulch without making it look dirty?**

     A. Rent a leaf blower and blow them out. Raking leaves crumbles them into small bits which lodge between the stones and become very difficult to remove.

76. Q. **Can I use a mulch to delay flowering of mid-season tulips?**

     A. A mulch acts as an insulator of the soil. After the soil freezes, place a generous covering, five to six inches deep, of a mulch such as bark chips or nuggets over the planting bed. Do not remove the mulch until late spring. The ground under the mulch may still be frozen when the surrounding soil has already thawed. As the soil warms, the bulbs will emerge.

77. Q. **How can I stop weeds from emerging in a stone mulch bed without using chemical weed killers?**

     A. Use a weed barrier, such as black plastic or landscape fabric, underneath the stone mulch. The barrier mulch inhibits growth of seedlings. For aesthetic purposes, care should be taken to ensure a sufficient depth of decorative mulch to cover the barrier mulch.

78. Q. **Can I use a mulch on the soil of large house plants to create a more decorative effect?**

     A. Yes. Pine bark mini-nuggets or washed gravel can be very decorative when spread over the surface of the soil of house plants. The mulch also reduces evaporation of moisture and lessens erosion caused by watering.

79. Q. **How can I protect my plants from a late frost in spring? I like to get an early start on my garden.**

     A. Depending on the severity of the frost, a lightweight row cover over the crop, or hot caps for individual plants, may be all that is needed. Uncover the plants after the sun has begun to warm the air in the morning.

80. Q. **Is there a difference between an antidesiccant and an antitranspirant?**

A. An antidesiccant is used to provide protection from dehydrating wind and sun during winter, and an antitranspirant is used to reduce the loss of water from the aerial parts of the plant during the growing season. The materials used may be the same, but the dilution rate for application is different.

VIII

INTEGRATED
PEST
MANAGEMENT
(IPM)

COMBATING GARDEN and PLANT PESTS

Before the ink has dried in this, the 3rd Edition of Ralph Snodsmith's *Fundamentals of Gardening*, there will probably have been the elimination of certain pesticides, the addition of new formulas, and the introduction of new techniques for pesticides and their uses.

If you have ever listened to the "Garden Hotline®" radio program, you have heard me say many, many times, "read the label and follow the manufacturer's recommended rates and directions." I use this phrase every time I talk about gardening products, particularly pesticides, whether they are organic or inorganic. Whenever I discuss an insecticide, a miticide, a fungicide, or a herbicide, I always caution callers to "read the label." I do this because most gardeners don't take time to read the label. Over the past few years, many callers have admitted they had never read the entire label. But, when they finally do, the label's strongly worded statements give way to dismay and horror. I insist you read the label each and every time you use a pesticide, to be aware of the formula's make-up, and the potency of its ingredients. Many gardeners conclude they could care for their plant problems with a less toxic product.

When gardeners ask how much of a certain pesticide formula they need to control a specific pest, my answer always is, "Read the label." The label is the law! Don't ask someone else; read the label for yourself. I cannot make even a general recommendation for the use of a pesticide if I don't know what the formula is, or what you <u>think</u> it is. Because of the many variables, pesticide formulations are labeled for specific uses and must be used accordingly. A pesticide's use, beyond what the label indicates, is prohibited. While I cannot recommend a particular pesticide -- for that you must read the label -- I can try to help you understand what the label says. I will also discuss alternatives for controlling pests.

Procedures and tactics for controlling invasions of insects, disease plagues, marauding weeds, and four- and two-legged trespassers, have changed more dramatically in the past few years than has any other gardening practice. Many of the beetles, blights, and invaders are the same, but the controls are different.

A LITTLE HISTORY

Following World War II and the development of DDT as a "miracle" insecticide, the philosophy of complete elimination was adopted for combating pest problems. Most people in the agriculture industry and most home gardeners used the "chemical" approach. Billions of research and development dollars were spent by the chemical industry to experiment with the many present-day chemi-

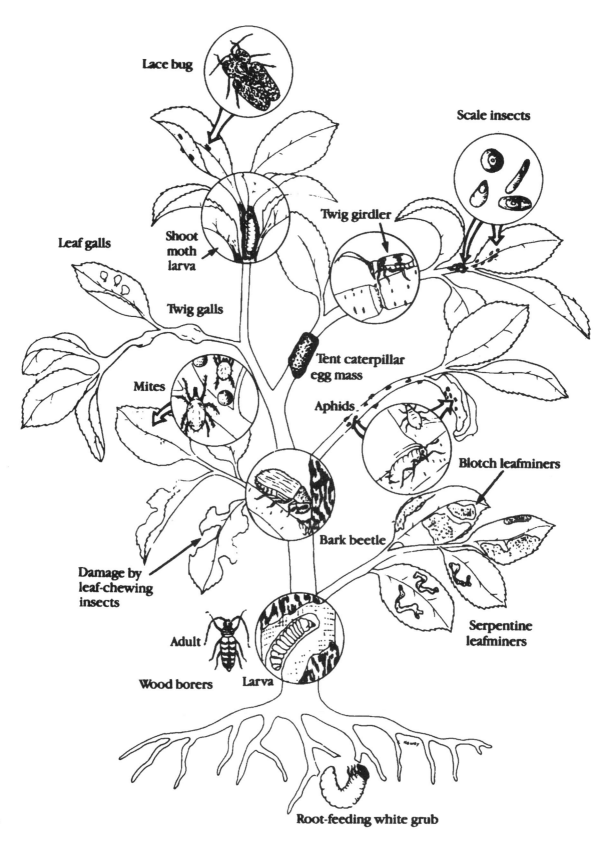

Lace bug

Scale insects

Twig girdler

Leaf galls

Shoot moth larva

Twig galls

Tent caterpillar egg mass

Mites

Aphids

Blotch leafminers

Bark beetle

Damage by leaf-chewing insects

Serpentine leafminers

Adult

Wood borers   Larva

Root-feeding white grub

Insects and Injury

cals which eradicate weeds, fumigate soil fungi, and kill flying insects. During that time, little research effort went to natural or biological controls. The intentions of the chemical approach were probably good, but the results, in some cases, spelled disaster. Some chemical pesticides did much more than control the intended pest; they also affected the biological balance of many other living organisms, including people, animals, and other microbes in the environment. Many long-term consequences were not realized until later. Today, after knowing some chemical pesticides caused harmful imbalances in the micro and macro biology of our environment, we have abandoned the philosophy of complete elimination, with one exception which will be discussed later in this chapter under Exotic Pests - Asian Longhorned Beetle ALB. It is not beneficial or to our advantage to attempt absolute control. Actually it is counterproductive to eliminate the pest entirely, for when a few pests of a particular species remain as a host, biological controls have a chance to develop.

Before undertaking the task of controlling pests in our gardens, we must understand what the problems are, and the reasons for trying to suppress them. If you understand the life cycle of a particular pest, controlling it may be unnecessary. Some pest problems disappear on their own and some never develop to a level that calls for containment. It is important to realize that one insect does not mean you have an invasion.

IDENTIFYING THE PEST

Identifying and diagnosing plant disorders can be as easy as observing a caterpillar eating holes in a rose leaf, or as difficult as trying to figure out why a plant is wilting when there are no visual clues. Don't feel discouraged if you can't identify the problem yourself. Any one of thousands of different pests could be the problem. For accurate analysis it might be best to consult a professional, such as the agricultural agent (or educator) at your Cooperative Extension office or the horticultural diagnostician at a local garden center. Your problem could be Eastern tent caterpillars chewing holes in the foliage of a flowering cherry tree, spider mites sucking the life out of tip growth of a fragrant gardenia, or slugs and snails devouring cabbage and lettuce leaves. You could have a scourge of fungi, viruses, or bacterial

blights infecting tomatoes, eggplants, and peppers. Crabgrass and dandelions are pests when they grow in a finely manicured Kentucky bluegrass lawn or when they invade a closely-clipped bentgrass putting green. Uninvited four-legged critters, like woodchucks who lunch on broccoli, Brussels sprouts, and cabbage, are also in the pest classification. Domestic four-legged friends, like the neighbor's cat or dog, are real pests when they dig up a tulip bed or use your garden as their litter box. By studying a plant and its potential enemies, you can take a much more intelligent approach to combating problems.

KEEPING GARDEN RECORDS

One of the most impossible gardening tasks, from year to year, is remembering how you have cared for a particular plant. When was it planted? When was it fed? When was it sprayed? And, with what? These are just a few of the questions you will need to answer before a plant problem can be diagnosed. If you have kept close tabs on garden activities you have eliminated the mind-boggling chore of having to remember. If you have just a few plants, making notes on a calendar may suffice, but if you have an entire landscape or plant collection to maintain, a notebook is in order. Organize your "garden diary" by the year.

GETTING THE FACTS

Questions to ask yourself and information to record should include:
General facts and questions about the plant and environment
a. What variety of plant is it? Is it a tree, shrub or ground cover in the landscape; a flower in the annual or perennial garden; turfgrass; an edible vegetable, herb or fruit; a window box of colorful annuals; a flowering or foliage house plant?
b. When was it planted?
c. What is the general growing environment?
d. Is the plant in the sun, shade, wind, etc.?
e. What are the moisture conditions of the soil? In other words, is the soil sandy, clay, or organic in content?
f. What is the pH of the soil?

Ways Insects Injure Plants

Chewing—devouring, notching, or mining leaves; eating wood, bark, roots, stems, fruit, seeds. *Symptoms:* ragged leaves, holes in wood and bark or fruit and seed, serpentine mines or blotches, wilted or dead plants, presence of "worms."

Sucking—removing sap and cell contents and injecting toxins into plant. *Symptoms:* usually off-color, misshapen foliage and fruit.

Vectors of diseases—carrying diseases from plant to plant, e.g., elm bark beetles are vectors of Dutch elm disease, various aphids are vectors of certain virus diseases. *Symptom:* wilt; dwarf, off-color foliage.

Excretions—honeydew deposits lead to the growth of sooty mold, and the leaves cannot perform their food-manufacturing functions. A weakened plant results. *Symptoms:* sooty black leaves, twigs, branches, and fruit.

Gall formation—galls may form on leaves, twigs, buds, and roots. They disfigure plants, and twig galls often cause serious injury.

Oviposition scars—scars formed on stems, twigs, bark, or fruit. *Symptoms:* scarring, splitting, breaking of stems and twigs, misshapen and sometimes infested fruit.

Injection of toxic substances—*Symptoms:* scorch, hopper burn.

Examples of insect injury to plants are shown on page 184.

Ways Infectious Diseases Injure Plants

Destroy or injure leaves —Examples: brown patch disease of turf, early blight, anthracnose. *Symptoms:* black, brown, red, or yellow spots on leaves; leaves that drop off earlier than normal.

Interfere or block water conduction inside stems —Examples: Dutch elm disease, Verticillium wilt. *Symptoms:* yellow, wilted, and/or brown leaves; brown, dark streaks inside the stem.

Destroy or injure roots —Examples: Pythium root rot, club root, root knot nematode. *Symptoms:* black or brown roots, galls on roots, stunting of the plant, yellow or brown leaves.

Destroy or injure flowers, fruit, or food products —Examples: fire blight, apple scab, potato scab. *Symptoms:* dead flowers, black or brown spots on flowers or produce.

Destroy or injure stems or shoots —Examples: Diplodia tip blight, Botrytis blight, Nectria canker. *Symptoms:* dead shoots or stems; cankered areas on branches; brown, shriveled, clinging leaves; brown inner bark.

Gall-forming diseases disrupt normal cellular organization —*Symptoms:* unusual growths on flowers, leaves, twigs, or roots.

Symptoms of injury to plants from infectious diseases are shown on following page.

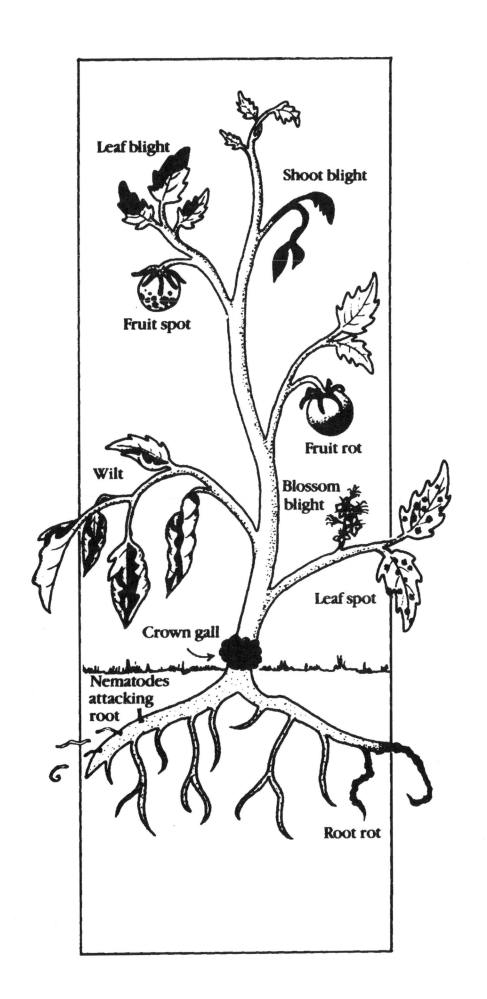

g. Has lime or sulfur been added? If so, when and how much?
h. Has a complete soil test for nutrient content been performed?
i. If the plant is growing in a container, what soil mix was used?

Questions and answers concerning maintenance practices
a. What have been the feeding practices and what fertilizer was used?
b. Were nutrients applied according to the label's directions? If so, how much and how often?
c. What have been the watering practices? Is the plant kept moist or is it allowed to dry between waterings?
d. Have pesticides been used? Always record the type of pesticide used against the targeted pest. Was an insecticide, fungicide, or possibly an herbicide, used? Information concerning application of the pesticides should include the Brand name, product name, manufacturer or formulator name and web-site including e-mail address, chemical name, date, time of day, air temperature, light conditions (sunny or cloudy), rainy or dry season, application rate, and frequency of use, and the company's 800 number given on the label for contact with the formulator or manufacturer in case a problem or question arises.
e. When was the problem first observed? This information will be useful next year if you choose to continue growing the same species and variety of plant, as it will be a clue as to when to start watching for a possible problem the following year.
You can see that the list of questions and answers could be endless, depending on your commitment to becoming an involved plant person. The most successful gardener still hasn't tapped all the potential knowledge about plant culture.

INTEGRATED PEST MANAGEMENT – IPM

As stated earlier, insects, diseases, and weeds haven't changed, but the controls have. During the late 1960's a new term emerged for controlling pests in the home and garden and in general agriculture too. That term is Integrated Pest Management (IPM). It is a complex approach employing many different procedures to keep pest problems to a minimum, acceptable level. Again, it is appropriate to remind everyone that "one insect does equal an invasion." If you see what you believe to be a problem, don't panic. First, identify the problem. Is it an invasion of weeds, an aphid or caterpillar infestation, or a pathogen like a fungus or bacteria? Is the problem related to general gardening practices like watering and/or feeding? IPM starts with a good dose of common sense. Any well-cared-for plant will be far less susceptible to insects and diseases, whether it is a potted croton on a sunny windowsill, or a broccoli plant in the vegetable patch.

New York State Department of Environmental Conservation established a definition for IPM as of January, 2000, as follows:

Integrated Pest Management (IPM) means a systemic approach to managing pests which focuses on long-term prevention or suppression with minimal impact on human health, the environment and nontarget organisms. IPM incorporates all reasonable measures to prevent pest problems by properly identifying pests, monitoring population dynamics, and utilizing cultural, physical, biological or chemical pest population control methods to reduce pests to acceptable levels.

Before discussing the important steps to an IPM program, let's review pesticides in general and find out what they are.

WHAT ARE PESTICIDES?

The word "pesticide" means "killer of pests." The word suffix "-icide," is derived from the Latin cida, to kill. Thus, "pest" plus "icide" is "pesticide."

According to Miscellaneous Bulletin 74, *1991-92 Guide to Pest Management around the Home*, published by Cornell Cooperative Extension, a pesticide is "any substance or mixture of substances intended to prevent, destroy, repel, or mitigate any insects, rodents, nematodes, fungi, or weeds, or other forms of life declared to be pests and any substances or mixture of substances intended for use as a plant regulator, defoliant, or desiccant." According to *Webster's New World Dictionary* a pesticide is "any chemical used for killing insects, weeds, etc." In its broadest sense, even water could be a pesticide if used to drown soil

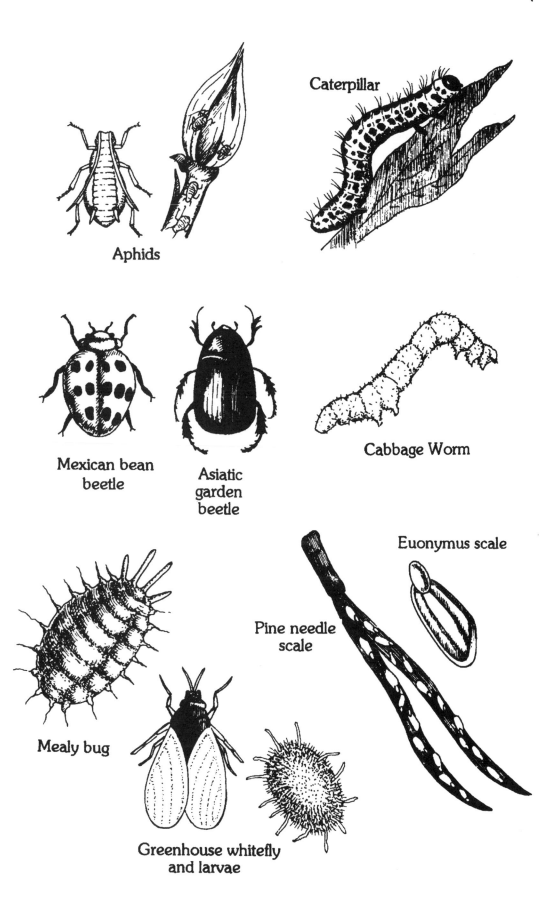

Caterpillar

Aphids

Mexican bean
beetle

Asiatic
garden
beetle

Cabbage Worm

Euonymus scale

Pine needle
scale

Mealy bug

Greenhouse whitefly
and larvae

insects, or even granules of table salt if sprinkled on slugs to cause desiccation.

Let me relate an experience I had as an agricultural extension agent attending pesticide legislation hearings. During the mid-60's beer became a recommended control for mollusks such as slugs and snails. At that time, laws governing pesticide labels would have required beer manufacturers to include a pesticide label on every bottle and can. I could just imagine the effect of a pesticide label on beer sales and consumption. What fun to pick up a can or bottle of beer and "read the label." Would you drink a beer that doubled as a molluscicide? To put it mildly, beer brewers strenuously objected and their protests were heard. No pesticide labeling was required for beer. You may find a Caution: Don't drink and drive.

PESTICIDE CLASSIFICATION

It is imperative to know what pesticide you are using, and whether its origin is chemical, organic, or biological. Read the label carefully before selecting a pesticide. There may be precautions related to potential allergic reactions. To legally and safely use a pesticide on edible crops, it must have passed tests and be registered for such use.

Many new pesticides carry the letters OMRI on the label. OMRI refers to Organic Materials Review Institute, a non-profit service established to provide verification that the products used by organic growers, including the active and non-active (inert) ingredients, comply with the National List established by the USDA's National Organic Program (NOP). Inert ingredients used in pesticides (ingredients other than pesticides) must be considered by the U.S. Environmental Protection Agency (EPA) to be inerts of minimal risk as found in EPA List 4A or 4B.

Following is a list of pesticide classifications and their use in gardening. The reference to the pesticide and pest problem is for example only, and not a recommendation. For specific uses, read and follow the recommended rates and directions on the label.

Bactericides Bactericides, such as streptomycin and terramycin, are used to protect crops from bacterial diseases, such as fire blight and bacterial spot.

Fungicides Fungicides are used to suppress fungi growth on the surface of plant tissue or within the plant cells. Fungicides such as Bordeaux and sulfur are inorganic compounds used to protect plants from such fungal infections as apple scab and downy mildew. Organic compounds, folpet and captan, are used as a protective fungicide and provide a very broad spectrum control of fungal diseases. Maneb, a carbamate compound, is used as a foliar fungicide to control and prevent such diseases as early and late tomato blight, grape black rot, and black spot on roses. Chlorothalonil, Daconil 2787, available as Ortho® Garden Disease Control is recommended for a wide spectrum of diseases affecting garden and landscape plants.

Methyl thiophanate, available as Topsin® M is a systemic fungicide, one that controls fungus diseases from within the plant tissue. It provides a very broad spectrum fungal control on many registered crops. Serenade® Garden, by AgraQuest, Inc., Davis, CA., an OMRI listed bio-fungicide prepared from microorganisms, QST 713 strain of Bacillus subtilis bacteria, is 100% certified organic for use in organic gardening and recommended for control and suppression of a long list of diseases including, but not limited to, powdery mildew, Downy mildew, anthracnose, botrytis, black spot, fire blight, rusts, leaf spots, and scab.

Biochemical A completely new classification or type of product to the agricultural industry is neither a fungicide nor fertilizer. It is harpin protein, produced as a harmless by-product of some plant disease organisms. Identified by Dr. Zhongmin Wei and colleagues at Cornell University during the early 1990's, Dr. Wei, now chief scientific officer with Eden Bioscience Corp. of Bothell, WA., developed the harpin product Messenger®. Messenger acts like an immune booster and stimulates even greater and more efficient use of nutrients in plant tissue. As indicated by the EPA Harpin Protein (006477) Fact Sheet issued 3/31/03 "Harpin does not act directly on the disease organism, nor does it alter the DNA of treated plants, but instead activates a natural defense mechanism in the host plant, referred to as systemic acquired resistance (SAR). This new active ingredient is currently the only broad-spectrum, proteinaceous elicitor of SAR commercially available. Harpin is effective against certain viral diseases for which there are no other controls or resistant plant varieties. It also protects against soil-borne pathogens and pests, such as certain nematodes and fungal diseases, which have few effective controls except for methyl bromide, which has adverse human health and environmental impacts. In addition to its ability to protect plants against diseases, Harpin protein also reduces infestations of selected insects and enhances plant growth, general vigor, and yield of many crops, including vegetables, traditional agronomic crops and ornamentals."

For two consecutive years in my garden, Messenger, applied as a foliar spray as recommended on the label at .12 oz of active Harpin protein at 3.0% /gal H20 at 21 day intervals starting with the emergence of new pink shoots (6-to 9-inches tall) of 30 varieties of Peonies, and continued through bloom in late May resulted in absolutely no symptoms of botrytis disease, blackened buds and mottled foliage with one exception. There was one blackened bud on one plant during the second year. In addition to no disease symptoms, the flowering mechanisms on all treated varieties were as much as 50% larger compared to those not treated. An equivalent experiment was conducted at three week intervals on Beefmaster VFN Hybrid, Tiny Tim, and Sweet 100 Hybrid Tomatoes. The first treatment with Messenger was applied at transplanting into the garden when the plants were 6- to 8-inches tall. All varieties were in flower within 2 weeks after the first application of the Harpin protein and set fruit within 3 weeks. Normally, my tomato crop shows a few yellow leaves on the lower parts of the plant by the end of June. We call that early blight. By late July, the yellowing has progressed half way up the plant. We call that midseason blight. By the end of the growing season, yellowing has progressed through out the plant. Late season blight. On the plants treated with Messenger, there were absolutely no yellowed leaves for the entire season. No tomato anthracnose on a single fruit. The fruits, with the exception of Tiny Tim, were almost one-half larger than normal for the variety. The foliage on all varieties was much greener in color and thicker and heavier than normal.

Herbicides Herbicides kill unwanted vegetation, selectively or non-selectively.
Pre-emergent □ Tupersan®, a very selective pre-emergent herbicide, is used to stop crabgrass seeds from germinating without affecting other desirable grass seeds. Treflan® chemical name trifluralin, also a pre-emergent control is non-selective in that it inhibits germination of most all seeds. An organic pre-emergent crabgrass control, Corn gluten meal was discovered by accident by Dr. Nick Christians, Professor of Horticulture at Iowa State University. Corn gluten meal works by letting the weed seed or any seed actually sprout, but inhibits root develop. The weed plant simply fades away. 50-60% of the crabgrass will disappear the first year. By the third year of use, weeds in the lawn that grow from seed (annuals) will not be a factor. Precaution: Do not use corn gluten meal on turf that has not been established for at least 60 days. For research articles on line, go to www.gluten.iastate.edu Renaissance® 10-0-0 is 100%corn gluten meal. As the formula indicates, the breakdown of the 10% nitrogen supplied by the corn gluten meal provides nitrogen nutrition for established plants, consequentially it is a weed and feed.

Post-emergent Selective broadleaved control, Trimec®, a combination of 2,4-D, MCPP, and dicamba, available under several trade names, kills only broadleaved weeds like clover, chickweed, and dandelions. The synergistic effect of the combination of the three chemicals allows for a far less concentration of the chemicals as compared to their use individually. This formula is used on bluegrass, rye and fescue lawns without damage to turfgrass. 2,4-D, MCPP, and dicamba are available as individual chemical ingredients for broadleaved weed control under several brand names. Non-selective post-emergent weed killers include: herbicidal fatty acids Concern® Fast-Acting Weed Killer and Safer® Brand Moss & Algae Killer® that kill contacted vegetation by desiccation, with no residual effect; 25% citric acid -- Burnout® by St. Gabriel Labs and Nature's Glory Weed & Grass Killer® by Monterey Lawn and Garden Products, Inc.; glyphosate, a post-emergent, translocated herbicide Roundup® and glyphosinate ammonia Finale®, with no residual effect; and prometone Pramitol 25E®, a pre- and post-emergent, long-residual control for use in noncrop areas.

Insecticides Insecticides are used to protect plants from damage by insects, such as aphids, caterpillars, and beetles. Insecticides may be biorational; that is, they may cause a disease in the target insect population. Examples: *Bacillus popilliae* (milky spore disease) bacterium sold as Milky Spore by St. Gabriel

Labs, infects Japanese beetle grubs in the soil. *Bacillus thuringiensis* (var. kurstaki (Bt)) sold under the label of DiPel® and Safer® Brand Caterpillar Killer causes disease bacterium in the eastern tent caterpillar and the cabbage-worm. Chitin protein stimulates soil organisms to produce enzymes that destroy pest nematodes. One of the latest introductions but one dating back Centuries in use to the biorational insecticide group is azadirachtin, the active ingredient found in oil extracted from seeds produced by *Azadirachtin indicia*, the neem tree of India. Neem oil has three modes of action: (1) It acts to regulate growth by reducing the levels of juvenile hormones, when ingested by immature insects, and disrupts the molting cycle, thus causing death. (2) Sprayed on foliage, it works as a repellent, causing the insect to avoid the plant. (3) It works as an anti-feedant, which stops the insect from feeding on the treated plant.

Another insecticide which has gained in popularity, partially because of its non-toxic rating to humans, pets, and many beneficial insects, is the potassium salt of fatty acid, called insecticidal soap, available under several Brand names. It is an organic compound recommended for control of adelgids, aphids, mealy bugs, mites, whiteflies, soft scale, and any other insect pests listed on the label. Some plants have a sensitivity (phytotoxicity) to insecticidal soap, so it one must be careful if using it on plants not listed on the label. Insecticidal soap has no residual effect. For it to provide control, it must contact the target insect at the time of spraying.

Hot pepper wax spray, another recent introduction has become extremely popular. The product—Hot Pepper Wax®—blends hot cayenne pepper juice with a highly refined, food-grade wax, to make an effective, convenient garden-greenhouse spray. Hot Pepper Wax's special, patented encapsulation process keeps the ingredients consistent and ready to use, without a lot of mess, stirring or mixing. It comes ready-to-use in a convenient pump-spray bottle, or in economical concentrate form that mixes with water.

In studies conducted by the University of California and others, Hot Pepper Wax was proven effective on a wide range of common garden pests including aphids, whiteflies, mites, thrips, mealybugs, codling moths, leaf-hoppers, scale, lace bugs and army worms. It's nontoxic to humans and pets, and it causes no phytotoxic damage to plants or buds.

The active ingredient—capsaicin, which gives hot peppers their heat—attacks the bug's nervous system and metabolism, while the wax slows and smothers them like a summer oil. The few insects that remain after the treatment are disoriented and deprived of their food source by the Hot Pepper Wax coating.

Hot Pepper Wax is most active and effective in the first week after application. However, tests have shown that the repellent activity continues for up to thirty days, depending mostly upon weather conditions. The wax will not wash off with rainfall after twenty-four hours, but may be less enduring in very warm weather. So, depending upon the hot summer days, follow-up treatment every two or three weeks might be most effective.

Effectiveness has been demonstrated on a wide variety of plants ranging from the delicate orchid to fruit trees, citrus, vegetables, roses and ornamentals. Indoors and out, Hot Pepper Wax has proven its repellent value to horticultural professionals and home gardeners. At last, a responsible approach to insect control! And in addition to its value as a repellent, Hot Pepper Wax acts as an antitranspirant. The wax component in Hot Pepper Wax® spray is now available as Moisture Guard® which leaves a very thin wax coating that protects and enhances the appearance of the plant, prevents the rapid loss of moisture and can be especially valuable in times of drought. The transparent film also provides a protective shield against many airborne diseases.

Horticultural oils are highly refined petroleum oil substances e.g., Sunspray®, Scaleicide®, Volck® used as insecticides because of their suffocating action. They have long been used to control over-wintering insects and egg masses during the dormant season. Today's horticultural oils are "superior" oils, so improved that they are now recommended as summer oils such as Bonide® All Seasons Horticultural & Dormant Spray Oil, if environmental conditions are right, for use on insects and mites infesting plants in full leaf. However, foliage may be damaged if the plant system is feeling water stress.

A recent addition to the oil family is Organocide®, an organic, insecticide/fungicide by Organic Laboratories, Stuart, FL, a formula containing Sesame oil as the active ingredient recommended as an insecticide for the control or suppression of eggs, nymphs, adults of scale insects and small soft-bodied insects such as mites, aphids, whitefly, fungus gnats and others, and, as a fungicide, to suppress or control black spot on roses, powdery mildew, helminthesporium and greasy spot on citrus. Organocide also acts as a repellent and a physical trap with its sticky, micro-film residue. This film, undetectable to humans, is repellent to egg-laying females for about 2 weeks.

The chemical makeup of an insecticide can be natural or synthetic in origin. Just because the active ingredient in a pesticide is derived from a plant does not mean it is non-toxic. Insecticides produced from nicotine extracted from the tobacco plant are more toxic than many of the synthetically produced pesticides. Pyrethrin and rotenone are two more naturally occurring botanical chemicals from tissues of specific living plants. Pyrethrin comes from the pyrethrum plant, *Chrysanthemum cinerariaefolium*, and has contact, stomach-poison, and fumigating killing action. If you, or a member of your family, tend toward allergic reactions, use caution before selecting pesticides containing pyrethrin. Rotenone, produced in the roots of two specific genera of legumes, *Derris* and *Lonchocarpus*, though harmless to plants is highly toxic to fish, and especially effective as a pesticide against caterpillars. A waiting period between time of application and time of harvest of a food crop is not required. Resmethrin is a synthetic-pyrethroid used as a selective, contact insecticide.

Some synthetically produced chemical insecticides familiar to the gardener include carbaryl, malathion, and RESTRICTED-USE PESTICIDEs such as imidacloprid and chlorpyrifos to name a few.

Carbaryl, best known under the trade name of Sevin®, is a carbamate insecticide with contact and stomach-poison action. Malathion is an organic-phosphate insecticide-acaricide with both contact and stomach killing action. Imidacloprid, best known under the trade name Merit™, is a systemic insecticide used in the Asian longhorned beetle eradication program, chemically related to the tobacco toxin, nicotine. Chlorpyrifos insecticide is an organic phosphate insecticide acting primarily as a contact and stomach-poison.

Chemical insecticides often act on a very wide spectrum of insect species. In many cases they can be just as harmful to beneficial insects as to those you want to control and may have residual effects. An insecticide with residual characteristics means that it continues to work for a period of time after being applied. So, once again, read the label and follow the manufacturer's recommended rates and directions.

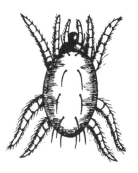

Red Spider Mite

Miticides Miticides or acaricides are used to protect humans, plants, and animals from microscopic spider-like animals called mites. Mites are not true insects since they belong to the animal class *Arachnida*, which includes spiders, scorpions, and ticks. They have four pairs of legs instead of the three required to fit the insect classification. Their piercing-sucking mouthparts extract sap from plant cells, leaving a stippled look to plant tissue. Miticides include hot pepper wax, horticultural oils, both dormant and all season, sulfur compounds, insecticidal soaps, Organocide® sesame oil, pyrethrin, and chemical compounds such as permethrin and malathion. The recent introduction of several species of predatory mites has made possible biological control of two-spotted spider mites. This mite leaves its telltale webbing on many home and office plants such as gardenias, scheffleras, Ficus benjamina, and citrus. Certain species of predatory mites are also effective against thrips, which attack cucumbers and peppers when they are grown as greenhouse crops.

Molluscicides Molluscicides are substances used to kill the many species of snails and slugs, another non-insect group of pests. A slug is merely a snail without a shell, or with a much smaller, internal shell. Biological predators control these pests, so look with a

Snail   Slug

kind eye on frogs, reptiles, ducks, and many other species of birds. Diatomaceous earth – a fossilized silica shell remains of diatoms – and wood ashes, if dry, act as barriers to the slug or snail. Both products, upon contact, cause desiccation of the pest. C-M PowderGard®, an organic, OMRI-listed and EPA-Exempt insecticide is made from a rare form of limestone with microscopic sharp edges which destroys the outer layer and scars the exoskeleton causing the insect to dehydrate. Chemical controls for slugs and snails include the carbamates, carbaryl and methiocarb. They are available in ready-to-use formulations for garden use. And, as we stated earlier in the introduction of this chapter, beer, although not labeled as such, is a recommended molluscicide.

The recent introduction of a new technology for slug control is the application of a formula of iron phosphate, sold under the trade name Sluggo®, by Monterey Lawn and Garden, Fresno, CA. A by-product of Sluggo is its end product of nutrition, iron and phosphorus. The bait that is not consumed by the slugs and snails will degrade and become part of the soil.

Nematicides Nematicides are used to combat plant-parasitic nematodes (microscopic worms known as root-knot nematodes), which are usually associated with the roots of the plant. Nematodes work in secret because their damage is below ground. Wilting in the plant's upper parts might be the first symptom, but by then it is too late for control. To date, soil fumigants are the most effective controls against nematodes. Fumigants are not, however, recommended to the home gardener because they are very expensive and must usually be applied by a certified applicator. Controls that are recommended for the garden are removing all infested plants and crop rotation. Research is currently underway, testing the potential biological controls, neem and *Bacillus penetrans* as nematicides.

Rodenticides Rodenticides are used both indoors and outdoors to kill rats, mice, and other rodent pests. For home and garden use, bait formulations are the safest chemical controls. Many rodent species have become immune to pesticides and require the development of ever-new formulations of Rodenticides. RESTRICTED-USE rodenticides must be handled only by those with proper accreditation, that is, licensed, certified pest-control professionals.

Other classified pesticides
Other substances falling into the broad classification of pesticides are disinfectants, growth regulators, defoliants, desiccants, repellents, attractants, pheromones, and chemosterilants (some of which have become quite popular in IPM, with good reason).

Growth regulators disrupt the life cycle by inhibiting the insects ability to change (molt or pupate) from one stage to another. For example: An insect treated with a growth regulator cannot grow up and complete the life cycle by laying eggs or having live born. Examples of growth regulators include diflubenzuron (Dimilin) used to inhibit the Gypsy moth caterpillar instar (growth stages) and the slow-acting hexaflumuron (Recruit*), Sentricon® Termite Colony Elimination System.

KNOW YOUR WEAPON

"I sprayed the plant with a *chemical*," says a caller, "but the problem didn't go away." When I ask what chemical, the caller doesn't know.

"I sprayed my roses with malathion and the black spot and mildew disease didn't stop," says another caller. Clearly, this gardener did not read the label! A fungicide, not an insecticide such as Malathion, suppresses black spot & mildew disease.

These questions reveal how important it is to *know what pesticide is being used*. In these two cases, the problem pest or disease became a secondary problem when the wrong chemical was used against it. That is, the callers used the wrong product.

UNDERSTANDING THE LABEL

Let me stress once again -- "Read the label!" You must follow the manufacturer's recommended rates and directions.

The label on a pesticide container can be very intimidating and frightening, what with all of big chemical names and "signal words" stating its toxicity to humans. You may be advised to wear protective clothing such as gloves, mask, and a respirator. The label may appear to be a jumbled mess of technical words and statements but it gives you information essential to succeeding with the product.

Before a pesticide can be sold, the Environmental Protection Agency (EPA) must have approved the uses listed on the label, by crop and by pest. The list of uses must be registered with the EPA. An EPA registration number does not imply or guarantee a particular pesticide is safe. It means only that the statements on the label have been reviewed and registered for these particular uses.

Specific information on the label, not safety, is required by law. Users are prohibited from using the product in any other way than what is indicated; the pesticide's use must be consistent with the labeling. So, read the label; it is the law. And, before purchasing or using a pesticide in your area, insure that product is registered for use in *your* state and/or your community. Local and State regulations vary from community to community and state to state. As pesticide registration must be renewed every two years, it is the responsibility of the applicator to check the registration status of each pesticide they use.

Parts of the Label

1. Brand, product or trade name of the pesticide.
2. Type of pesticide -- example: Fungicide, Insecticide, Herbicide, etc., and general use or purpose.
3. Classification (if applicable) -- If it is a restricted-use pesticide, the top of the front label panel must state: "RESTRICTED-USE PESTICIDE. For sale and use only by certified applicators or persons under their direct supervision and only for those uses covered by the certified applicator's certification."
4. Ingredients:
   a. The official chemical names and/or common names of active ingredients, and their percentage.
   b. Inert ingredients need not be named but must identify the percentage they comprise.
5. Hazard statement, including signal words: "CAUTION"; "WARNING"; or "DANGER-POISON!" "DANGER-POISON!" is always accompanied by the skull and crossbones. "KEEP OUT OF THE REACH OF CHILDREN" must appear on every label.
6. Statement of practical treatment (may be included in the precautionary statement)

   a. If swallowed
   b. If inhaled
   c. If on skin
   d. If in eyes
   e. Note to physicians
7. Precautionary statements
   a. Hazards to humans, domestic animals and wildlife.
   b. Environmental hazards.
   c. Physical or chemical hazards.
   d. Protective wear required.
8. Environmental Protection Agency registration and establishment number.
9. Name and address of manufacturer or formulator.
10. Amount contained in the package.
11. General information and directions for use.
    "It is a violation of Federal law to use this product in a manner inconsistent with its labeling."
    a. crops - if for an edible crop, the pesticide must be registered for that specific crop.
    b. pest.
    c. days to harvest (if applicable) - listing of the number of days from the last application to the day of harvest.
12. Storage and disposal.
13. Statement of liability.

PARTS OF AN IPM PROGRAM

An IPM program may call for the use of resistant varieties, sanitation, mechanical controls, soil sterilization, natural enemies, insect repellents, biological and organic pesticides, and, as a last resort, chemical pesticides.

Resistant varieties A look at any catalog confirms the existence of many garden seeds and plants which are pest-resistant varieties. The description, depending on species, may include not only a full representation of flowers, vegetables, trees, and shrubs, but also words like "resistant to." A particular seed or plant may be resistant to: Downy mildew, powdery mildew, tobacco mosaic (T), nematodes (N), verticillium wilt (V), fusarium wilt (F), black spot, cucumber mosaic, etc. Even for vegetables grown in containers on the deck, patio, or backyard, diseases can spell disaster. If your tomato plants have ever been infected with verticillium (V) or fusarium (F) wilts, you know them to be recurring problems, often related to gardening in the same location year after year. As a defense, change to varieties which are V/F-resistant. This does not mean that V/F-resistant plants will be immune to the problem. Pest-resistant varieties do promise, at the least, a better chance of success.

Turfgrass has historically been plagued with the diseases of brown patch, dollar spot, leaf spot, etc. In answer, a multitude of disease-resistant varieties of bentgrass, Bermuda grass, bluegrass, ryegrass and fescue, have been developed. Insect-resistant varieties mark the most recent advancement in turfgrass management. Certain varieties of perennial ryegrass have shown resistance to above-ground insect damage from chinch bugs, billbugs, cutworms, sod webworms, and others. A naturally-occurring fungus called an endophyte, within the plant cells, affords this resistance. Certain varieties of perennial ryegrass and Kentucky-31 (a variety of tall fescue) contain naturally-occurring endophytes. Not all varieties of grass contain this beneficial fungi but many can be inoculated with the repellent. These grasses are then referred to as "endophyte enhanced" varieties. Many varieties of perennial ryegrass, Chewings fescue, and fine-leaf fescue are endophyte-enhanced with natural insect resistance. It must be noted that root-feeding insects, such as white grubs, are not repelled or controlled by the endophyte or endophyte-enhanced varieties.

Sanitation The old saying that "cleanliness is next to Godliness" is most assuredly true when it comes to growing plants and keeping them healthy and productive. Sanitation is a very important front-line defense in the IPM program. Keep your plants and garden clean. For houseplants, such as gardenias, dwarf citrus, croton, and zebra plants which are infested with spider mites, use running water to rinse both the top and bottom of the foliage and wash away mites. Out in the garden, a hose with an adjustable spray nozzle can remove rose chafers from rose blossoms. A gentle stream of water will dislodge critters from flowers and flush them to the ground.

Another sanitation practice is to remove debris that could become hiding places for insects. Slugs and snails love to hide under empty seed flats or any containers left lying around in the garden. Weeds can be a breeding ground for pests too. Whitefly often rests in tall weeds during the day and returns to desired crops during the evening and overnight. The solution is to get rid of the weeds. Pull them out and dispose of them before they go to seed.

Disinfectants are used to sanitize containers, tools, growing benches, and potting tables infested by insect-type pests or infected with fungi and bacteria. Common household bleach diluted with water (check with your Cooperative Extension educator or Master Gardener for dilution rates and cautions) will eliminate many problems while the problems are still small. Clean everything thoroughly. Even a minute number of insects or a few spores of a disease can reinfect a growing area.

Mechanical controls Traps, music, reflectors, inflated plastic owls, barriers, and even electric fencing are all mechanical controls. Some work and some do not. You might find aluminum pie-tin reflectors flapping in the breeze next to staked tomatoes and pole beans to scare crows away from ripening fruits. Right before harvest time, a radio tuned to a loud conversation might drive raccoons away from a corn patch. (Supposedly raccoons do not like confused noise.) The scarecrow – attached to a garden hose and sprinkler □ deters visitors such as deer, rabbits, dogs, cats, and two-legged pests with a motion detector.

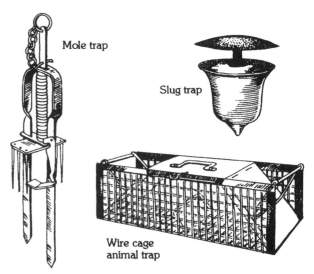

Mole trap

Slug trap

Wire cage animal trap

When disturbed, the sprinkler is set in motion and showers the invaders. Traps, including the live-bait type, are used to relocate wildlife that invade the garden. I have used these traps against woodchucks that do damage to my broccoli, Brussels sprouts and cabbage. Always check with the local animal control au-

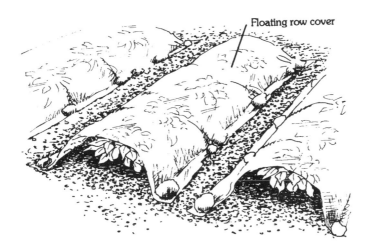
Floating row cover

thorities before using such a trap. Local laws may specify their use and forbid transporting wildlife by anyone other than certified, wildlife handler. Trap size is a significant considera- tion. If trapping skunks is the goal, use the small live-bait trap with an opening and cage of no more than six inches. The larger trap, twelve inches by twelve inches, is usually for raccoon and woodchuck.

Many flying insects, such as fruit flies, fun- gus gnats, and whiteflies, can be caught with yellow sticky traps, available as Seabright Yel- low Aphid/Whitefly Trap®. If the traps are in place early enough in an insect invasion, their use may be enough to quell the problem with- out further controls. The traps are pieces of brightly colored, yellow plastic coated with a sticky residue. Lured to the traps by the bright yellow color, flying insects entangled themselves in the sticky coating. Such traps can be purchased commercially or can be homemade. I have constructed traps for the garden using the bright yellow plastic lids from a certain brand of ground coffee by coat- ing the lids with petroleum jelly. When many insects have been trapped, I wipe them off and reapply another coating of petroleum jelly.

Lure traps have been criticized by many gardeners because they work so well. They attract target insects from other areas to the trapping area. Sometimes lures are used to monitor pest populations in fruit production regions. Lure traps for the Japanese beetle have a pheromone (sex) and floral scent to at- tract both the male and female adult beetles. The idea of the traps is to get "mom" and "pop" before they have a chance to reproduce. Basi- cally, it is birth control for insects. Read the directions very carefully before installing lure

traps because success depends largely on their location and time of installation. Set out Japanese beetle traps at least two weeks be- fore adults normally emerge. I suggest placing traps at the outer edge of the vegetable patch to draw adult beetles out of the garden. By the time you see adult beetles in the garden, it may be too late for traps to do any good.

One mechanical method to scare away dis- couraging invasions of our "feathered" friends is to display an inflatable owl. Just before the crop ripens, put the owl in a visible spot on the branch of a peach, apple, or pear tree. Blackbirds and crows do stay away.

Floating row covers made of spunbonded polypropylene were first intended to extend the growing season by protecting seedlings from frost in both spring and fall. They have also proven themselves beneficial as a barrier to insect damage. The light-weight covers, loosely placed over a newly seeded crop of car- rots or transplants of cabbage and trenched in around the crop so that invaders are barred from the plants, provide excellent control of the carrot rust fly, the cabbage maggot, and the cabbage looper. The cucumber family, in- cluding squash, pumpkins, melons, and cu- cumbers, can be protected from the adult egg- laying moth of the squash vine borer by laying a row cover over the plants after spring plant- ing. Keep them covered until the plants begin to flower. Once flowering starts, the cover must be removed to allow pollination. Bees and other pollinators must have access to flowers to gather pollen from the anthers of the male blossoms and carry it to the stigma of the female flowers.

Cutworms are nocturnal caterpillars that attack many seedlings and new transplants in

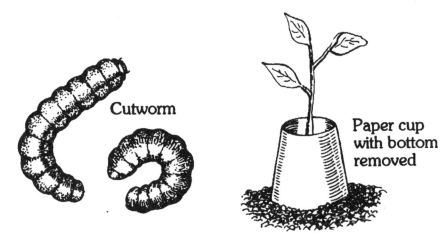

Cutworm

Paper cup with bottom removed

Cutworm Collar

Barrier Fencing

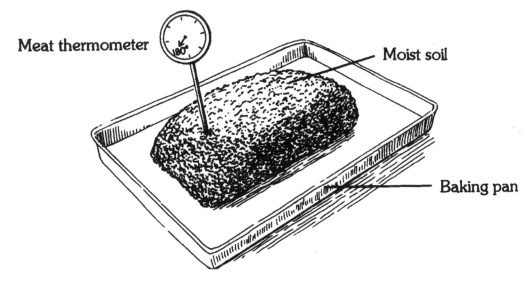

Meat thermometer

Moist soil

Baking pan

the flower and vegetable garden. It might look like someone clipped or sawed off the plant right at ground level; the upper part of the plant may be completely detached from its root system. Cutworms are voracious larvae of several inconspicuous moths. They live in the soil and can be controlled by constructing a barrier, called a "cutworm collar," from cardboard-type paper cups. Remove the bottom from each paper cup to create a cylinder and slip it over the transplant at least one inch into the soil. The cutworm can't crawl over or under the cup. If you know cutworms are a problem in your garden, install cutworm collars on the very day you plant seedlings. A few years ago I planted broccoli and cabbage seedlings late one afternoon. By the very next morning, *all* of my new, tender transplants were cut off at ground level.

Fencing often is not a practical control or barrier deterrent. I installed a four-foot high, split rail fence to keep deer out of my vegetable garden but, of course, they jumped over it. I dug a trench six inches deep around the bottom of the split rail barrier, and put a chicken-wire fence into the ground to discourage woodchucks and rabbits, but they dug under it. The fence has helped to a limited extent but, when I consider its cost, the per-pound price of my vegetables is very expensive.

One mechanical "trick," recommended to me by a gardening friend to stop woodchucks from eating my broccoli, was a six-foot-long, inflatable snake. I was instructed to place the inflated plastic snake between the plant rows. When the woodchucks saw it they supposedly would be frightened away. About three days later, I only wish my camera had been loaded with film. I would have taken a prize-winning photo, I'm sure. Out there in the vegetable patch was Mr. Woodchuck, standing on the snake, devouring my broccoli! The snake, as a mechanical deterrent, does *not* work in *my* garden.

Soil sterilization The container gardener or propagator has no worry about sterilized soil if he uses one of the many soilless mixes or pre-sterilized soils on the market today. Sterile growing and propagating mixes eliminate weed seeds, soil insects, and most pathogens. Store any opened bag of prepared mix sterile in a dry environment protected from outside elements. I use garbage cans with tightly fitting lids.

Homemade houseplant soil can be sterilized by baking it in the oven. On a cookie sheet, make a large "meat loaf" of slightly moist soil.

Insert a meat thermometer. Keep the oven temperature at 225° degrees until the meat thermometer reaches 180° degrees. Then reduce the oven control to 180 degrees for thirty minutes. When the soil has "cooked" for thirty minutes, remove it and let the soil cool. Be forewarned, though. One possible and unpleasant outcome of the cooking process is a rather foul smell from ammonia being released from the soil. Don't worry, just open the window and let in fresh air.

To sterilize garden soil which may harbor a weed problem, plant a cover crop of buckwheat (2 to 3 lbs. of seed per 1000 sq. ft.) as soon as the soil begins to warm in the spring. Let it grow until mid-summer, and then till it under. Immediately replant another buckwheat crop at the same rate. This type of cover crop will inhibit annual weeds and crowd out even the most stubborn perennial weeds, such as quack grass. Buckwheat grows so thickly that light cannot penetrate to the soil.

In commercial agriculture, soil sterilants are used to eliminate weed seeds, soil nematodes, grub populations, and soil fungi. Most soil sterilants are "RESTRICTED-USE PESTICIDES", and must be handled by appropriately certified personnel.

Natural enemies A major component of IPM is reliance on the natural enemies of pests. These enemies could be parasites, predators, or even something as subtle as a change in weather. A parasitoid is one insect that parasitizes another insect. Examples: The braconid wasp whose larvae feed on the tomato hornworm, the tiny *Trichogramma* wasps that parasitize egg masses of the Gypsy Moth, and the parasitic nematodes that attack termites in moist soil. Grubs in the lawn and garden, including those which attack the roots of Rhododendrons, azaleas, holly, etc., can be controlled with an application of predator nematodes *Steinernema* and *Heterohabditis*. These are two of the best beneficials which are effective in controlling grubs, fleas, cutworms, fungus gnats, thrips, bagworms, leaf minors and over 200 other pests. It is imperative that you follow the manufacturer's directions when using the predator nematodes. They must be fresh, live nematodes, and applied after the soil temperature reaches above 55° F and be inundated into the soil with water.

Other parasites include *Aphytis melinius* for Armored scale, *Metaphycus helvolus* for soft scale, *Lindoris lophantae* for black, brown, California red, cottony cushion, cottony maple, purple, hemispherical, white peach, white prunicola scale. Thrip and spider mite predator, *Amblyseus cucumeris,* provides good to excellent prevention and protection when released in a timely fashion on infested plants like peppers and gardenia. Whitefly parasites *Eretmocerus californicus* are scattered throughout affected areas as soon as infestations are noticed.

Predators are animals that attack and feed on other animals. Lady beetles are probably the most famous of all garden predators. They, depending on their many species, can eat hundreds of insects in a lifetime, including spider mites, mealybugs, aphids, and scales. *Pseudoscymnus tsugae*, a non-described ladybird beetle, described and named in 1992 by Drs. Mark S. McClure and Hiroyuki Sasaji after Dr. McClure collected samples from adelgid-infested hemlocks throughout Honshu, Japan is now being cultivated as a biological predator of the hemlock woolly adelgid Adelges tsugae (Annand). Each beetle larva consumes about 500 adelgid eggs or from 50 to 100 adelgid nymphs during its development. Adults, living for up to a year or more, may consume about 50 adelgid nymphs each week during times of peak feeding activity. Since 1995 more than 100,000 adult beetles have been raised and released in infested forests of New Jersey, Connecticut, and Virginia to evaluate the potential of control.

The praying mantis, *Tenodera sinensis*, another predator found in many gardens, consumes both the good guys and bad guys, unlike lady beetles which are more specific in that they target mostly mealybugs, aphids or scale insects. One egg case of the praying mantis hatches forty to one hundred mantises.

Birds are probably the most beneficial and pleasing predators, since they provide color and song as they consume insect eggs, beetles, and grubs. A wren can snatch up hundreds of insects in just one afternoon. The Baltimore oriole dines on tent caterpillars, and the cheery chickadee eats aphid eggs all winter.

Weather changes can be a very effective natural control for pest problems. In my growing area, it is not unusual to have an early hatch of springtime caterpillars if a prolonged period of warm weather arrives prematurely. Early one spring, arborists and pesticide applicators prepared to battle Gypsy Moth caterpillars because the egg mass counts reported by the State Department of Forestry were astronomically high. There were thousands of egg masses per acre and each cluster contained as many as a thousand eggs. When this huge population of caterpillars emerged, deciduous trees and shrubs in the infested areas would be stripped of foliage. Trees and shrubs, because of insufficient time to manufacture food, are weakened. Excessive growth of underbrush also creates a fire hazard. A Gypsy Moth caterpillar eats for up to ten weeks before it pupates into the adult moth. Thus, foliage would be missing for at least one-half of the growing season. That spring we were in all-out alert for the Gypsy Moth invasion. During March, temperatures rose to the high 80's for two consecutive weeks and the overwintering egg masses hatched. However, immediately following this unusual warm spell, came bitter cold temperatures, as low as 10° F. The newly hatched caterpillars froze to death and no sprays were needed. In fact, many other springtime caterpillars, such as inch worms and canker worms, were also eliminated as a pest problem that year. No spray program could have been more effective.

Weather changes – from cloudy, humid, and rainy to sunny, drier and breezy conditions – can reduce or stop fungus infections. Water droplets on the leaf surface and high humidity in the air around the leaf present an excellent medium for incubation of fungal diseases. Fungus spores of powdery mildew germinate under conditions of low light and/or darkness if moisture is present. This is one reason we do not recommend wetting foliage (*especially* for rose varieties susceptible to powdery mildew) in the late afternoon or evening.

Repellents Repellents work because of their taste and/or odor. Some are affective – and some are not. Four-legged pests, such as raccoons, squirrels, woodchucks, and deer, have become so numerous in some areas that they literally over-run many gardens and landscapes. Humans are building homes and shopping malls on land that once provided food and shelter for these animals and where, now, few or none of the natural controls are present, such as predatory animals, disease, famine, etc. Controls for our four-legged "friends" now depend largely on repellents and/or barriers.

I have found it pays to alternate repellents, particularly if they are based on *one* primary ingredient; do not use the same product for more than a few months at a time. If deer adapt to a specific repellent halfway through a season, that repellant no longer serves its purpose.

Deer Off® Deer, Rabbit and Squirrel Repellent, manufactured by Woodstream, Lititz, PA, a liquid formulated to work by taste and smell, applied as a spray to the foliage of plants on a two to three month schedule under normal deer pressure, incorporates several ingredients as repellents including putrescent whole egg solids, capsaicin and related compounds, and garlic. Sprays prepared from *Capsicum* (hot peppers) repel through their taste. The "hot" pepper sauce, in contact with taste buds on the pest's tongue, drives the pest somewhere else to eat. Deer Off is cleared for use against deer, rabbits, and squirrels attacking edible crops, flowers, grasses, bulbs, seedlings, trees and shrubs.

Another liquid repellent, *Shot-Gun® Repels-All® Animal Repellent,* by Bonide® Products, Inc. Oriskany, NY, lasting up to 60 days, includes armadillos, beavers, birds, cats, crows, chipmunks, deer, groundhogs, mice, porcupines, rabbits, raccoons, rats, skunks, shrews, and voles on its list of pests deterred. Ingredients include dried blood, putrescent whole egg solids, garlic oil, acetic acid, potassium salt, cloves, fish oil, onions, meat meal, seaweed, vanilla, vitamin E, wintergreen oil and water. When an animal touches, tastes, or smells Repels-All®, it triggers the natural instinct to escape, avoid and/or leave the area.

Dried blood – a by-product of the slaughter houses and available from garden supply stores – when scattered on the soil around tulips and other spring flowering bulbs has been recommended for repelling squirrels, rabbits, and chipmunks. Repellents for these small garden pests usually work through odor.

Milorganite®, a specific turf fertilizer manufactured in Milwaukee, Wisconsin, is processed sewage sludge has an additional benefit, other than plant nutrition. I have experienced that if applied at the turf fertilizer rate, just as the bulb foliage emerges from the soil and reapplied at six week intervals through bloom, Milorganite repels browsing deer. When the deer bend their necks to browse the tulip foliage, they get the fragrance of the sludge and back away.

Deer Scram™ Americas Finest Deer and Rabbit Repellent™, Enviro Protection Industries Company Inc., Binghamton, NY is more than just an offensive scent or unpleasant taste to foraging deer and rabbits. Blended from selected organic components, Deer Scram's round-the-clock, 100 percent guaranteed protection is based on a non-toxic, proprietary, granular formula that has no foul odor to humans but through the deer's uncanny sense of smell, it convinces deer that trouble is nearby. Deer Scram's principal active ingredients take advantage of two internal defense mechanisms, both genetic and biological: 1) the fear and flight reactions that deer and rabbits employ to avoid predators; and 2) the fear of disease from dead kin. This granular product, applied in a strip 16 to 18-inches wide at the perimeter of the area or plants to be protected according to the label directions, provides the barrier of fear for 30 to 45 days.

Another barrier deterrent to deer is *PLOTSAVER Yard & Garden™,* Messina Wildlife Management, Inc., Chester, NJ, OMRI listed, incorporates a deer repellent with an obstructive, yet effective, 3-D physical and sensory barrier that deer will not cross. The PLOTSAVER Yard & Garden system uses black ribbon attached at a recommended height of 30 inches above ground to black posts to seamlessly blend into the shadows of landscape plants for year long protection. Instructions are to treat the ribbon with the proprietary, odor based liquid PLOTSAVER repellent every 30 days.

Sprays prepared with a thiram (fungicide) and/or rotten egg base, along with a spreader/sticker, are applied to landscape foliage to repel browsing deer.

Two-legged thieves have become a problem in some areas, stealing the tops out of landscape evergreens to use as Christmas trees. This has caused some growers of specimen evergreens to resort to spraying their trees with a vile smelling chemical mixture -- a vile odor that becomes even more revolting when exposed to room temperature. A pesticide used in this manner is classed as a repellent.

I must tell you an experience I had with a commercially prepared repellent "that worked." As I said earlier, always read the label and follow the manufacturer's recommended rates and directions.

I purchased a three-pound container of repellent that worked via the olfactory senses: i.e., it stank! I went into the garden, spread the repellent at the rate called for on the label, came indoors, and washed my hands. *But*, for three days, I couldn't hold my hand anywhere near my nose. I had missed one very important statement on the label – the one that advised me to wear gloves.

Remember what I say: "Always read the label and follow the manufacturer's recommended rates and directions" – and that means *all* the directions.

Pesticides A properly selected pesticide can be very beneficial and have a positive influence in our home or garden A pesticide might be used to prevent, destroy, repel, or eliminate insects, fungi, bacteria, weeds, rodents, nematodes, or even two-legged thieves. In an IPM program, a pesticide should be used only as a last resort. Only when the pest has been identified and its damage is excessive is the use of a pesticide in order. I repeat, sometimes a pesticide is just not necessary.

PESTICIDE FORMULATIONS

Commercially, pesticide preparations for home and garden use are available in several different formulations. The more common formulas include emulsifiable concentrates (EC), flowable (F), wettable powders (WP), dusts, horticultural oil, and granules. For spray applications, emulsifiable concentrates (EC) are the most popular formulation. They are made of a concentrated oil solution of the technical grade material (the pesticide) with enough emulsifier to make the concentrate mix readily with water. Many liquid concentrates found on the pesticide shelf at the garden center are EC's.

Flowables (F) are formulations of pesticides that are neither water nor oil soluble. They are a blend of fine particles of the pesticide in a liquid to make a flowable liquid or paste. For use, the flowable liquid must be diluted and mixed with water. A sprayer with an agitator must be used to keep the particles in suspension.

Wettable powders (WP) are essentially concentrated dusts of technical material (the pesticide) combined with a wetting agent to facili-

tate mixing of the powder with water. They must be diluted and mixed with water for application. Agitation during spraying will reduce the settling of the pesticide particles in the sprayer. DO NOT USE WETTABLE POWDERS AS A DUST. Wettable powders contain too high a concentration of the pesticides active ingredient to be used in dust form.

Dusts are ready-to-use, diluted formulations of the dry active ingredient for use in dusters. They are not to be confused with wettable powders which must be diluted with water before use.

Horticultural oil sprays are liquids of highly refined and distilled petroleum products. Recent advances in distillation processes have expanded their use from only winter dormant sprays to also include all season or summer oil sprays for plants in active growth.

Granules are pesticide-impregnated, inert particles, such as clay, vermiculite, or ground corncob, used to deliver the pesticide in a dry formulation. An advantage of granular application is that fertilizers and pesticides can be applied at the same time. They are sold as weed-and-feed or insect-and-feed combinations.

EQUIPMENT FOR APPLYING PESTICIDES

Selecting equipment for application of a pesticide depends on the formulation and the size of the job to be accomplished. The pesticide may be in the liquid, granular, or dust formulation and the job size may range from one single plant to many acres. The equipment I have selected for applying pesticides to my garden and landscape plants includes a trigger sprayer for house plants; 2, 1 gallon compressed air sprayers, one for insecticides and fungicides, and the other for weed killers in the outdoor landscape and garden; a 3 gallon backpack sprayer with a hand regulated pump for pressurizing; a hose-end sprayer for small fruit trees, shade trees, and shrubs; a centrifugal spreader for granular lawn fertilizers, insecticides, fungicides, and herbicides; and a plunger duster for fine coverage of foliage where leaf chewing pests are working. There are many more types of equipment for applying pesticides. Whatever equipment you choose, follow the manufacturer's directions for operating the unit, and read and follow the directions on the pesticide label as well.

Let me tell you the reasons I chose the equipment I did to maintain my garden and landscape.

Trigger sprayer You are probably familiar with the trigger sprayer because it is sold with many ready-to-use (RTU) formulations -- window-cleaners, furniture polish, household grease removers, and home and garden pesticides. For the garden you will find formulations of RTU insecticides, miticides, fungicides and herbicides. The trigger sprayer unit, with its adjustable nozzle, is an ideal way to apply pesticides to house plants and plants on the deck and patio. The adjustable nozzle enables you to direct the stream of spray to one specific spot or to thoroughly cover a plant with a fine mist. The RTU sprays are one of the most expensive formulations (pressurized aerosol bombs being the other), but when you have only a few plants to treat, they are the most convenient. If the container is not reusable, follow the manufacture's recommendations for disposal of the empty container. If you purchase a trigger sprayer container to apply spray mixes you prepare yourself, <u>do not</u> use the same trigger sprayer for both insecticides and herbicides. It is possible that traces of an

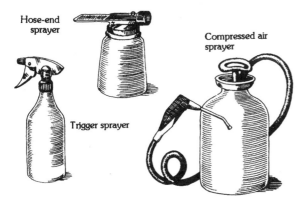

Hose-end sprayer

Compressed air sprayer

Trigger sprayer

herbicide will remain in the container and damage sensitive plants. To remember which sprayer is for herbicides, write on the container with an indelible marker "FOR WEED KILLERS ONLY."

Compressed air sprayer The compressed air sprayer is the most convenient unit I have found for applying liquids and wettable powders to treat only a few plants, or where my garden hose will not reach. I use a sprayer with a one gallon capacity and a 3 gallon backpack compressed air unit (various capacity sizes are available). This allows me to mix the pesticide in relatively small quantities.

When using wettable powders it is necessary to shake the container frequently to keep particles suspended in the water. If they are allowed to settle for even a short period of time, the particles may sink to the bottom of the tank and clog the spray nozzle.

If weed killers also are to be used in the compressed air sprayer, purchase an additional unit for that purpose only and label it "FOR WEED KILLERS ONLY." Using a single sprayer for both weed killers and other pesticides is begging for trouble. As I mentioned earlier, it is terribly difficult to completely clean the herbicide residue from internal parts of the sprayer. Even the slightest trace of a weed killer in the sprayer could wreak havoc on flowers, vegetables and ornamentals.

Hose-end sprayer The hose-end sprayer is basically a siphon operated by water pressure from the garden hose (generally from 50 to 60 pounds household pressure).

The pesticide concentrate, in either liquid or wettable powder form, is placed in a jar attached to a spray-gun-metering jet which, in turn, is attached to the garden hose. Water delivered from the garden hose mixes with the pesticide concentrate, diluting it to the proportions set by the metering jet. With good water pressure from my water system, I can spray as high as 25 to 30 feet, which makes it possible to reach the top of my semi-dwarf fruit trees. Be sure to purchase a hose-end sprayer with an anti-siphon device to prevent contamination of your water supply. In fact, make it a practice to install an anti-backflow valve, available from most plumbing supply or hardware outlets, between the water source, the faucet, and the garden hose connected to the spray unit. The backflow valve will inhibit the mixing of a chemical or fertilizer into the water supply due to an inadvertent pressure drop. This anti-backflow valve will eliminate contamination of your water supply. One drawback to the hose-end sprayer is its reach; you can work only as far as your garden hose is long.

Centrifugal spreader For the lawn and large garden areas where I want to apply granular pesticides and/or fertilizers, I prefer the centrifugal or cyclone-type spreader. Compared to the drop type spreader, which applies the granules in narrow strips usually 18 to 36 inches wide, the cyclone spreader disperses the granules in strips 8 to 10 feet wide, in a surprisingly accurate delivery pattern. I have applied granular materials to my lawn in

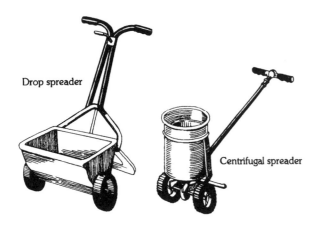

Drop spreader

Centrifugal spreader

less than one-third the time required by the drop type spreader. To maintain a spreader, whether it is a drop type or cyclone, always follow the manufacturer's directions for cleaning and storage. Chemical fertilizers and chemical pesticides can corrode metal parts, rendering the spreader inoperable.

Plunger duster I prefer using the plunger duster to apply diatomaceous earth or C-M PowderGard® pulverized limestone for controlling slugs, cutworms, and leaf eating caterpillars in the flower garden and vegetable patch. The duster can be adjusted to deliver a heavy dust pattern to the soil around a plant, or a fine cloud to cover the plant's foliage. Other pesticides, such as fungicides and insecticides, are available in dust formulation. CAUTION: When using any duster, wear protective clothing, goggles, and a respirator or disposable paper mask. The mask must be capable of screening out micron-sized particles.

EXOTIC PESTS

If you have been listening to the Garden Hotline® radio program you know I have refused to answer questions about plants and seeds which travelers have "snuck" back into the United States from overseas. Why? The answer is simple. By "sneaking" plant material or seeds onto this continent we could inadvertently be bringing in insects and diseases that, if not stopped, could destroy our agriculture production and environment.

Earlier in this chapter I said it is recognized that the complete eradication of a pest is not recommended, and in most cases not possible, but in the case of "exotic" pests, pests which are non-native to an area with NO natural

Asian Longhorned Beetle
Body approx 1" to 1-1/2" long
Antenna may be 2" long

controls in the local environment must be eradicated.

Asian longhorned beetle

The latest and newest exotic insect to arrive on the scene, *one that could spell unbelievable disaster*, environmentally and economically, *if not eradicated* from the North American Continent, is the Asian Longhorned Beetle (ALB) (*Anoplophora glabripennis*).

It is believed that the beetle arrived in North America, particularly in the United States in raw, untreated lumber used to make wooden pallets and crating for cargo shipped from China and possibly in the untreated, timber bracing found in the hold of cargo ships. Interceptions have occurred in some 34 warehouses throughout the United States.

After the discovery of the ALB in August, 1996, in several trees in the Greenpoint sec-

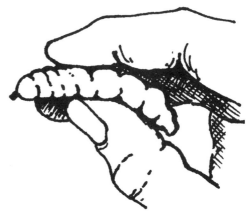

Larva of Asian Longhorned Beetle

tion in Brooklyn, New York, the U.S. Secretary of Agriculture's declaration of an *extraordinary emergency* made it possible to combat the infestation with regulatory and control actions. Within weeks, the beetle was discovered on Long Island in Amityville, NY. It was learned that infested wood had been taken there from the Greenpoint infestation area to Amityville. Since that time, additional infestations were discovered in Queens County, Nassau County and Suffolk County, NY, all part of Long Island, and in trees in and around Central Park and in street trees in lower Manhattan, NY.

In 1998, the ALB was found in Ravenswood, a suburb of Chicago, Illinois, and in New Jersey, in Hoboken/Jersey City in October, 2002, and Middlesex/Union counties, the Borough Carteret, the Avenel section of Woodbridge Township, and in the nearby cities of Rahway and Linden, NJ in 2004. The beetles found in the Hoboken/Jersey City infestation were identified through DNA testing to have come from the infestation in lower Manhattan. Possibly they hitchhiked on a vehicle through the Lincoln Tunnel or were blown across the lower Hudson River when Hurricane Floyd blew through on September 17, 1999.

The Canadian Food Inspection Agency, Plant Products Directorate, Plant Health Division established a Regulated Area (quarantine) in Woodbridge, Toronto, Ontario, Canada in 2003, and subsequently found the ALB in the City of Toronto and the City of Vaughan. To eradicate this infestation, complete areas of potential host trees are being totally destroyed. In the U.S, all of the infested areas have been placed under Federal and State Quarantine and eradication efforts are under way, as well. A Quarantine is absolute. If you live, garden, or work in an ALB Quarantine area, you must adhere to the rules completely: www.aphis.usda.gov/ppq/ep/alb/regs.html

Regulated Articles
The regulated articles for ALB include the following:
1. The Asian Longhorned Beetle (Anoplophora glabripennis) in any living stage of development.
2. Firewood all hardwood species.
3. All host material living, dead, cut or fallen inclusive of nursery stock, logs, green lumber, stumps, roots, branches, and debris of half inch or more in diameter of the general listed in Appendix 1.

Regulated Establishments
Establishments placed under regulations for ALB within a quarantined area include:
1. Landscapers
2. Tree pruning companies
3. Tree removal companies
4. Firewood dealers
5. Pallet distributors
6. Nurseries
7. Sanitation workers, as well as other municipal or community services and associated contractors.

Eradication may cost over 300 million dollars and take beyond 2009 to complete. According to a research study conducted for the USDA Interagency Research Forum, January, 2001 "The estimated maximum potential national urban forest impact of the Asian Longhorned beetle is a loss of 34.9% of total canopy cover, 30.3% tree mortality (1.2 billion trees) and a value of $699 billion."

Host trees are hardwoods including several species of Maple (Norway, sugar, silver, and red maples), box elder, horsechestnut, buckeye, elm, London plane, birch, poplar, and willow.

The Asian longhorned beetle is easily recognized from its shiny, coal black body which is 1 to 1 1/2 inch long with multiple white spots on each wing cover. The antenna colored with multiple black and white bands protrude even longer than the body of the beetle. The beetle adults emerge from large 1/2 inch diameter round holes in the branches, trunks, and roots during mid-May with peak activity between mid-June and October. The ALB usually has one generation per year. The female adult, after emergence, feeding and mating, chews out an oval spot (oviposition site) in the bark where she lays one egg in the cambium layer. Within 10 to 15 days, the egg hatches into a tiny larva, feeds in the cambium layer, then tunnels as a larva through the sapwood and enters the heartwood to feed and mature. The larvae, just before pupation into the adult, may be as large as your little finger. The female has the capability of laying 35 to 90 eggs. Infestation is certain death to the tree. In several Quarantine locations, uninfested host trees within an ALB quarantine are being injected or soil treated with the systemic chemical insecticide, Imidacloprid®. Unfortunately, the only method of stopping the beetles in an infested tree is the complete removal of the tree, chipping, and burning the remains.

Since few natural biological controls are known for ALB in China, the beetle's home environment, U.S. scientists are conducting surveys to identify previously undiscovered beneficial insects and pathogens that could be developed for management. In addition, research is being conducted with the use of sound detection, extremely sensitive listening devices, to identify the presence of the beetle within the woody tissue of a tree. The USDA Eradication team includes Federal experts along with representatives from each States' Agricultural Department, Forestry Department, Department of Environmental Conservation, Environmental Protection Department, Parks Department, Sanitation Department, etc. The Eradication Team is just that, a team effort to eradicate the ALB. Survey crews are active in each Quarantine area inspecting potential host trees by ground inspectors along with professional, certified arborists with climbers and bucket trucks, and climbers from the National Forest Service (smoke jumpers.).

If you should find or suspect that you have identified an Asian longhorned beetle, capture the beetle in a glass jar, put it in the freezer, record the location where you found the beetle specimen and IMMEDIATELY call in New York: 866-265-0301, New Jersey: 866-BEETLE1, Illinois: 800-641-3934 or your State Agricultural Department, State Forester, Cooperative Extension educator, or USDA APHIS PPQ representative. Go to www.aphis.usda.gov. It would be better to have a false alarm, than no alarm at all.

Emerald Ash Borer (Agrilus planipennis)

Another new exotic beetle from Asia was discovered feeding in ash (*Fraxinus* spp.) trees in southeastern Michigan. Identified in July 2002 as Emerald Ash Borer (EAB), the beetle's larvae feed in the phloem and outer sapwood, producing galleries that eventually girdle and kill branches and entire trees. Though this killer pest has not been found in New York, Connecticut or New Jersey to date, it has been established in Michigan for at least five years and has killed over 5 million ash trees. In my opinion it won't be long before we discover infested trees over the entire East coast. Infestations of EAB can be difficult to detect until canopy dieback begins and can easily be confused with the ash dieback we are experienc-

ing today. Evidence of infestation includes D-shaped exit holes 1/8 to 1/4 inches in diameter on branches and the trunk. Callus tissue produced by the tree in response to larval feeding may cause vertical splits 5-10 cm in length above the gallery. Infested branches in the canopy die when they are girdled by the serpentine tunnels excavated by the larvae. The tree is often killed after 2-3 years after being infested. In Michigan, this borer has been observed only on ash trees, green ash (F. pennsylvania), white ash (F. americana), and black ash (F. nigra) as well as several horticultural varieties of ash.

For more detailed information on the EAB visit the UDSA Forest Service at: www.na.fs.fed.us/spfo/eab/index.html

Gypsy Moth

Another insect which arrived in America, legally though, is the Gypsy moth *Lymantria dispar* now identified as the European Gypsy moth because of the introduction of the Asian Gypsy moth. The European Gypsy moth discussed earlier in this chapter, brought to America by a French naturalist, who intended to interbreed them with silkworms to obtain a superior silk strand, unknowingly unleashed a disaster on the northeast United States and Canada. In 1869, a number of the imported gypsy moths escaped into the natural environment in Medford, Mass. Since that time the gypsy moth has spread to Michigan, Virginia and the entire Northeast states. One egg mass, a velvety, beige colored blob 1 1/2 inch long and about 3/4 an inch wide, can hatch up to a thousand caterpillars with an appetite for over 500 species of trees and shrubs, preferring oaks and alder. The adult female Gypsy moth is unable to fly. When loaded with eggs, she's like a 747 with too much luggage. The male moth can fly. The caterpillar, in its first two to three instars, spins a silken thread which serves as a mode of transportation. Caught in the wind, the caterpillar on its thread can travel several miles to a new location.

Integrated approaches for suppression and eradication are now used in all efforts to combat Gypsy moths. Quarantines, inspections, releases of predators and parasites, traps, and the release of sterile-male adults are just some of the recommended controls. *Bacillus thuringiensis* (B.T.) a biological control, diflubenzuron (Dimilin) a growth regulator, and carbaryl (Sevin®) a chemical control, are all effective in suppressing Gypsy moth caterpillars if applied as recommended on the label.

The Asian Gypsy moth (Lymantria dispar ssp.), differs from the European Gypsy moth in that the female does fly up to 20 miles with each life cycle. The Asian strain, native to Asia, was first identified in North America in late 1991 near the Port of Vancouver in BC, and since then found in traps in WA, OR, and BC and has probably arrived on ships infested with egg masses from eastern Russia. According to the Animal and Plant Health Inspection Service (APHIS) and the U.S. Forest Service has a great potential for colonization in Pacific Northwest forests. The same control efforts are in effect for the Asian species as for the European species.

Egg masses are laid on trees, stones, walls, logs, lawn furniture, and other outdoor equipment including mobile campers and trailers. If you are visiting an area where either the European or Asian species of the Gypsy moth are laying egg masses, you may run into inspection teams checking for deposited egg masses. Be cooperative.

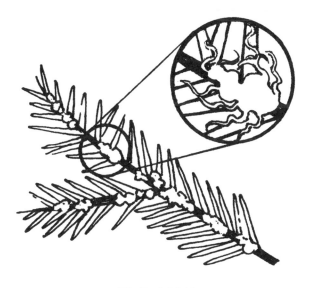

Woolly Adelgid

Hemlock Woolly Adelgid

Hemlock woolly adelgid *Adelges tsugae* (Annand) is a small aphid-like insect, introduced in the 1920's from Japan, that has become a serious pest problem of eastern hemlock, *Tsuga canadensis*. This pest is easily recognized on the young hemlock twigs by the presence of a dry, white woolly substance that covers its body and egg masses. Hemlock

woolly adelgid (HWA) is parthenogenetic (all individuals are females) and completes two generations of development each year. The injury, bud kill, desiccation of twigs, and death of major limbs as well the entire tree is caused by the sucking of sap and the injection of a toxin in the saliva while feeding. Death often occurs within 4 years.

Understanding the life cycle, an integral part of IPM, is essential when considering HWA suppression. I say suppression because this pest is virtually impossible to eliminate. HWA may be introduced to a landscape by wind, and/or birds, squirrels or other wildlife. Under nursery and landscape conditions, careful monitoring, enhancement of tree vigor, and discouragement of pest invasions with cultural practices either natural or chemical is a must. During March and April, adults of the overwintering generation lay about 100 eggs each in the cottony mass on the young twigs. Nymphs (also called crawlers) hatch from these eggs during several weeks in April and May. Within a few days, they start feeding with the insertion of piercing and sucking mouth parts. This spring generation matures by mid June and lays eggs which hatch into nymphs in early July starting the second generation. The nymphs lay dormant in the cottony masses until mid October when they start feeding and over winter to mature in early spring.

The suppression of the hemlock woolly adelgid by the homeowner can be accomplished with applications of sprays of dormant oil, soaps, and/or chemicals. Chemical controls labeled for hemlock woolly adelgid provide residual killing action where as soaps and oils must make contact at the time of application. Check with your Cooperative Extension educator for the recommended chemical control. Read the label.

Biological controls such as beetles, flies and lacewings are occasionally predators of the HWA but provide little control. The ladybird beetle (*Pseudoscymnus tsugae*), referred to earlier, provides hope for managing HWA in our forests as well as nurseries, and commercial and home landscape areas.

Termites

Although not an "exotic" pest problem, great advance has been made in termite suppression. In fact, a barrier treatments with chemical termiticides may be a thing of the past. Millions of dollars of research have culminated in the development of termite baits for suppressing the life cycle of the termite. James R. Lofton, Termite Specialist for Dow AgroSciences, provides an update of The Sentricon* *Termite Colony Elimination System*: "Signs of termite swarming in the spring are one indication of a termite problem. Termites cause more than $750,000,000 in damage to homes across the U.S. That's more than is caused by all fires and storms combined (not including Hurricanes Katrina and Rita).

Granted, the damage caused by termites isn't as dramatic as a fire or tornado. And it may not be discovered for years. But eventually it can lead to sagging floors, loose trim, cracked plaster, severe structural problems, and more. Eventually, major repairs may be necessary. Termites are tough, determined, highly efficient and, chances are, you'll see no evidence of their work until structural damage has already been done. Subterranean termites – the most common kind – live in colonies in the soil. Each colony is built around a king and queen whose sole job is reproduction. The swarmers or "flying black termites" are the adults, attempting to establish a new colony. Less than 1% are successful. While a nuisance, these termites do no damage but do indicate there a problem that needs looking into.

Most of a termite colony is made up of worker termites. These small white termites are the *real* problem. They are the ones that do the damage as they 'commute' between the colony and sources of food which includes wood fibers and other forms of cellulose which they eat, digest and share with other colony members. These workers rarely break the surface of the wood; instead they hollow it out from inside. The vast majority of the structural damage remains invisible ☐ until something suddenly gives way.

Traditionally, to control termites the soil around a structure was treated with a termiticide, producing a barrier to keep termites out. While generally effective, structural limitations, soil disturbance and eventual termiticide degradation could produce gaps that termites can get through. Now there's a better way to control termites—The Sentricon* *Termite Colony Elimination System*.

The Sentricon system offers an entirely new way to deal with termites. For the first time you can get to the source of the problem by totally eliminating a termite colony. Sentricon does not require a chemical barrier to block termites from entering a structure. Instead, foraging worker termites find, feed on and spread a unique, slow-acting insect growth regulator called Recruit* termite bait throughout their colony. Within months of the first consumption, the termite colony completely dies off. With the continued use of Sentricon, a structure can be permanently protected from future termite infestations.

Sentricon is an ongoing monitoring and baiting process — a radically different approach for termite control. Monitoring stations are placed around a structure by a trained pest control professional. When placed in the soil, these plastic stations resemble lawn sprinkler heads and are distributed around the property in intervals of 10-20 feet, about 2-3 feet from the building. When termites are discovered in the wood monitors inside the stations, the termites are removed and replaced in a Recruit baitube* that's inserted into the station. From there, the workers carry the bait back to the colony. Over time, the entire colony is affected by the bait. As its members die off, the colony can no longer support itself, and dies.

Recruit* termite bait, used in the Sentricon* system has proven to be effective against all species of subterranean termites. Years of university research and global field testing have shown the long-term effectiveness of this product. It has been used throughout the world, including France, Japan, Australia and the United States. The active ingredient in Recruit bait has an extremely low toxicity rate for mammals and was the first product registered by the EPA as a Reduced Risk Pesticide.

The bait is only used in the stations that have termites and only while they are present. Once the termite colony has been eliminated, the bait is removed and your pest control professional returns to monitoring. The wood monitoring devices in the stations are checked monthly until colony elimination and are checked once per quarter after elimination to protect against future attacks from new termite colonies.

In addition to in-ground station placement, the Sentricon system includes an above the ground bait station, Recruit*AG, that can be used indoors in situations where actively foraging worker termites are located in the wooden structure or mud shelter tubes. These stations are only used when termites are found above ground and the stations are removed after elimination.

The Sentricon system can even be used as a termite 'alarm' for structures that don't have an identified termite problem or a known infestation. The old saying goes, "There are two types of house: those that have termites, and those that will." With Sentricon, you can monitor for termite activity, treat when found and after elimination return to protective monitoring.

The Sentricon system has received significant national press over the past three years. Sentricon has been used to protect many well known structures, including The Statue of Liberty. The Sentricon system is even being used to treat entire city blocks in New Orleans' historic French Quarter district."

Reference for Products:

The mention or reference to products is not a personal endorsement by this author.

Hot Pepper Wax®, www.hotpepperwax.com 800-627-6840
Moisture Guard®, www.hotpepperwax.com 800-627-6840
C-M PowderGard™ Desiccant Dust, www.cmpowdergard.com
Serenade® Garden, www.agraquest.com 800-962-8980
Organocide®, www.organiclabs.com 772-286-5561
Messenger®, Eden Biosciense, www.messenger.info 888-522-5976
PLOTSAVER®, www.messinawildlife.com 888-411-3337
Deer Scram™, www.deerscram.com 877-337-2726
Deer Off® Deer, Rabbit and Squirrel Repellent, www.deeroff.com 800-DEEROFF
Bonide®, www.bonide.com
Milorganite®, www.milorganite.com 800-304-6204
Safer® Brand, Woodstream Products, www.saferbrand.com
Sentricon®, Dow AgroSciences, Inc., www.dowagro.com
Renaissance®, 10-0-0 Renaissance Fertilizers www.organicfertilizers.com 800-395-4769
New Jersey Department of Environmental Protection, Trenton, NJ. www.state.nj.us/dep/
New York State Department of Environmental Conservation, Albany, NY www.dec.state.ny.us/
University of Connecticut, www.canr.uconn.edu/ces

QUESTIONS AND ANSWERS

1. **Q. Something is digging up big chunks of turf in my lawn. What is it and how can I stop this from happening?**
   A. Chances are the digging is by a skunk looking for grubs. Grubs are the larval stage of beetles. Check with your local Cooperative Extension entomologist for the grub control recommended for your area.

2. **Q. How can we get rid of moles? Their tunnels seem to run everywhere—through the lawn, the flower garden, and the vegetable garden.**
   A. Moles can be controlled by mechanical traps, poison baits, mechanical vibrators, and by limiting their food supply.

3. **Q. I saw several miniature windmills on a front lawn. I was told they are for mole control. Could that be right?**
   A. Windmills, with a foot that mechanically thumps the ground, causing vibrations, are said to drive the moles away. In order for the vibrations to occur, you must have wind to move the mill blades.

210 • FUNDAMENTALS OF GARDENING

4. **Q. Is there anything that can be done to prevent birds from digging up and eating the corn seed when it is planted?**

    A. You can protect corn seed from corn-pulling birds and animal pests by treating the seed with a repellent before you plant it. There are products available that will repel birds such as crows and blackbirds, and animals such as squirrels and moles. Check with your Cooperative Extension Educator for an up-to-date list of repellents for treating seeds.

5. **Q. We live in the country and have a problem with deer getting into the vegetable and flower gardens. Is there anything that we can do to keep them out, besides building a fence?**

    A. There are commercial products available that one can spray on, or around, the plants to be protected. Some work by creating an odor that deer dislike or that frighten them, and others work by creating a very hot sensation in their mouths every time they take a bite. Sometimes only one bite will make them go elsewhere to browse. If you are planning to use a repellent in the vegetable patch, it must be one that can safely be applied to edible crops. A fence to keep out deer must be very tall, because deer are capable of extremely high jumps.

6. **Q. We don't have any dogs but the neighbors' dogs seem to enjoy our property better than their own. Is there anything we can do to keep them away from our gardens and shrubs?**

    A. Special repellents that work on olfactory senses have been developed to repel dogs. Check with your garden center or Cooperative Extension Educator for a listing. An inexpensive fence would work well around a vegetable or flower garden.

7. **Q. Are there any plants we can grow in our garden that will keep dogs away?**
    A. Yes. Plant pot marigolds, Calendula.

8. **Q. I love gooseberry pie, but every year, the birds eat my gooseberries before I manage to get more than a handful. What can I do?**

    A. A very effective protection is plastic netting, put over the bushes just before the berries begin to ripen. You could also use cheesecloth or tobacco cloth. Other suggestions, but usually less successful, are the well-known scarecrow figures or flashy glass or aluminum pie tins tied to the bushes where they will move with the wind and reflect sunlight.

9. **Q. Every spring, I have trouble with rabbits eating on rose bushes. I would like to plant more, but not until the rabbit problem is eliminated. What can I do?**

    A. Rabbits eat the bark and leaves of the rose in early spring when other sources of food are scarce. A low fence (one foot high) will keep rabbits out of a garden. You might also consider sprinkling dried blood around the plants, which will be useful as a fertilizer, as well as a rabbit repellent.

10. **Q. What is "dried blood"?**
    A. Dried blood is a by-product of slaughter houses. It is blood that is dried and ground into a powder. Dried blood is available in five-pound packages at garden-supply stores.

11.. **Q. My potted schefflera plant has little brown specks on its stem. If this is a disease, I would like to know what to do about it before I bring the plant into the house for the winter. Can you help me?**

    A. It sounds as if your schefflera plant is infested with soft brown scale, an insect that can eventually weaken or destroy your plant. Carefully wash or scrape off as many of the "brown spots" as you can and then spray the plant thoroughly with insecticidal soap or Hot Pepper Wax Spray. Repeated applications of the insecticide will likely be necessary; be sure to read the label first.

12. **Q. During late winter, my gardenia collection develops a very fine webbing over the leaves and flower buds. What causes this?**

A. The webbing is probably due to an infestation of spider mite, a tiny arthropod with eight legs. During the latter part of the heating season, the air in our homes becomes dry enough to encourage rapid population development.

13. **Q. How can I test my plants for spider mites? The population seems to get out of hand before I recognize the symptoms.**

A. Hold a suspected plant up to the light. If you see a fine webbing developing amongst the leaves and flowers, the population is probably building. Hold a piece of white paper under the foliage and tap the leaves vigorously. Gaze at the "dust" that falls onto the paper. If it moves, it is likely spider mite.

14. **Q. The colorful foliage on my croton has developed a chlorotic look. It almost looks as if something is sucking the life out of the leaf. What could be the cause?**

A. Croton are highly susceptible to spider mite, a tiny insectlike critter that pierces and sucks the life from the living plant tissue. The spider mite feeds on cell sap by inserting its mouth parts into the plant tissue and sucking the liquid content. This action results in the bleached-out appearance of the foliage.

15. **Q. How can I control spider mites on my house plants?**

A. I know of no complete control of spider mites, but you can keep them in check by keeping the plants clean, using predatory mites, changing the environmental conditions, and/or using miticides.

16. **Q. Can I wash my miniature roses to get rid of spider mites?**

A. Sanitation goes a long way in reducing the population of spider mites. Rinse the foliage, both tops and bottoms, with lukewarm water on a weekly basis.

17. **Q. I have tried to wash the leaves on my gardenias by giving them a bath in the kitchen sink. Every time I tip the plant to wash the underside of the leaves, soil falls out of the pot. What can I do?**

A. To keep soil from falling out of the pot when you turn the plant upside down, moisten the soil and then wrap the pot and soil surface with a plastic wrap right up to the plant stem. Hold your fingers over the plastic wrap when you tip the plant.

18. **Q. Will increasing humidity reduce the buildup of spider mites on my schefflera, which is growing just inside a bright, sunny, warm window?**

A. Dry air and warm temperature makes an ideal environment for an explosion of the spidermite population. Lower the temperature by moving the plant away from the sunny, warm location and increase the humidity.

19. **Q. Can I use insecticidal soap as a miticide on my roses?**

A. Read the label. Insecticidal soap will give partial control of spider mites. The important consideration is the coverage; the spray must thoroughly coat all surfaces of the plant. Any leaves or stems left untreated will host insects that will reinfest the plant. Repeated applications may be necessary.

20. **Q. The Dutch use predatory mites to control spider mites and other mites on greenhouse crops of flowers and vegetables. Will that work for me?**

A. Predatory mites do reduce the population of parasitic mites. In order to obtain the right predator, you need to know the species of mite you are trying to control. Check with your Cooperative Extension entomologist for proper identification. There are several species of predatory mites available commercially.

21. **Q. Recently my poinsettia developed what I have been told were whiteflies. Every time I touched the plant, a "white cloud" of them rose into the air. A short time after noticing the whiteflies, all of the leaves curled up and fell off the plant. All I have left now are stems sticking out of the pot. Can I contain this problem and revive the plant?**

    A. The leaf drop probably did you a favor. If you discarded the dropped foliage and cleaned up the area where the plant was growing, this probably reduced the population to next to nothing. You should clip back the stems by as much as fifty percent, feed and water regularly, and place the pot in a sunny window. Use a yellow sticky trap, according to the label directions, in order to detect and identify the early emergence of a whitefly problem. A small parasitic wasp, Encarisa formosa, is available for biological control. Apply Hot Pepper Wax Spray according to label directions.

22. **Q. My tropical hibiscus develops a case of whitefly each year, just before I am ready to set the plant outside for summer. The infestation is not enough to kill the plant at this point. How can I contain the whitefly?**

    A. Whiteflies can be difficult to control on hibiscus. As insecticidal soap may damage the foliage, wash the underside of the leaves with the insecticidal soap and then rinse thoroughly. Hang a yellow sticky trap among the branches to catch the adult, and, while the plant is indoors, vacuum it to remove as many of the whiteflies as possible. An alternate control would be Hot Pepper Wax Spray.

23. **Q. Our tomato plants succumb to an invasion of whiteflies every summer, just as we start picking a ripe crop. If you brush up against the plants, a white cloud arises. What can we do to possibly overcome the problem?**

    A. Start with early detection. Set out yellow sticky traps so you can be alerted as to when the invasion starts. As soon as you notice even just a few adults, apply insecticidal soap as a spray, or Hot Pepper Wax Spray, making sure you thoroughly coat the bottoms of the leaves. Use a sprayer with enough force to apply a heavy mist that will penetrate the dense foliage. Repeat the application as needed.

24. **Q. I have tall weeds that grow along our property line; they always seem to be full of different insects. Do weeds house vegetable garden pests?**

    A. Weeds can be a wonderful home and hiding place for both beneficial and destructive insects. If there are any weedy areas adjacent to your garden, cut them or pull them out. One major garden pest, whitefly, congregates in the tall weeds during the day and returns to your tomatoes, eggplants, peppers, cucumbers and squash in the evening.

25. **Q. I grow geraniums in a sunny window during the winter, but they always become invested with whiteflies. Can I use a mechanical control as a defense?**

    A. Put the hose attachment on the vacuum cleaner, place two mothballs in the dust bag, turn on the suction, and touch the plant to make the adults rise. Suck up the adults that fly. Repeat the vacuum treatment on a daily basis for at least fourteen days. The mothballs in the dust bag act as a fumigant to kill the adults whiteflies.

26. **Q. My spider plant has little brown bumps on the leaves and stems. The windowsill and floor below the plant is sticky. What is the problem?**

    A. If the brown bumps can be moved or flicked off stems and leaves without leaving a hole, the soft brown bumps are likely scale insects. The sticky substance is the honeydew secreted by the feeding scale. If not controlled, they can cause sufficient damage to kill the plant. Spider plant foliage is easily damaged, so carefully wash the leaves and stems with soap and water to remove as many of the adults and eggs as possible. Apply insecticidal soap or Hot Pepper Wax Spray according to the label directions during the crawler stage of the insect. You will need a strong household cleaner to remove the honeydew from the windowsill and floor.

27.   **Q. My lilac shrub has a grayish-white, flaky substance on the bark of the main stems. Is this a fungus?**

   A. From your description, the grayish-white flaky substance is probably scale insects. Apply a dormant oil spray before new growth begins in spring and prune out the heaviest infested stems after bloom. During the growing season, apply insecticidal soap. Repeat the dormant oil spray each spring. It is very important to coat the stems thoroughly with the pesticide. Spraying must be done from all sides of the plant and sprayed to drip. Mechanically, you can put on a pair of gloves and rub them off. Once a scale has been rubbed off, the mouth parts are destroyed and it dies.

28.   **Q. What does it mean when you say "spray to drip?"**

   A. Basically, it means to apply the pesticide until it runs off the plant. Pesticides with no residual controlling power must come in contact with the pest at the time of spraying. A "spray to drip" application helps ensure a thorough coverage.

29.   **Q. What are some beneficial or friendly insects I can release in my garden to help control aphids and mealybugs?**

   A. Lady beetles (commonly, but wrongly, called ladybugs) lunch on scale, aphids and mealybugs. Green lacewing is a general predator of aphids, psyllids, mealybugs, moth eggs and larvae.

30.   **Q. Last summer, on my tomato plant, I found a large, about two-inch-long green caterpillar with white stripes, and a horn sticking up from its back end. Several of the leaves were almost completely devoured. What type of caterpillar was it— and can you suggest a control?**

   A. The green caterpillar you described was probably the tomato hornworm, but could also have been the tobacco hornworm. Generally, hand picking is the only control needed; you seldom find more than a couple of them in a small garden. A biological control that can be applied to tomatoes as a spray is Bacillus thuringiensis var. kurstaki (BTK)—and be sure to read the label.

31.   **Q. The day after I set my broccoli transplants into the garden, I found several of them snipped off right at the point where the stem emerged from the ground. The upper part of the plant was still there. I could find no insects. What critter caused this?**

   A. The likely critter was one of many cutworms that live just below the surface of the soil. The safest, easiest, nontoxic control is a cutworm collar. Tear the bottom out of a paper coffee cup and slip the cup down over the transplant so the leaves stick up through the top. Work the base of the cup one inch into the soil. The cutworm can't crawl under or over the barrier. If cutworms have been a problem in your garden, always install cutworm collars on the same day the transplants are put in the ground.

32.   **Q. Japanese beetle adults have attacked my roses, asparagus, zinnias, tomatoes, and just about every other plant in my landscape. Will it help to use the beetle trap?**

   A. The traps need to be in place before you see the emergence of the adults. The idea behind the trap is to get both mother and father into the trap before eggs are laid. Check your garden records for the date when you first saw the adult beetles last year, and set the traps out about two week prior to that date. Also, follow the directions on placement of the traps. They should draw the adult beetles away from the crop being protected.

33.   **Q. I have been told that the biological control for grubs does not work 100 percent. Is it worthwhile to inoculate my lawn with milky spore disease to suppress the invasion of Japanese beetles? The grubs are getting worse each year.**

   A. Estimates of control vary depending upon whom you talk to. We know that the bacillus does not provide anywhere near a complete control. As part of integrated pest management, a biological control such as bacillus is a good investment.

34. **Q. During April, I saw one of the most interesting caterpillars at work on my mugo pine trees. The needles looked as though they were moving. In fact, upon closer examination, I saw the needles were gone and, what looked like needles, were actually caterpillars. When I touched the tree, the caterpillars froze in position. Do I need to spray this year?**

A. The caterpillar or larvae of the sawfly was the culprit. The caterpillar has, as part of its camouflage, the ability to masquerade as a needle. When a vibration occurs, the caterpillar freezes in position. Most likely the adult sawfly has laid eggs, for this year's crop, on the branches of the mugo pine. Apply a biological insecticide Bacillus thuringiensis according to the label directions.

35. **Q. What is the pest that builds a massive web in the fork of my weeping flowering cherry tree just after it starts to leaf out in the spring? I don't see any insects.**

A. The pest that is building the massive web is the tent caterpillar. The reason you see no insect is they are nocturnal in feeding habit. If you open the web with a stick, you will find thousands of caterpillars inside. Apply Bacillus thuringiensis at the first sign of web development.

36. **Q. During midsummer, junipers planted on the south side of my house develop a yellowing of the needles with a very fine webbing. I think I see something moving in the webbing. What could it be?**

A. The pest is spider mite. This arthropod is piercing and sucking the sap from plant tissue. The environment produced by the hot summer sun on the south side of the house is ideal for their growth. According to the label directions, a thorough spray of insecticidal soap will suppress the pest. Repeated applications may be necessary.

37. **Q. The flower buds on my geraniums have holes in them and the foliage is covered with what looks like large grains of pepper. What pest is causing the damage?**

A. The holes in the geranium flower buds are probably caused by a nocturnal caterpillar called the bud worm. The "large grains of pepper" is the waste from the caterpillar. Apply Bacillus thuringiensis as a biological control at the first sign of damage. As an alternate, if you have only a few plants, pick the caterpillars off by hand.

38. **Q. What is eating the foliage of my cabbage plants? The leaves have great big chunks taken out of them.**

A. The damage to cabbage leaves is caused by either the cabbage looper or the imported cabbageworm. They are both common pests of cabbage, cauliflower, Brussels sprouts, and kale. Apply Bacillus thuringiensis according to the label directions.

39. **Q. The foliage of my bush beans, planted midsummer, often becomes encased in very fine webbing. I can see microscopic red dots moving in the webbing. What is it?**

A. The beans are being attacked by two-spotted spider mites. Rinse the plants early in the day with a hard stream of water, or spray them thoroughly with insecticidal soap formulated for fruits and vegetables. Repeat applications as necessary.

40. **Q. The label on the tomatoes I purchased had "V/F resistant" printed next to the variety name. What does V/F resistant mean?**

A. "V" is the abbreviation for verticillium wilt and "F" represents fusarium wilt. The word resistant means just that. The plant variety is resistant to, but not immune to, verticillium and fusarium blight.

41. **Q. My cucumber seed packet stated the variety is tolerant to CMV, PM, and DM. What does this mean?**

A. CMV are the initials for "cucumber mosaic virus"; PM represents "powdery mildew"; and DM is "downy mildew." The variety can tolerate an infection of these diseases and continue production.

42. **Q. My zucchini, melon, and cucumber plants collapse during the heat of summer. The base of the stems look rotten. Is this from lack of water?**

A. No, not likely. The "rotten" stem is caused by the squash vine borer, a white grub with a dark head that enters the stem near the base of the plant and eats away the water-conducting tissue inside. At the first sign of wilting, look for a hole about the size of a pencil lead, near the base of the stem. There may be a wet sawdust oozing from the stem. Split the stem longitudinally with a sharp blade and remove the borer. After the surgery, pile moist soil over the wounded stem. If you get to the borer problem before severe collapsing occurs, you may save the crop.

43. **Q. I have been told to start applying a deer repellent to my shrubs by the end of summer. I don't see them eating any of my plants at that time. Why start then?**

A. The reason for using a deer repellent in late summer is to teach the deer that they do not like your plants from the very first time they browse your shrubs. If you wait until you see them eating, they will already have set their browsing pattern. All you are doing is encouraging the deer to eat somewhere else.

44. **Q. There are several different brands of deer repellents at my local garden center. Do commercial deer repellents work?**

A. Deer repellents do work, but to a limited extent. Repellents basically work on either taste or smell. It is best to alternate the use of repellents, because deer seem to get used to one specific control. Before purchasing a deer repellent, read the label for crop use; not all deer repellents can be applied to all crops.

45. **Q. I have a few dandelions in my lawn each year, but not enough to warrant applying a broad-leafed weed killer. I have tried digging them out, but each time I do, two or more come up in their place. What can I do?**

A. You have the right idea in digging, but when you say you are getting two or more dandelions in their place, you are just not digging deep enough. When cutting a dandelion from the lawn, use a sharp, long-bladed knife or digging tool. Cut the tap root at least three inches below the surface.

46. **Q. My roses have hundreds of little green pear-shaped critters, about an eighth of an inch long, all over the new growth. The tips appear stunted and wilted. What are they and what is a biological control?**

A. The little green pear-shaped critters are most likely aphids. Depending on their species, they come in green, black, beige, brown, pink, yellow, and red. Aphids pierce and suck the sap from individual cells. Most of them prefer the youngest, most succulent tissue. Biological controls include predators: lady beetles, lacewings, and the cecidomyiid fly. Insecticidal soap as a spray is also effective as a natural control.

47. **Q. My African violets are developing hard, curled leaves in the center of the plant. The new growth is just not expanding. What caused this?**

A. A very close examination is in order. Pinch out one of the hard, curled leaves and unroll the specimen. With a 20X lens, look for a very tiny, white or beige-colored mite. The pest is probably the cyclamen mite. Sanitation is the best control. Discard infested plants and clean the growing area.

48. **Q. I purchased several new ferns for my apartment only a few weeks ago and now there are little black gnats all over the windowsill near where I have them growing. The ferns are growing in a peat moss soil. Are these pests coming from my plants?**

A. The little black gnats are probably fungus gnats enjoying the dampness of the soilless potting mix. The larvae feed on fungi in the peat moss mix, but can cause some damage to the plant root system. Removing and discarding the growing media and repotting in a sterile mix can reduce the pest. A yellow sticky trap, placed next to the plant, will attract many flying adults as well.

49. **Q. My prize jade plant, which I have been growing on a patio of a fourteenth-floor apartment, has suddenly developed little white cottony blobs all over the stems and leaves. What are they, where did they come from, and what can I do?**

    A. The cottony blobs are probably mealybugs. They may have come in on another plant you added to your collection or been brought to the fourteenth floor by a flying insect. The little cottony blobs can contain hundreds of eggs. If a flying insect landed on an infested plant, it could pick up a few eggs and then land and deposit them on your jade plant. Sanitation is the first line of defense. Quarantine the jade plant and, using a soft brush, give it a complete bath with a mild soapy water solution. Repeat the bath as necessary. Cottony blobs can also be removed with a cotton swab that has been dipped in rubbing alcohol. If an insecticide is used, read the label; jade plants are sensitive to some insecticides.

50. **Q. I have noticed a sticky residue on the hardwood floor and windowsill where I grow most of my house plants. Where is it coming from?**

    A. The sticky residue is probably coming from an insect infestation on one or more of your plants. Look for spider mites, scale insects, aphids, and/or mealybugs. A thorough bath, and further examination of your house plant collection, may be in order.

51. **Q. I purchased a potted dwarf orange, loaded with fruit. Can I use them to make orange marmalade?**

    A. Most of the dwarf orange varieties produce a rather bitter fruit. They do make a delicious, tart marmalade. I would not use the fruit that were on the plant at the time of purchase. You have no way to knowing what pesticides might have been used on the plant. After the fruit has been cultured under your care, make your marmalade.

52. **Q. My neighbor has been using an antitranspirant spray on his roses to reduce black spot and mildew. Does it really work?**

    A. Recent research indicates that an antitranspirant does reduce infection of both black spot and mildew on roses. The antitranspirant works by forming a barrier between the infective disease spore and the plant tissue. Repeated applications are necessary, because new growth emerges unprotected.

53. **Q. Why do some pesticides contain a wetting agent?**

    A. Wetting agents, or surfactants, are used to make water wetter, ensuring even coverage of a pesticide and increasing penetration of the pesticide to the insect.

54. **Q. Can I till all of the garden residue into the soil in late fall when I am cleaning up the garden?**

    A. It is highly recommended that you compost garden residue, including both the roots and the shoots, before using it as an organic additive to the soil. Composting destroys much of the disease problems, whereas tilling infected plant material into soil may just reintroduce the pathogen again next year.

55. **Q. Hosta plants, which I am growing along a shady walkway, are magnificent, but they end up with big holes in their leaves by mid-season. I have not seen the pest that is causing the problem. Any ideas?**

    A. The holes are probably created by slugs. They are a nocturnal pest that love hosta beds because of the dampness of the shady environment. No matter what slug control you use, start the control early, just as the hosta plants are emerging, early in spring. Do not wait until damage appears. Check with your Cooperative Extension entomologist for the slug or snail control recommended for your locale.

56. **Q. My lawn has several light-green stripes running parallel to each other. Could this be a disease that is being spread with the wheels of my fertilizer spreader?**

    A. The "disease" is not a disease but, instead, it is a problem with the application procedure of the fertilizer. Ensure overlapping of the rows when applying fertilizer; the light green stripes probably are where no fertilizer was applied.

57. Q. **What is a multipurpose fruit spray mix?**
    A. A multipurpose fruit spray usually contains an insecticide, a miticide, and a fungicide. Such a mix is used in a "shotgun" approach to controlling multiple pest problems on fruit crops. The label may list directions for use on several different species of fruit. Read the label.

58. Q. **Why use a spreader-sticker when applying chemical insecticide?**
    A. A spreader-sticker acts as a wetting agent and "glues" the pesticide to the leaf surface. Its use can prolong the effectiveness of a pesticide and reduce the overall need for reapplication. Spreader-stickers prevent washing away of the pesticide in rainy weather.

59. Q. **My neighbor lent me a live-bait trap for use in trying to catch the woodchuck that is devouring my broccoli. Are there any tricks in making it work?**
    A. First, check with your local or state officials regarding any regulations toward its use. Some regulations prohibit their use by anyone other than a licensed, wild-animal handler. To increase the probability of getting the woodchuck into the trap, rinse the trap with water to remove any human scent. Put on rubber gloves to reduce the possibility of leaving human scent on the bait. Fresh cabbage leaves are a favorite of woodchucks. Good luck.

60. Q. **I saw a slimy residue on the surface of the soil and on the foliage of coleus plants in my flower garden. The leaves on the coleus also have large holes in them. What is causing the problem?**
    A. The slimy residue and holes in the coleus leaves are probably caused by garden slugs. Apply a dusting of diatomaceous earth to the soil surface around each plant. Diatomaceous earth kills by desiccation and abrasive action. It is necessary to reapply the dust after irrigation or rain; the powder cakes and becomes ineffective in dampness. Do not use diatomaceous earth prepared for swimming-pool filters, because it has been chemically enhanced and heat treated, which makes it a respiratory hazard.

61. Q. **What causes the spitlike substance on strawberry plants? It makes harvesting very unpleasant.**
    A. The frothy substance is from the nymph stage of the appropriately named spittlebug. Insecticidal soap spray or pyrethrum insecticide spray may be applied according to the label directions, up to, and including the day of harvest. Read the label.

62. Q. **When I water a potted tropical hibiscus, tiny white insects jump around on the soil surface. After watering they disappear. What are they?**
    A. The tiny jumping insects are probably springtails. They inhabit the organic matter in the soil mix. They are basically harmless, but often a nuisance. Submerge the growing pot in warm water for an hour or so to flush them from their hiding place. Also, insecticidal soap, as a soil drench, is a recommended control.

63. Q. **Just before peony blossoms open, large black ants appear on the buds. Should they be controlled?**
    A. The ants are feeding on sugary materials secreted by the developing buds and not on the buds themselves. Except for the possibility of spreading botrytis blight, there is no reason to try to control them.

64. Q. **My potato plants are devoured by a black-and-yellow-striped beetle. I used "Bt," but to no avail. What to do?**
    A. You probably applied the wrong variety of Bt. Bacillus thuringiensis var. san diego and var. tenebrionis are the recommended Bts for Colorado potato beetle. Hand picking the adults, larvae, and egg masses from the leaves may be all that is necessary in a

small garden. The Colorado potato beetle has become immune to many of the chemical controls.

65. **Q. In the corner of the greenhouse where I grow dwarf citrus and gardenias, there is a black sooty substance that develops on the topsides of the leaves, stems, and flowerpots. It is almost impossible to wash away. What caused this?**

A. The black sooty substance is called sooty mold, a fungus that grows on the honeydew secreted by insects. Examine your plants carefully for spider mite, scale insect, aphid and mealybug infestations. Control the pest and the sooty mold will not reappear.

66. **Q. What does the term RTU mean when referring to pesticides?**

A. Ready-to-use (RTU) is a formula of a pesticide (insecticide, fungicide, miticide, or herbicide) that is premixed for immediate application. The RTU formula is more expensive than the concentrate of a specific pesticide, but often more convenient to use.

67. **Q. My calendula, which I am growing for salads and to ward off asparagus beetles, are covered by midseason with black aphids. What can I use to control the aphids and still be able to use the flowers in my salad?**

A. Apply insecticidal soap according to the label directions, to rid the calendula of the black aphid. Repeated applications will be necessary, as calendula is highly prone to the pest.

68. **Q. Can you tell me a few herbs I can grow in my garden to repel insects?**

A. Although no herbs repel 100 percent of the pests, here are some suggestions: Summer savory repels the Mexican bean beetle; basil deters flies; pot marigold repels asparagus beetles; and mint discourages cabbage pests.

69. **Q. My carrot tops get a blight about mid-season that virtually wipes them out. What can I do to avoid the problem?**

A. The only control for leaf blight on carrots is to plant resistant varieties.

70. **Q. What is an entomophagus nematode and what plants is it used on?**

A. An entomophagus nematode is a beneficial parasite that feeds on certain larvae and adults of the beetle family. These beneficial nematodes are used to suppress populations of black vine weevil on rhododendron, azaleas, taxus, and holly.

71. **Q. What does parthenogenetic mean when referring to insects?**

A. Parthenogenetic means there is development of the egg without fertilization. No male insect is needed for reproductive purposes.

72. **Q. A moss and algae growth develops on the sides and bottoms of all of my clay pots. Is there something I can use to stop its growth?**

A. Moss and algae are developing because of the favorable, moist environment. Allow the container to dry a little more between waterings, and increase air circulation. Potassium fatty-acid, the moss and algae killer formulated for structures, is recommended for use on flower- pots—be sure to read the label.

APPENDIXES

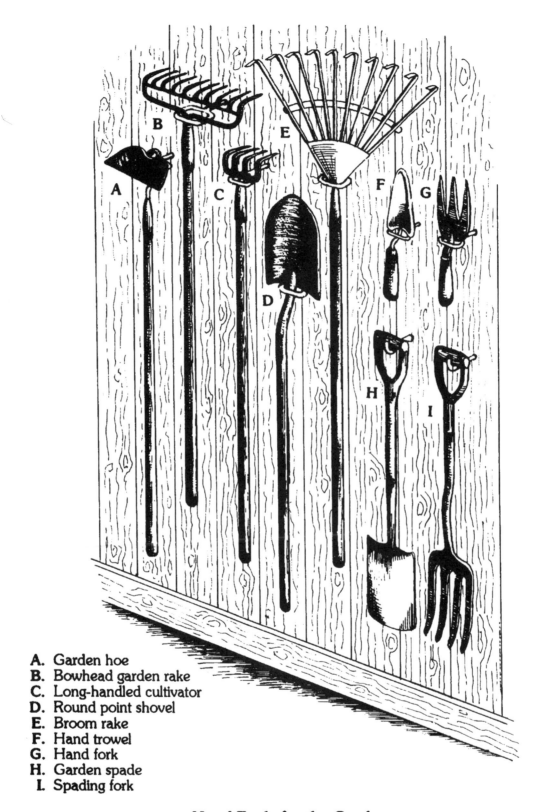

A. Garden hoe
B. Bowhead garden rake
C. Long-handled cultivator
D. Round point shovel
E. Broom rake
F. Hand trowel
G. Hand fork
H. Garden spade
I. Spading fork

Hand Tools for the Gardener

II

METRIC EQUIVALENTS

LINEAR MEASURE

1 centimeter		0.3937 inches
1 inch		2.54 centimeters
1 decimeter	3.937 in	0.328 foot
1 foot		3.048 decimeters
1 meter	39.37 inches	1.0936 yards
1 yard		0.914meter
1 dekameter		1.9884 rods
1 rod		0.5029 dekamenter
1 kilometer		0.621 mile
1 mile		1.609 kilometers

SQUARE MEASURE

1 square centimeter	0.1550
1 square inch	6.452 sq. centimeters
1 square decimeter	0.1076 square foot
1 square foot	9.2903 square dec.
1 square meter	1.196 square yards
1 square yard	0.8361 square meter
1 acre	160 square rods
1 square rod	0.00625 acre
1 hectare	2.47 acres
1 acre	0.4047 hectare
1 square kilometer	0.386 sq. mile
1 square mile	2.59 sq. kilometers

MEASURE OF VOLUME

1 cubic centimeter		0.061 cu. inch
1 cubic inch		16.39 cubic cent.
1 cubic decimeter		0.0353 cubic foot
1 cubic foot		28.317 cubic dec.
1 cubic meter		1.308 cubic yards
1 cubic yard		0.7646 cubic meter
1 stere		0.2759 cord
1 cord		3.624 steres
1 liter	0.908 qt. dry	1.0567 qts. liq.
1 quart dry		1.101 liters
1 quart liquid		0.9463 liter
1 dekaliter	2.6417 gals	1.135 pecks
1 gallon		0.3785 dekaliter
1 peck		0.881 dekaliter
1 hektoliter		2.8375 bushels
1 bushel		0.3524 hektoliter

WEIGHTS

1 gram	0.03527 ounce
1 ounce	28.35 grams
1 kilogram	2.2046 pounds
1 pound	0.4536 kilogram
1 metric ton	0.98421 English ton
1 English ton	1.016 metric ton

APPROXIMATE METRIC EQUIVALENTS

1 decimeter	4 inches
1 liter	1.06 quarts liquid, 0.9 qt. dry
1 meter	1.1 yards
1 kilometer	5/8 of a mile
1 hectoliter	2 5/8 bushels
1 hectare	2 1/2 acres
1 kilogram	2 1/5 pounds
1 stere, or cubic meter	1/4 of a cord
1 metric ton	2,204.6 pounds